THE PEACE REVOLUTION

CONTRIBUTIONS IN PHILOSOPHY

The Peace Revolution

Ethos and Social Process

John Somerville

Contributions in Philosophy
Number 7

Greenwood Press
Westport, Connecticut ● London, England

JX
1952
.S 734
1975

Library of Congress Cataloging in Publication Data

Somerville, John, 1905-
    The peace revolution.

    (Contributions in philosophy   ; no. 7)
    Includes bibliographical references and index.
    1. Peace. I. Title.
JX1952.S734   1975   327'.172   74-5993
ISBN 0-8371-7532-1

Library of Congress Catalog Card Number: 74-5993
ISBN: 0-8371-7532-1
First published in 1975

Greenwood Press, a division of Williamhouse-Regency Inc.
51 Riverside Avenue, Westport, Connecticut 06880

Manufactured in the United States of America

To Those Who Are Making

the Peace Revolution

Contents

Preface

At times during the recent past people have wondered whether the peace movement was over. If the peace movement actually came to an end under present conditions, it would not be long before the human race would come to an end, because the "normal" course of operation of present social institutions and the prevalent habits of thought and action would inevitably lead to increasingly destructive wars. It is obvious that the war game is still central in policy-planning, though it is morally on the defensive as never before in human history, and requires more public hypocrisy than ever before on the part of those who plan it, those who carry it out, and those who profit by it. The war problem will grow, and the peace movement will grow with it, not only because of Indochina, or the Middle East, or any other particular theatre of war, and no matter who is President of the United States, or sits at the top in other countries. The only thing that can be decisive is that which needs to be done by people, even if their governments have good intentions. A revolution in ways of thinking and habits of acting must take place both among leaders and the general public if the all-too-final war to end all wars is to be avoided. To define that revolution and to understand its process of growth is the purpose of this book.

What we call "détente," always welcome in itself, is not a solution of the war problem. It is not even a diagnosis of the problem. It is a mood, the mood in which one has decided to discuss the problem with the other party in an atmosphere of outward cordiality. Our effort in this book is to show what such a détente must lead to if the problem is to be solved.

The "peace movement" is disturbing to many people, to most established authorities, and to all governments. The people suffer from underdeveloped imagination and lack of education; established authorities and governments from overdeveloped love of power and fear of losing it. The "movement" is thus felt as "disruptive," as an irrational breach of normalcy, an unjustifiable intrusion, an intolerable violation of law and order. It is only natural, therefore, that sighs of relief should be heard from all around at the slightest diminution in peace activities, at any momentary decrease in such things as protests against war, mass demonstrations, sit-downs, strikes, occupations of premises, destruction of property, civil disobedience, and moral confrontations. At the slightest indication that such phenomena are "dropping off," one is immediately told by all sorts of established moralists, academic spokesmen, media commentators, and government authorities that the worst is over, the mood has changed, the youth have quieted down, and now we can all get back to normal life, i.e., saying the right thing about peace and doing the old thing about war, without any disruptions. The established and the unimaginative comfort themselves with the conjecture that maybe the "peace movement" was only a fad and is now disappearing.

But is is hardly likely that this is the case. The reason is not simply that all deeply disturbing and disruptive social movements of the past, like abolitionism, trade unionism, and women's rights were also at first treated as temporary aberrations. What is decisive is that the modern "peace movement" has become something more than a movement. Even if it were only a movement, a period of calm at the surface would not be sufficient grounds for concluding that it had ceased to exist. One must in any case examine what is going on underneath, what are the root forces at work, and how and why they grow. The peace thing is like the ecology thing, or the population thing: the less that is done to *counteract* presently accepted patterns of action, deeply ingrained habits, and widely dominant ways of thinking, the closer will we approach the point of total disaster from which recovery is physically impossible. What are at stake in ecology and population are the quality of the natural environment and standards of human life. Present practices could proceed "normally," though with increasing misery, for decades. What is now at stake in war is the survival of life itself in any form whatsoever; and the present underlying habits and attitudes could bring total extinction in a few years.

There is a further important difference between the "movement" to do something about peace, and "movements" to do something about the environment or population. This is what was referred to above in saying that the "peace movement" has become more than a movement. It has grown into a kind of continuing rebellion—more exactly a series of rebellions—constituting part of a wider social phenomenon which may be growing into a revolution, violent or non-violent.

In any case, this series of rebellions is a deep-rooted and many-sided process, in terms both of the variety of social institutions and human attitudes it has confronted and the variety of means and methods it has employed. The institutions and attitudes stretch over the whole spectrum of social life—politics, economics, education, morality, life-style. The means and methods likewise run the gamut—legal, illegal, political, religious, educational, propagandistic. Paradoxically (which in this context means hypocritically), in historical moments of the kind we are now living through, even leading representatives of established power will *say* we need a revolution, usually adding, with every evidence of sincerest conviction as regards *this* point, that, of course, it must be kept entirely peaceful, within the established channels of law and order, in complete obedience to all who wear official uniforms and carry institutionally issued weapons. In short, revolution without disruption of the status quo; no violence save what those in power decide is necessary.

Thus Richard Nixon himself declared that we need "a new American Revolution," and that he would lead it, of course. In *Mein Kampf* Adolf Hitler candidly confessed that he chose the color red for Nazi party purposes because it was the color of his strongest political opponents, the Marxist socialists, whose terminology he also appropriated, so that he could pass off his fanatical nationalism as "national socialism." Louis XV and various French nobles are reported to have said, "Après nous le déluge"; they saw what was coming, but felt safe for their time. Dostoevsky, the most realistic of Christian novelists, was convinced that there had to be a revolution in Russia (that was always the inner focus of his work), and that the only question was whether it would be a Christian or a nihilistic (scientific-communistic) revolution. (This counterposing of the Christian to the scientific spirit was always the inner weakness of his philosophy.) From another angle Otto Kahn, the international investment banker, vetoed a Wall Street loan to Tsarist Russia during World War I, when Russia was weakening and becoming a liability as an ally, on the ground that that country needed a revolution. He said he would not be against a loan *after* the revolution. Revolutions can be wanted or unwanted, but they are never unexpected.

The point is that the present is a part of history, which means that the present can only be understood as a *process.* History is demarcated by revolutions, and each one is a long and wide process. To understand a process going on at present it is necessary to look backward and forward, to extrapolate from the past and project into the future. This is the precondition of doing anything sensible about the present thing that is "going on." We must know *what* it is and *where* it is going. In this case we need to identify the major components of the series of rebellions, punctuated by periods of relative quiescence, that we are living through, to determine where they are headed, and to indicate what it would be sensible to do about them.

THE PEACE REVOLUTION

1

Revolution and Peace

In the decade of the sixties a new and startling social phenomenon came to the fore, not only in the United States, but all over the world, in varying degrees and forms. It has been called by many names, the most frequent of which is youth rebellion. In any case its essence was and remains a challenge and a resistance to unjust authority, no matter how firmly established in tradition or how physically powerful in fact. The kinds and levels of authority that have been denied, flouted, scorned, ridiculed, weakened, or defeated represent an astonishing catalogue: police and government authority, religious and moral authority, educational authority, parental authority, and the authority of established standards of "good taste" in lifestyle, i.e., manners, speech, dress, undress, sex relations, choices in the use and abuse of stimulants and narcotics.

Police were repeatedly interfered with and physically prevented from making arrests and carrying out other duties, by spontaneous crowd action as well as the organized action of small groups, going as far as armed attacks upon police stations. Draft, tax, and other laws were systematically violated on a national scale in accordance with openly published declarations, arguments, and discussions which circulated throughout the country. Religious services taking place in large, richly appointed churches attended by wealthy congregations were invaded and interrupted by small groups of articulate members of oppressed minorities from poverty-ghetto areas, who proceeded to lecture the rich congregation, demanding, on religious and moral grounds, financial reparations and indemnities of various kinds, some of which have been granted. Hundreds of universities, including some of the largest, oldest,

3

and most influential institutions, experienced student strikes, seizures of buildings, forced occupations of offices, libraries, and other facilities, and the burning and bombing of laboratories and buildings connected with war contracts and military training. Blood flowed on dozens of campuses, students were shot dead on several, and mass arrests took place on many. Numerous high university officials found their posts untenable, and in the great majority of cases, if not in all, the university in the end granted at least some of the demands of the students. Parents as well as educational administrators have been forced to accept, contrary to their original principles and wishes in the great majority of cases, all sorts of permissive arrangements regarding men's and women's dormitories, annulling age-old restrictions on unchaperoned visits by students of opposite sexes to each other's rooms, and abandoning other age-old attempts to police student behavior. In similar fashion amazing defeats have been suffered by general public opinion in matters of male hair styles, male and female nudity, racy speech and print, and the like.

Of course, things of this kind have happened, *to a certain extent*, in every generation. But the point is that the extent to which they happened in this generation was greater than anyone had seen in America since the Civil War. Moreover, as something that was happening on a world scale, in some kind of causally interconnected fashion, these events may well be of historically unprecedented extent.

WHAT IS A REVOLUTION?

But is this a revolution? When is it proper to apply the term revolution to events of this kind? Revolution, like many other words—for example, health, sickness, wealth, poverty, intelligence, stupidity—stands for something that is a matter of degree, unlike such terms as circle, triangle, citizen, alien, quadruped, biped. If someone asks simply: Is this man healthy? Is he wealthy? Is he intelligent?, we recognize that in each instance the question is too general, that it is treating something that is a matter of degree as if the degree of it didn't matter. To give a yes-or-no answer, without qualification, would be of little value and might lead to serious misunderstanding. The only way to express the truth about such things is, in each case, to state an amount or degree. For a man can be (and in fact usually is) healthy in some respects and not so healthy in others, wealthy compared to some and poor compared to others, intelligent in some respects and not so intelligent in others. Exactly the opposite is true of the second set of terms mentioned. To treat *them* as matters of degree would lead to misunderstanding, for their meaning is absolute and fixed, in a recognized context. Thus the question whether a given figure is a triangle may be answered yes or no without qualification. There is nothing relative about it. It is not a matter of degree, for quantitative comparison does not enter. The figure is a triangle if and only if it has just three sides and three interior angles. Of course, there are large and small triangles, but the point is, the larger ones are not more *triangular*. What makes them all triangles has nothing to do with size, and the same is true of circles.

The term *citizen* might at first appear to be relative, since different countries have different conditions for citizenship, but the point is that in any one country the standard is fixed; a person having citizenship there cannot have more citizenship there than another person who has citizenship there. But a person who has health, wealth, or intelligence there can have more health, wealth, or intelligence than someone else there. Quadrupeds are clearly absolute in their quadrupedality. An animal species is either four-footed or not four-footed. There is no such thing as a degree of four-footedness, and a biped is not a small quadruped.

To make sense of revolution, we must talk about it in the way we talk about health, wealth, and intelligence. We must keep in mind that it *is* a matter of degree. Then the problem of defining it becomes properly focused, and we immediately ask the right question: Degree of what? If wealth means degree of capital, or of something negotiable in terms of capital, and health means degree of normal physiological functioning and growth, and intelligence means degree of ability to solve problems, what is revolution a degree of? In a very broad sense one might say, change. But that would be too broad, for it is understood that we are not in this context speaking of revolutions in the sense that would include mechanical motions of wheels, astronomical orbits, and the like. We are speaking of socio-political revolutions, so that it is not the degree of change in general, but the degree of socio-political change that is here the defining factor.

But we must be still more specific, for the term *socio-political change* itself needs clarification in its relation to revolution. That which defines a socio-political revolution is the specific kind of socio-political change that represents an overthrowing of the principles (this includes both theory and practice) of established authority. We lay stress upon the *principles*, for sometimes a mere change of the *personnel* of the authoritative or governing group is referred to as an overthrow of established authority, e.g., when, in the political arena, a ''palace coup'' occurs. In this event the top leaders of the government are forcibly removed and replaced by other persons who, however, have no desire to change materially the principles—the basic laws, the economic order, and the cultural norms—of the society or state. This type of ''revolution'' is therefore recognized to be without substantive revolutionary significance. Expressed as a definition, then, any set of events is a socio-political revolution to the extent that it changes the principles and practices of established authority, or (what is the same thing) the prevailing institutions of the society. The term *rebellion* is usually applied to small-scale revolution, or attempts at revolution.

The extent of socio-political change must be measured primarily in two respects: *the number of social institutions or areas* in which such change takes place, and the *amount of the change*. It will be readily agreed that a revolution which changes only political institutions is, other things being equal, not as much of a revolution as one that also changes economic institutions, and that a revolution which changes only certain aspects of these institutions is not as much of a revolution as one which makes equal changes in those aspects and makes changes in other aspects as well. In other words, one of the factors we are talking about is the *range* of socio-political change; the other is the *depth*.

The range is usually easier to measure than the depth. For example, it is not difficult to see that the range of the American Revolution of 1776 did not extend to the institution of slavery, that is, it did not abolish legal slavery or the slave trade. Neither did this revolution directly make any significant changes in the position of women and children, in the attitude toward the native Indian population, in the methods of education, in art forms, in moral standards, sex mores, and lifestyles. The main changes that were directly and immediately brought about were in the political, economic, and religious institutions.

While it is not as easy to measure the depth of changes as it is to measure their range, it is possible to make certain kinds of quantitative judgments and comparisons as to depth even at this relatively early stage in the development of social and behavioral sciences. For example, while the American Revolution immediately brought about numerous economic changes, especially in regard to taxation, revenue, and existing restrictions on production and foreign trade, these changes did not extend so deeply as to alter the basic, pervasive nature of the economic system as a whole, as a system of private capitalism. While the political changes loomed largest of all, they did not go so far as the enfranchisement of women, or the removal of property qualifications for voting in the case of men. Religious institutions were changed to the extent that the principle of a state church was explicitly abolished and outlawed (the first instance of explicit constitutional separation of church and state). But churches as such were not abolished or outlawed, and the predominant religion—Protestant Christianity—remained predominant.

Within limits, it is possible to compare revolutions in respect of range and depth. We can see, for instance, that the Russian (Bolshevik) Revolution of 1917 immediately and directly affected a wider range of social institutions than did the American Revolution of 1776. The former made large-scale changes not only in economic, political, and religious institutions, but in the position of women, children, primitive and semi-primitive ethnic groups, in methods of education and health care, in art forms, moral standards, sex mores, and life-styles. Within most of the institutional common ground affected by these two revolutions the evidence indicates that the changes made by the Soviet Revolution (whether one agrees with them or not) were deeper in some respects. In the political area, women were enfranchised; in the economic, the system of private capitalism was abolished; in the religious area, church schools as well as public pro-religious propaganda were outlawed.

A distinction that can be helpful in these matters is one between quantitative and qualitative changes in social institutions. One way of expressing the difference is to say that quantitative change is that which is restricted to increases or decreases in the *amount* of functioning of certain components in certain established relationships within a social institution, without changing the basic character of the components themselves or the basic nature of their roles in relation to one another, whereas qualitative change is that which alters the basic character of the components themselves or the basic nature of their relationships. In these terms one would say that the American Revolution changed economic institutions quantitatively, whereas the Soviet Revolution changed them qualitatively.

That is, the American Revolution did not try to change radically the basic nature of the economic components—private owner, private employer, private buyer, private seller, open market, individually planned production, and the like. Nor did it try to change the roles of these components in relation to one another; the differing power potential of propertied and unpropertied, buyer and seller, landlord and tenant, creditor and debtor remained substantially the same. However, the Soviet Revolution drastically altered the components, and made a new one—the state itself—the legal, overall economic agent, as owner, employer, production planner, and market controller, at the same time changing the basic nature of the old economic relationships to the point of outlawing private ownership of the principal means of production, and making it a criminal offense to hire workers in order to obtain a private profit out of their labor.

A point which needs strong emphasis is that, though most sociopolitical revolutions have included large-scale violence, this is not a necessary element in the concept of revolution. Whether a certain set of events is a revolution or not depends on the nature and amount of the change brought about in social institutions, not on the amount of violence involved in making the change. We must remember that in all human history so far physical force and violence have played a large part in the normal functioning of an established social order, as well as in the replacement of one social order by another, and that there has been more violence in the former than in the latter. In the case of the established order, the violence is massive and institutionalized on a permanently operating basis, in the local police forces, and all the many branches of the national armed services. The fact that it is legal does not alter the fact that it is violence, i.e., force applied with the intent to bring about bodily injury or death. Revolutionary violence is relatively transitory, and usually of a less organized and more spontaneous character.

At the same time we must also remember that changes which we rightly call revolutionary can be and have been brought about without precipitating violence on the scale of civil war. Indeed, sometimes the same sort of change is carried out peaceably in one place and violently in another. For example, in America the emancipation of the slaves came about as part of a bloody and protracted civil war, while in Russia the liberation of the serfs took place without such a war, though there were many localized instances of violence. For decades, Gandhi in India carried on a revolutionary movement based on the philosophy, strategy, and tactics of non-violence, a movement which played the main role in accomplishing the objective of national independence and sovereignty, an objective usually gained principally by violence.

Let us now try to apply these considerations concerning revolution and its meaning to the overall contemporary situation. In relation to the problem of war and other social problems, we have witnessed, principally in the decade of the sixties, a series of rebellions which, although of remarkable range and unusual depth, have not yet reached the scale of a revolution. The seventies ushered in a period of relative quiescence, though the roots of the problems that had called forth the rebellions were not removed. Our thesis is that the series of rebellions will not come to an end until the problems are solved, and the rebellions will have to grow into a revolution in order to solve them.

TODAY'S REVOLUTION AND THE REVOLUTION OF 1776

In pursuing this thesis, let us put before ourselves two questions: (1) What makes this series of rebellions that may be growing into a revolution different from, and similar to, past revolutions with which we are familiar? (2) Do we need a revolution of this kind? In regard to the first question, let us take our original American Revolution for the purpose of comparison. A difference and a similarity immediately stand out: the difference has to do with the composition of the social group mainly active in each; the similarity has to do with some of the main demands and protests put forth by the dissatisfied groups. The difference is an obvious age contrast. Though persons of all ages could be found active in both sets of events, there is no doubt that the contemporary series of rebellions, at least so far, has been primarily a phenomenon of youth, while the earlier revolution did not have this distinctive character.

The similarity, which in the end may be far more important than the difference, comes to light when one checks through the list of specific grievances, demands, and protests that the signers of the revolutionary

Declaration of Independence carefully set down in that document. They number about twenty-nine (the numerical reckoning depends on how one subdivides several of the longer passages.) Of the twenty-nine, the majority (around twenty) are directly political, and half of these have to do with complaints about war: the oppressiveness of military policies and impositions, the injustices, cruelties, and barbarities of war, and the like.

In the political aspect of the contemporary rebellions two things have stood out very prominently. The first is the centrality of a moral approach: repeated emphasis on human rights, the rights and dignity of the individual, civil rights, human justice, social justice, love as a supreme value. The second is the prominence of the war problem as a source of grievance and protest. Both these traits manifested themselves strongly in our Founding Fathers. The very first grievance set down against the British King in the Declaration of Independence is: "He has refused his assent to laws the most wholesome and necessary for the public good."[1] The third grievance is: "He has refused to pass other laws for the accommodation of large districts of people, unless those people would relinquish the right of representation in the legislature, a right inestimable to them, and formidable to tyrants only." The fifth is: "He has dissolved representative houses repeatedly for opposing with manly firmness his invasions on the rights of the people." This moral emphasis is carried over and applied with particular force to the grievances connected with the war problem. The twelfth has an uncannily contemporary ring: "He has affected to render the military independent of, and superior to, the civil power." The eleventh also suggests contemporary issues: "He has kept among us in times of peace standing armies without the consent of our legislatures." The thirteenth goes further along this line with a specific statement suggestively applicable to things we have witnessed in our own day. This grievance, which refers once again to "the large bodies of armed troops," charges the British monarch with "protecting them by a mock trial from punishment for any murders which they should commit on the inhabitants of these states." Finally, the twenty-fifth grievance sounds a dire note all too familiar to those who have lived through the years of "Vietnamization," "military aid," and the like. "He is at this time transporting large armies of foreign mercenaries to complete the works of death, desolation and tyranny already begun with circumstances of cruelty and perfidy scarcely paralleled in the most barbarous ages, and totally unworthy the head of a civilized nation.'' It is not only in this moral and political emphasis on the war problem that we see remarkable common ground between contemporary rebellions and the original American Revolution. What is even more remarkable is that the common ground extends also to the accompanying phenomenon, or complex of phenomena, to which we refer today as the "credibility gap," with all its attendant charges of duplicity and hypocrisy. Thus the twenty-seventh grievance states: "In every stage of these oppressions we have petitioned for redress in the most humble terms: our repeated petitions have been answered only by repeated injuries." This cannot but call to mind the numerous occasions on which, in vain, suits were instituted in the courts to test, by due process of law, the constitutionality of the Executive's action in initiating and escalating large-scale war in spite of the fact that the Constitution of the United States gives to Congress, and to Congress alone, the power to initiate such war. [2]

The courts which have the legal power and responsibility to rule on matters of constitutionality all refused to make any direct ruling whatsoever, affirmative or negative, on this issue, closing the door to a normal, judicial determination of the question, and allowing the Executive to multiply its war actions unhindered. What makes this situation even more grievous is the fact that the U.S. Constitution, as if in recognition of the importance of such matters, provides for a second way to test the legality of such actions on the part of the Executive: a proceeding of impeachment, initiated by action of the House of Representatives, and decided by a two-thirds vote of the Senate. In 1968 petitions for a proceeding of impeachment to test President Johnson's right to carry on an undeclared war in Vietnam were duly submitted by a group of constitutional lawyers to the Speaker of the House. The petitions were received by the Speaker, and passed on to the House Committee on the Judiciary for its consideration and recommendation. No recommendation of any kind, one way or the other, ever came from this Committee. No hearing was held; no testimony was taken. When President Nixon later ordered his invasion of Cambodia without prior authorization of Congress, similar petitions for an impeachment proceeding were filed with the same House Committee, but again were never acted upon nor reported out. Only in 1974, after the Watergate revelations, did this Committee give serious attention to impeachment.

This is the sort of situation that breeds cynicism towards government, generates a crisis of confidence, and creates the credibility gap, especially when the issues at stake are matters of life and death to the people, in this case especially the younger people. The feeling increases that the government is not being open and honest with the governed, that it is not respecting their basic rights, that it is eroding and destroying the safeguards laid down for the protection of those rights in the Constitution which the officers of government have all taken a solemn oath to uphold. This feeling that the government is not respecting established principles, though pretending to do so, that it is assuming and usurping powers not legally given to it, thereby violating its contract with the people who create it, and whom it exists to serve, is the very feeling that pervades the Declaration of Independence in its statements both of specific grievances and of general principles.

Thus the fourth grievance says of the King: "He has called together legislative bodies at places unusual, uncomfortable, and distant from the depository of their public records, for the sole purpose of fatiguing them into compliance with his measures." And in the fifth: "He has dissolved representative houses repeatedly." And in the sixth: "He has refused for a long time after such dissolutions to cause others to be elected." And in the eighth: "He has obstructed the administration of justice. . . ." Though the ways mentioned in which the King has been guilty of these offenses are not the same as those complained of today, the same underlying feeling is present—that the goverment's measures and tactics are tricks, hypocritical evasions, pious frauds, forms of stalling, administrative dodges, gimmicks by means of which the people are denied their rights, and the Executive authorities gain their own way.

THE RIGHT AND DUTY OF REVOLUTION

This repeated violation of rights is what the Declaration identifies as "despotism" and "tyranny": "But when a long train of abuses and usurpations, pursuing invariably the same object, evinces a design to reduce them under absolute despotism, it is their right, it is their duty to throw off such government, and to provide new guards for their future security. . . . The history of the present King of Great Britain is a history of repeated injuries and usurpations, all having in direct object the establishment of an absolute tyranny over these states. To prove this let facts be submitted to a candid world.''

The facts which the Declaration then submits are nothing more nor less than the grievances which we have just examined. In respect of them, we can hardly avoid observing that those complained of today are of far greater magnitude and gravity than the earlier ones. The costs of war to the people who must bear the burdens were high enough then, but they are incomparably higher now. The risks of war were great then, but they are infinite now, so far as human beings, human civilization, and the future of the human race itself are concerned, because the weapons now available have the potential of total destructiveness, total annihilation not only of man and his works, but of all forms of life whatsoever that exist in the world along with man and within his reach.

This means that the waging of war, the decision to bring the weapons of war into play, is charged with immensely greater gravity today than it was in the eighteenth century. Therefore, any usurpation of the war-making power, any illegal use of it, is a far graver crime against the people than was the case earlier in history. This means in turn that any continued refusal on the part of the government in power to have its actions in this regard submitted to the judgment of the laws and the people by due and peaceful process is an infinitely more dangerous despotism than anything that was possible in the eighteenth century. *This* credibility gap could become a bottomless pit into which everything disappears; *this* fraud could be the last ever practiced on humankind; *this* hypocrisy could transform the planet into mushroom mist. Is it any wonder, then, that there is rebellion?

The moral and political principles of the Declaration are unmistakable in their revolutionary import:

We hold these truths to be self-evident: that all men are created equal; that they are endowed by their Creator with certain in-alienable rights; that among these are life, liberty and the pursuit of happiness; that to secure these rights, governments are instituted among men, deriving their just powers from the consent of the governed; *that whenever any form of government becomes destructive of these ends, it is the right of the people to alter or abolish it,* and to institute new government, laying its foundations on such principles, and organizing its powers in such form as to them shall seem most likely to effect their safety and happiness. Prudence indeed will dictate that governments long established should not be changed for light and transient causes; and accordingly all experience hath shown that mankind are more disposed to suffer while evils are sufferable, than to right themselves by abolishing the forms to which they are accustomed. But when a long train of abuses and usurpations. . . . [Our emphasis.]

Evidently, both then and now there were principles involved, expressed by and for Americans once and for all in their Declaration of Independence, their only birth certificate as a sovereign nation. The central revolutionary principle enters at exactly the point where the official (contemporary) Jefferson Memorial in Washington suddenly, as if in fright, breaks off its marbled quotation of Jefferson's "self-evident truths," and omits the one in which all the others culminated: ". . . that whenever any form of government becomes destructive of these ends, it is the right of the people to alter or to abolish it. . . ." This is the God-given right of revolution, if the word Creator in the Declaration signifies God. Indeed, it is declared more than a right; it is, under certain conditions, declared a duty; and it is the only one of the rights that is referred to also as a duty. Thus, the Declaration goes on to say that when any government confronts the people with "a long train of abuses and usurpations," "it is their right, it is their duty to throw off such government," of course, violently if necessary; and violence was evidently necessary in this instance.

Writers and spokesmen disposed to protect contemporary government from any possibility of revolutionary action have sometimes argued that this principle of revolution became outmoded, so far as America is concerned, after we gained our independence, that the government which was then set up provided, and continues to provide, channels of law and order for peacefully carrying out the will of the people and for protecting their rights from being violated. These writers and spokesmen seem to forget that such channels are not self-operating, that they operate only if the government itself uses them, and allows them to be utilized by the people. A government becomes a tyranny or a despotism not only by proclaiming at the doctrinal level the principles of autocracy and explicitly denying those of democracy. It can become a tyranny or despotism just as effectively by professing principles of democracy (and perhaps practicing them in some matters) while acting the part of a despot in that which most concerns the people's welfare. In a sense, this is even worse than the case of the sincere and consistent autocrat because it adds hypocrisy to the offense, insult to injury. This is precisely the feeling that is strong in the contemporary rebellions.

We must remember that it was strong also in the original American Revolution. The British government was the government of our Founding Fathers, and that government, though monarchical in form, was already in large part under the control of an elected House of Commons. The principle of *absolute* monarchy had long since been whittled away, modified beyond recognition by new governmental institutions and laws that had become well established. Of course a revolution, by no means bloodless, had been required to bring this about in Britain, a fact which lent added aggravation to the sense of injury felt by the American revolutionaries of the eighteenth century. The colonists were being denied rights, privileges, and powers possessed by other Britons; the colonists were being treated by the King and his ministers as if the seventeenth-century revolution had never taken place. In these circumstances, the King and his ministers could have legally been called to account by a parliamentary majority. The channels were all there, but they were not used. They were closed off and blocked up, so far as the colonies were concerned, much as the channels so wisely provided by the Constitution of the United States in regard to the war-making powers, and the correction of abuses and usurpations of those powers, were closed off and blocked up. In our day, where the problem of war is concerned, the Executive and Judiciary often act as if the Constitution of the United States had never been written, and the Congress often seems to give tacit consent.

In such circumstances the central questions always are: Has the government become a despotism, a tyranny? And, who has the right to decide what the answer is? Jefferson makes the position of the Founding Fathers very clear: only the people themselves, as distinguished from the government, have the right to decide, and they always have it. Whatever the time or place, they can never give it up, and it can never legitimately be taken away from them. That is what it means to say, as Jefferson did, that their right to alter or abolish their government, their right of revolution, is "inalienable." As we have seen, he speaks of "a long train of abuses and usurpations," and he sets down a common-sense caution that will hardly be disputed by anyone: "Prudence indeed will dictate that governments long established should not be changed for light and transient causes. . . ." However, what is perhaps more significant in this connection is that, immediately after sounding this note of caution, he draws attention to a fact of history and human nature which must be taken into account in order to put the caution in proper perspective, in order not to exaggerate the caution: ". . . and accordingly all experience hath shown that mankind are more disposed to suffer, while evils are sufferable, than to right themselves by abolishing the forms to which they are accustomed." In other words, there is no great danger that people will ever overdo revolution. The danger is rather that the opposite will happen.

This judgment about the practice of revolution, like the concept of the right of revolution itself, was well established in the traditions of British political thought. Jefferson's philosophical and political guide and mentor, John Locke, had pointed out before the end of the seventeenth century, in a passage which Jefferson must have studied carefully, that

revolutions happen not upon every little mismanagement in public affairs. Great mistakes in the ruling part, many wrong and inconvenient laws, and all the slips of human frailty will be borne by the people without mutiny or murmur. But if a long train of abuses, prevarications and artifices, all tending the same way, makes the design visible to the people—and they cannot but feel what they lie under, and see whither they are going—it is not to be wondered at that they should then rouse themselves and endeavor to put the rule into such hands which may secure to them the ends for which government was at first erected. . . .[3]

Masses of people may be slow to rebel, but when they do rebel, the cause is never the seditious advice of a few agitators, and the preventive is never the repression of free speech or the calling upon school, church, and family to teach respect for established authority. Locke drives home this point with characteristic realism:

> For when the people are made miserable and find themselves exposed to the illusage of arbitrary power, cry up their governors as much as you will for sons of Jupiter, let them be sacred and divine, descended or authorized from heaven, give them out for whom or what you please, the same will happen. The people generally ill-treated and contrary to right, will be ready upon any occasion to ease themselves of a burden that sits heavy upon them. They will wish and seek for the opportunity, which in the change, weakness and accidents of human affairs seldom delays long to offer itself. He must have lived but a little while in the world who has not seen examples of this in his time, and he must have read very little who cannot produce examples of it in all sorts of governments in the world.[4]

What is, in fact, the best preventive of rebellion, as Locke saw it? It is none other than the widespread recognition of the right of rebellion itself. In a remarkable passage he says:

> . . . this power in the people of providing for their safety anew by a new legislative when their legislators have acted contrary to their trust by invading their property [one must always remember that in Locke's usage ''property'' includes human rights] is the best fence against rebellion, and the probablest means to hinder it. For rebellion being an opposition, not to persons, but to authority, which is founded only in the constitutions and laws of the government, those, whoever they may be, who by force break through, and by force justify their violation of them, are truly and properly rebels. For when men by entering into society and civil government have excluded force, and introduced laws for the preservation of property, peace and unity amongst themselves, those who set up force again in opposition to the laws do *rebellare*—that is, bring back again the state of war—and are properly rebels; *which they who are in power (by the pretense they have to authority, the temptation of force they have in their hands, and the flattery of those about them)*

being likeliest to do, the properest way to prevent the evil is to show *them* the danger and injustice of it who are under the greatest temptation to run into it.[5]

In other words, the main problem of law and order is not so much that of the people obeying the government, as that of the government obeying the constitution which set it up, and keeping to the terms and within the bounds of the contract which it (the government) made with the people who created it, and who must remain its master. Rebellions of the people, when looked at closely, usually turn out to be counter-rebellions directed against a government which has broken its compact with the people, resorted to illegal force, and thereby placed itself in a state of war with the people. The really massive and most dangerous violence is a monopoly of governments, a monopoly which all too frequently leads them into sin and crime.

REVOLUTION, MAJORITY AND MINORITY

The classic case for the right of revolution, presented by Locke in the second of his *Two Treatises of Government,* includes as one of the preconditions, agreement of the majority of the people (though this term is not defined very closely) as the body with ultimate and final authority to make all binding political decisions and judgments, including the judgment whether any government has become a despotism or tyranny, and the consequent decision whether to take action against it, though how this judgment and decision are to be made under the disturbed conditions of a revolutionary crisis is scarcely entered into. It must be noted, however, that Jefferson did not dwell upon the concept of the majority even to the extent that Locke did. Not only is it not brought into the Declaration of Independence: on other occasions Jefferson went so far as to defend rebellions which were admittedly of a minority character, or even founded on misconceptions of oppression. His reasons are very interesting, and entirely in the spirit of Locke's realism.

Consider, for example, "Shays' Rebellion," named after its leader, Captain Daniel Shays of Massachusetts, who had fought with distinction in the Revolutionary War. The circumstances are summed up in the *Encyclopedia Americana* as follows:

The rebellion of 1786-87, in which he (Shays) was the directing figure arose . . . more particularly from special reasons for dissatisfaction in Massachusetts. Among these were the wastefulness in the costs of litigation, the high salaries attached to public offices, and above all the exorbitant land taxation. The time was one of financial depression. In the Fall of 1786 five or six hundred malcontents, under the command of Shays, gathered at Springfield, the purpose being to overawe the Supreme Court about to sit there, and prevent the finding of indictments. After a three days' session the court adjourned. In November, when the Court of General Sessions attempted to sit at Worcester, Shays filled the courtroom with an armed force, and no court could be held. . . . On 25 December, 1787 Shays, with 1,100 troops, made an attack on the Springfield arsenal. . . .

In the end, though the rebels were defeated, ''The greatest clemency was shown toward the leaders, and a very general amnesty proclaimed. Shays removed to Vermont, was pardoned and went thence to Sparta, N. Y., where he obtained a pension for his Revolutionary services.''[6]

At the time Shays was leading his rebellion, Jefferson was in Paris, conducting negotiations. Reflecting upon the events in Massachusetts, he wrote: ''God forbid we should ever be twenty years without such a rebellion.''[7] In explaining his judgment of the insurrection, he points out:

I say nothing of its motives. They were founded in ignorance. . . . The people cannot be all, and always, well informed. The part which is wrong will be discontented, in proportion to the importance of the facts they misconceive. If they remain quiet under such misconceptions, it is a lethargy, the forerunner of death to the public liberty. . . . And what country can preserve its liberties, if its rulers are not warned from time to time, that this people preserve the spirit of resistance? Let them take arms. The remedy is to set them right as to facts, pardon and pacify them.[8]

Thus in Jefferson's reasoning, freedom and the chances of a humanly decent government are threatened far more by ''lethargy'' (the silent majority?) than by rebellions. Where the former prevails, the government easily becomes a tyranny, and death takes over; the latter is a sign of the spirit of life, mistaken and violent though it may on occasion be. But its mistakes and violence are small, compared to those of tyranny and despotism. Hence, as Jefferson writes in another place, "I hold it that a little rebellion now and then is a good thing, and as necessary in the political world as storms in the physical." [9] There is little doubt that many persons of the present day would say that Jefferson goes too far in these judgments and evaluations, but there is also little doubt that, if the temper of mind of such people had prevailed in our history, we would have had no revolution in 1776, and perhaps would have no United States of America today.

DO WE NEED A PEACE REVOLUTION?

If we needed a revolution in 1776, is there any logical way in which it could be argued that we do not need one today? Indeed, the conclusion would seem inescapable that the need is greater now because what is at stake now is life itself. What was threatened then was recapturable liberty; what is threatened now is unrecapturable life. It is no accident that when Jefferson listed the inalienable rights, of which no government could legitimately deprive its people, he put life first and liberty second. It comes back to the simple and obvious truth that everything depends on life. There could not possibly be any greater crime, sin, immorality, stupidity, or evil than to bring the whole story of life to an end by destroying every living thing on earth, in the air and under the waters, down to the last cell. This is what war can now do, because of the new weapons with which wars can now be fought; and this is what war will do if people do not restrain the governments which they created.

Government leaders and spokesmen today all say that they understand the qualitatively new situation which exists in the world now that the stockpiles of thermonuclear and biochemical weapons are large enough to kill every living thing on earth many times over. They all speak movingly and eloquently of what could happen if such weapons were used. Some of the best things said about war and against war under the new conditions are said by the very statesmen (e.g., John F. Kennedy: "Man must put an end to war, or war will put an end to man") who evidently cannot refrain from playing the same old game of ultimata, threats to drop bombs, and documented readiness to use atomic weapons if the ultimata are ignored by the other party,[10] who also has a full arsenal of thermonuclear and biochemical weapons at his disposal. But we have "superiority": he can kill us only seven times over whereas we can kill him ten times over, or something of the sort. Thus an intellectual admission that no one can any longer win the war game is combined with a political-economic-psychological compulsion to go on playing this same game.

It is obvious that we desperately need a whole new way ot thinking about war and peace. We need a new politics in relation to war and peace, a new economics in relation to war and peace, a new moral and religious awakening in relation to war and peace. In short, we desperately need a peace revolution. If the only way that present governments and silent majorities can be made to confront the need is by disruption, civil disobedience, and public disorders, then these things are also needed. The rebellions of the present are still only rebellions. If those in power are capable of grasping their significance, the peace revolution that is needed may become also a peaceful revolution.

NOTES

[1]As the entire text of the Declaration of Independence comprises but four pages, of which three are the list of grievances, all passages quoted from it will be readily confirmable in any one of the many available editions.

[2]In 1848 Abraham Lincoln was a member of the House of Representatives which passed a resolution of censure directed against President Polk on the ground that the war against Mexico had been "unnecessarily and unconstitution-ally begun by the President of the United States." Lincoln voted for the resolu-tion, and his reasons for doing so, expressed in a letter to Herndon, read as if he were referring to Presidential actions in our day: "Let me first state what I understand to be your position. It is that if it shall become necessary to repel invasion, the President may, without violation of the Constitution, cross the line and invade the territory of another country, and that whether such necessity exists in any given case the President is the sole judge. . . . allow the President to invade a neighboring nation whenever he shall deem it necessary to repel an invasion, and you allow him to do so whenever he may choose to say he deems it necessary for such a purpose, and you allow him to make war at his pleasure. Study to see if you can fix any limit to his power in this respect, after having given him so much

power as you propose. . . . The provision of the Constitution giving the war-making power to Congress was dictated, as I understand it, by the following reasons: Kings had always been involving and impoverishing their people in wars, pretending generally, if not always, that the good of the people was the object. This our convention understood to be the most oppressive of all kingly oppressions, and they resolved to so frame the Constitution that no one man should hold the power of bringing oppression upon us. But your view destroys the whole matter, and places our President where kings have always stood.'' (Quoted in Francis D. Wormuth, *The Vietnam War: The President Versus the Constitution* (Santa Barbara: Center for the Study of Democratic Institutions, 1968), p. 11.

³John Locke, *An Essay Concerning the True Original Extent and End of Civil Government* 19, 225. In Somerville and Santoni, *Social and Political Philosophy: Readings from Plato to Gandhi* (New York: Doubleday-Anchor, 1963), p. 200-201.

⁴Ibid., p. 200.

⁵Ibid., p. 201. Emphasis added.

⁶*Encyclopedia Americana,* vol. 24 (New York, Chicago: Americana Corporation, 1950), p. 661.

⁷Letter of November 13, 1787, to Colonel Smith. In Somerville and Santoni, op. cit., n. 3, p. 259.

⁸Ibid.

⁹Ibid., p. 258. Letter of January 30, 1787, to Madison.

¹⁰See Robert F. Kennedy, *Thirteen Days* (New York: New American Library, 1969). This posthumously published account of the Cuban missile crisis, during which Robert Kennedy was his brother's chief representative in dealing with the Soviets, makes it insistently clear that President Kennedy was not bluffing in his ultimatum to the Soviet authorities. If they had not removed the missile bases (which they had every legal right to keep in Cuba, as we kept our bases in Turkey and in many other places), the President would have given the order to bomb them even though he "expected" that this action would begin World War III as a thermonuclear conflict. All the consequences were evidently faced by the President. Speaking of him, Robert Kennedy writes: "The thought that disturbed him the most, and that made the prospect of war much more fearful than it would otherwise have been, was the specter of the death of the children of this country and all the world—the young people who had no role, who had no say, who knew nothing even of the confrontation but whose lives would be snuffed out like everyone else's" (p. 106). The thought that most disturbs the reader, and the children as *they* learn to read, is that all this was deliberately risked to keep Soviet missiles out of Cuba while ours were in Turkey! Even more astonishing, in a sense, is the fact that Robert Kennedy assumes throughout that the Executive

alone would make this decision, without waiting for congressional approval or declaration. Though, as Attorney General of the United States, Robert Kennedy was the chief enforcement officer of the Constitution, he never makes mention of that document, nor gives the slightest hint that there would be any legal (or moral) problem involved, considering the fact that the Constitution gives the war-making decision to Congress. "These hourly decisions, necessarily made with such rapidity," he says, without explaining by what moral calculus decisions involving the death of the children of this country and all the world really had to be made with such haste, and why Congress had to be denied its legal role in a matter of such gravity, "could be made only by the President of the United States; but any one of them might close and lock doors for peoples and governments in many other lands. We had to be aware of this responsibility at all times, he [the President] said, aware that we were deciding, the President [sic] was deciding for the U.S., the Soviet Union, Turkey, NATO, and really for all mankind. . . ." (p. 99). It is sad but true that we are thus told, on the highest authority, not only that the decision to begin the war that would destroy the human race would have been made by a United States government, but that it would have been made by *one man* within that government, if the Soviets had stood on their legal rights. Quotations from *Thirteen Days: A Memior of the Cuban Missile Crisis,* by Robert F. Kennedy, © 1969. Reprinted with permission of W.W. Norton & Company, Inc.

2

The New Politics

NEW POLITICS AND OLD PRINCIPLES

Our task here is to identify the new political attitudes and tactics that came into being in the sixties, to determine why they came into being, and to define the conditions that must be fulfilled in order to attain the goal that is needed in relation to the contemporary problem of war. In descriptive terms what was politically new was the degree of civil disobedience, the frequency of the tactics of disruption, the extent of the sense that there was something wrong with the existing establishment *as a whole and at its centers,* the surprising penetration of philosophies and tactics of non-violence, the strength of the moral and physical courage manifested, the militance of oppressed minorities, and the number of revolutionaries evidently prepared to risk their liberty and lives.

All this never added up to an organizationally unified movement, to a consistent strategy or tactics, to a common philosophy or political credo. It was always full of the most diverse tendencies and contradictions: legal and illegal activities, violent and non-violent tactics, religious and anti-religious outlooks, communists and anti-communists, anarchists and anti-anarchists, and splinter groups of each. But in America all politics is characterized by diversities and contradictions; it is only that these were new and unusual ones, and their impact was more noticed.

Take, for example, our ''normal'' political parties. In the Democratic party one finds reactionaries of the Deep South alongside liberals and radicals of the North and East, disagreeing on every important issue save beating the Republicans. In the Republican party, ultra-conservatives and up-to-date liberals have in common only their enemy—Democrats.

We grow accustomed to contradictions of this type simply because they are so frequent and come in the respectable packaging of the Establishment.

Is there not the same situation within the established religions? We grow accustomed to a Christian church daily preaching a Gospel of brotherhood, while segregating its congregations along lines of skin-color, professing peace while supporting war, condemning the pursuit of wealth, while pursuing it with all its energy. Surely these are contradictions of serious magnitude. Sometimes they are defended or extenuated on the ground that the church "must not get involved in politics," as if accepting and conforming to the political *status quo* was not involvement in it and support of it. While these contradictions become habitual and seem respectable, we feel shocked when we learn that a few priests and ministers have broken into the offices of Draft Boards to destroy Selective Service records or spatter them with blood in order to dramatize their Christian protest against the wholesale slaughter called war. We are shocked to learn that nuns might become involved in conspiracies to disrupt the functioning of the war machine.

Those who are shocked by such events, as distinguished from being surprised, have not reflected seriously on the moral principles of Christianity. They have paid attention only to the customary behavior of priests, ministers, and nuns. They see only the contradiction between that behavior and the present civil disobedience; the gigantic contradiction between certain aspects of the old customary behavior and the central principles of Christianity escapes them. It does not occur to them that a nun who breaks a law to stop a war is a better *Christian* (perhaps in the final reckoning even a wiser politician) than a Cardinal who encourages the army to fight. Those who are shocked remember only one principle: customary obedience to established authority, but they forget that Christianity does not put that first.

Neither does democracy. The same people who are shocked by the civil disobedience of clergymen and nuns are equally shocked by the disruptive behavior and protest demonstrations of anti-war groups such as those at the Democratic National Convention of 1968 in Chicago. Yet who would be so bold as to say that the old-line politicians of the party machine ever had any intention of seriously facing the war issue? And who would be so bold as to say that the war issue was not, by all odds, the most important which then faced the people? What does a democrat do at a Democratic Convention in these circumstances? Does he tell himself that in the politics of democracy "law and order" come first, regardless of what kind of law it is, and no matter who is giving the orders? If that were the case, how could there have been a democratic revolution in 1776? Democracy, like Christianity, is born in *resistance* to certain "authorities," no matter how heavy their overlay of hypocritical respectability.

Is this, then, just another case of naive rebels demanding an honest politics? Do they not understand that politics is only the art of the possible, and can never be anything else? Are they really such idiots? The curious thing is that these rhetorical questions, which once had an aroma of realism, now exude only the sickening odor of death. For if anything at all is clear in the times in which we live, it is this: if the kind of politics in which we were traditionally brought up is continued, there will be bigger and bigger wars, and one or two bigger wars will certainly finish the human race completely. In these circumstances, who is naive? History has caught up with Christ, and Dostoevsky's *Idiot* is now the realist. The grain of truth in the statement that politics is only the art of the possible must now give way to the grain of truth in the statement that where there is a will there is a way. The former grain, in the sense it was understood, is no longer capable of bearing the fruit of life. Worldly wisdom has become the stupidity that destroys the world, and romantic idealism has become the only practical way to keep your feet on the ground, or more literally, to keep the ground under your feet. Paradoxically, the new politics, in a sense, is but the determination to *practice* some old principles.

THE POLITICS OF NUCLEAR PACIFISM

This determination is a powerful element of the common bond that unites the diverse and contradictory groups and forces in the new radicalism. Their greatest common enemy is war, and their greatest common detestation is hypocrisy, the life-style of injustice. How this determination is to be carried out in terms of a political movement is a staggering question, the answer to which has not yet been found. The actual role that this determination played—and the importance of this role could hardly be exaggerated—was to inhibit and obstruct the ''normal'' course of the old politics, so that it would not arrive at its most likely juncture of global war. All the rational people agree that global war would be the worst thing of *all*, that *every* alternative to it would be better, but, so far, only a minority of the rational people have had the courage to take the actions that are called for by these convictions.

What emerged was a sort of politics of the united front, always a politics of the short run, and usually a politics of desperation. It was certainly so in this case, for there was and is no alternative to it this side of disaster. Orthodox radical political movements like socialism, communism, and anarchism, are geared for the long run. Their theories, principles, and solutions are fixed on distant goals. They were almost as little prepared to deal with the problem of peace in the context of thermonuclear weapons as were the conservatives and liberals. The nineteenth-century founders of these movements, having no conception of thermonuclear weapons, naturally did not work out political or military strategies to deal with such a situation. In *practice*, the Soviet leadership did the intelligent thing in the Cuban missile crisis, entirely in the spirit of nuclear pacifism and the new politics: they avoided the ultimate contest of *force* that would have been World War III fought with thermonuclear weapons; they accepted a temporary *physical* defeat, a temporary loss of face as they yielded to the American government's ultimatum and took their missiles home. However, neither the official political leadership nor the ideological theoretical leadership in the Soviet Union tried to express the implications of this policy decision, or even acknowledged that there was anything new about it. They went on talking the same old language and thinking (apparently) in the same old concepts: there is a just war and an unjust war; good Communists are ready and willing to fight just wars. But there is an obvious contradiction between this traditional theory and the fact that the Soviet Union did not join the fighting in the just war in Korea, or in the just war in Vietnam, and took its missiles home from Cuba.

Is it not also obvious that the contradiction must be explained by the existence of thermonuclear weaponry? The operative principle can be readily inferred: to the extent that entrance into armed conflict is, under the concrete conditions, likely to precipitate thermonuclear war, such entrance is to be rejected. Considering the universal and total destructiveness that would result from a fight to the finish between major powers armed with thermonuclear weapons (admitted as a fact by everyone), the validity of the political principle that this is always to be rejected would seem self-evident. But apparently it is not self-evident, as arguments from the traditional left as well as from the right (often remarkably similar arguments in relation to this matter) testify.

However, none of these arguments is capable of surviving logical analysis. The most frequent is that acceptance of the political principle of thermonuclear pacifism by any government would lay that government open to "atomic blackmail," so that it would have to capitulate to every ultimatum delivered by any atomic power. Thus the blackmailed government would allegedly soon be reduced to impotence, and the blackmailing government would win an easy victory. In the context of contemporary events, the first thing that occurs to one is that if this argument were sound, the United States should have been able to win an easy victory in Vietnam (or in Korea), and the Soviet Union, after having "lost face," and taken its missiles home from Cuba, should not have dared to build up its military power in the Middle East. In other words, the argument is far too simple; it forgets the actual conditions that exist within nations and in the international arena.

In the first place, every government that wants to stay in power has to reckon with its own people. History may have to say that one cause, as strong as any other, for the failure of the United States to win a military victory in Vietnam was the opening up of the credibility gap between the American people and its government. Every escalation of the war widened the gap, and every widening of the gap made it more difficult for the government to be confident of staying in power while "winning" the war. But suppose the government had been disposed to take the risk with its own people, and had dropped a few thermonuclear bombs on North Vietnam. Besides the fact that there would still have been the Viet Cong in South Vietnam, there would have been the dilemma: either the destruction of life and natural resources in North Vietnam was so great as to render "victory" profitless and occupation unfeasible, or the destruction was less than that. In either case, the guerrilla war would have continued in South Vietnam, aided by China and the Soviet Union. Not only would that war not have been over (and experience shows that occupation of the North would simply have widened its theatre), but the American government, from the start, would have had to fear atomic retaliation by the Soviet Union, even if the Soviet Union had publicly proclaimed its adherence to the principle of never carrying on thermonuclear war, *and meant it without reservation,* for in politics no one takes the risk of banking on the honesty of his opponent where matters of great importance are concerned, especially not in anticommunist politics, the primary axiom of which is that Communists are liars by definition. In short, fear of unknown quantities such as what the American people would do, what the Soviets and Chinese would do, whether the American government could wisely try to undertake a vast occupation of a devastated and atomically polluted country (or countries) of Southeast Asia, whether the pollution and contamination could be contained—all these fears inhibited the decision-makers, preventing them from beginning the game of atomic blackmail in Vietnam.

The Cuban missile crisis is not a good case by which to judge the efficacy of atomic blackmail as a tactic, though it led our chief policy planner, Dr. Walt Rostow, into thinking so.[1] For, even though the destruction of the world was really and truly risked, in the sense that our government was fully prepared to initiate war which it expected to become nuclear if the Soviets did not comply with our ultimatum, as Robert Kennedy insisted, not without pride, in his authoritative account,[2] the gains were limited to the removal of the missiles from Cuba. (This must stand as the greatest risk for the smallest gain ever recorded in the history of the world.) However, if compliance with the ultimatum had had some such result as our sending an occupying force to take over and administer the territory and population of the USSR, this would simply have amounted to shifting the contest to another level, and to fighting it with other weapons.

It is one thing to march into a country, but it is quite a different thing to make your occupation a political and economic success, especially when the country is larger and more populous than your own. Then you are no longer dealing with the government which was willing to capitulate and resign in order to prevent the incineration of the human race. You are dealing face-to-face with a people numbering hundreds of millions who now naturally hate you with a bitter hatred and fight you with little weapons not capable of destroying the world but quite capable of denying you victory, on a kind of battlefield not only physical and not mainly physical, where they have every possible advantage over you. It was said in the nineteenth century that war is politics carried on by other means. Now that wars can be fought with thermonuclear weapons, politics must become war carried on by other means. Was this not the story of Vietnam? Politics became the guerrilla war which the best-equipped army in the world could not win.

POLITICS AND THE INALIENABLE RIGHT TO LIFE

The new politics goes back to some old premises, which, as it happens, were most pointedly expressed in the American tradition. No one ever structured the axiomatics of democracy better than Thomas Jefferson did in the Declaration of Independence, when he placed among the "self-evident" truths the fact that human beings have "inalienable rights," and listed the principal ones as "life, liberty, and the pursuit of happiness." The order is not accidental, and fits the contemporary situation like a glove. The primary right *is* the right to life, the right to live out one's normal life-span, for the undeniable reason that every other human value depends on life. In this, Jefferson was more right and more apt than he could have suspected. In the eighteenth century he must have thought of "the right to life" as it applies to individuals, and groups of individuals, but not especially to the human species as a whole, or to all species of life as a whole.

The reason Jefferson was not concerned to think in these wider terms is clear: no government had the physical power to threaten the life of the human species as a whole, let alone the life of all species taken collectively, down to the tiniest unicellular organisms. He was dealing with a situation in which, even though the most powerful armies on earth were to wage war for a century with the most destructive weapons that then existed, most of the human race and most of the plant and animal species would still be alive and flourishing when the war was over. Not only that, but it is at least conceivable that the prospects of the human race for its future happiness might have been improved as a result of the kind of maximum war that could then be fought. That is, the war might have ended in the defeat of some oppressive and tyrannical power which was making life miserable and short for the great majority of people, and in the victory of a power capable of contributing significantly to the opposite result. All this would be in a still existing world, with a still existing human race. In Jefferson's mind the political right of a government or a people to wage war was in principle qualified only by the answer to a single question: is the cause just? But the history of science and technology has now moved to a point where we are confronted by a further question which Jefferson, or anyone before 1945, did not have to consider: does any goverment or people have the right to wage war as a contest of weapons that will end the world, *even for a cause that is just?* The answer has to be in the negative because the least just of all possible outcomes is the one that destroys everything.

The logic of the new politics must take its point of departure from the fact that there are ways, times, and places of fighting for national liberation that do not carry the danger of precipitating thermonuclear warfare. Stated precisely, the principle is: To the extent that a given form of fighting would, under the given conditions, be likely to precipitate thermonuclear warfare, that form of fighting must be avoided under those conditions. That is the very least that can be said. It is not the principle of total pacifism espoused by many contemporary rebels; it is only thermonuclear pacifism, the irreducible minimum of principle that must exist in any form of contemporary politics that is not self-evident insanity.

But it would be cultivating illusions to imagine that this irreducible minimum could be attained by one grand stroke in the form of something like a nuclear disarmament treaty. Not that one would argue against such a treaty. On the contrary, it would be salutary to have such a treaty; it would do everyone good to think along these lines. But it could by no means be relied upon as a guarantee. Even if all present stockpiles of nuclear weapons were destroyed, one would have to assume that if war between major powers broke out, new weapons of this type would probably be produced. This means that political strategies must be thought out in advance in any case. Priorities must be decided, and alternatives must be explored. Life must come first, liberty second. Patrick Henry had the right to say, "Give *me* liberty or give *me* death." He would have had no right to say, "Give *me* liberty, or let the story of life come to an end right now.'' If we can believe Robert Kennedy, this was precisely the political logic used by his brother John: I would see everyone dead before I would let the missiles remain in Cuba.[3]

Does the principle of avoiding thermonuclear war at all costs mean that an oppressed people cannot take up arms and fight a war of national liberation against an atomic power, or against a foe who is backed up by an atomic power? It does not mean that, as the case of Vietnam shows. In the circumstances that existed in that country—a civil war in which the American government intervened—there was no reason for the Viet Cong or North Vietnamese to believe that continuing an armed struggle for national liberation would precipitate a thermonuclear war. They did not possess atomic weapons or even a significant air force, and everyone knew this. Thermonuclear war requires a confrontation between nuclear powers. Thus, resistance by a non-nuclear power is not a decisive factor. But this logic does not operate conversely. It does not mean that military intervention by a nuclear power against a non-nuclear power likewise carries no significant threat of thermonuclear conflict. In Vietnam it did, for the American government had to reckon with the very real possibility that if it intervened on one side, the Soviet Union, or China, or both (and both are very closely concerned, geographically and ideologically) might well intervene on the other side, as the Chinese had intervened in the Korean conflict, following American intervention, but a few years before. Nevertheless, American policy, carried out by presidential war in defiance of the Constitution, did not scruple to risk the thermonuclear confrontation. Truman, Kennedy, Johnson, and Nixon all took their unconstitutional stand on this infinitely risky ground, this thin crust over a bottomless pit.

Anyone seriously interested in the future of the human race, which now means, first of all, that the human race should be able to have a future, must understand that in its most urgent sense this is a question of the kind of politics that will be carried on in the immediate future, and that the kind which is still evident in the most powerful centers of authority can only be described as a politics of reckless desperation and madness. This is why the most basic of contemporary political problems, those concerned with the issue of thermonuclear war, have to be approached in the frame of mind of a psychiatrist dealing with mental patients in a hospital. One must, as calmly as possible, accept the fact that these people are making a great many decisions and plans and for some time will go on making a great many decisions and plans which are homicidal and suicidal because their thinking has become separated from reality, because, while reality has taken a sharp turn in an entirely new direction, their thinking has continued on along the same old line. One must first of all try to remove from these people's reach all objects that could be used as lethal weapons. This is very difficult, not only for the usual reasons, but because one discovers that some of these people are themselves administering the hospital, in posts of the highest authority. However, one must not panic. One must try to think out those patterns of action which are open to one, which, without directly challenging the physical authority of the most powerful maniacs at one stroke, tries to reduce their authority, obstruct their plans, and bring the thinking of the others back to reality.

This new politics of survival demands an unusual combination of involvement and detachment. One must never forget that one is dealing with madmen sincerely convinced that their madness is really patriotism, true religion, and freedom. At the same time one must never forget that the madness is curable, though some of its victims will not live long enough for a cure to be effective. Above all, one must avoid the temptation, however great the provocation, to return irrationality for irrationality, to answer suicide with suicide, genocide with genocide, and finally biocide with biocide. To call these things ''the right of self-defense'' is a madness as far from reality as any other. There must always be two parties to a thermonuclear conflict that would destroy the world. Suppose that in the thermonuclear conflict, A is in the right and B is in the wrong, but that B is too stupid to see that he is in the wrong, or too wicked to acknowledge it. If, then, A is asked, on rational grounds, to back away, and he angrily replies, ''Don't tell me to be rational; tell B, who is in the wrong,'' and refuses to give way, and the world is destroyed, A, who was originally in the right, would have become just as stupid and just as much in the wrong as B.

The new politics got its strength from three sources always weak in the old politics: honesty, courage, and moral concern. It was a reflex from hypocrisy, timidity, and greed. As a social and psychological phenomon, this had much in common with early Christianity, with the first American revolution, and the Russian revolutionary movement between 1905 and

1917. Historically, this can hardly be regarded as surprising, because there must always be human limits, different though these are under different social conditions, to the degree of tolerance of hypocrisy, timidity, and greed. In this case, the entire body of creative literature of the nineteenth and twentieth century—novels, plays, stories, poetry—is like an ever more detailed and extensive indictment of the massive penetration of hypocrisy and greed into the corpus of modern society. If sufficient people did not believe that there could be a politics which was honest and free from greed, or could not find the courage to act on this belief, the end of human society might already have been reached.

But history enters as another kind of witness to a stubbornly recurrent question. What happened, that the Christianity of Christ should take the form of the present church, that the Declaration of Independence should give to rise to the Smith Act and the Committee on Un-American Activities, that Lenin's politics of national liberation and self-determination should come to Stalin's internal repression and the invasion of Czechoslovakia? The new politics seeks the answer to that question, but certainly no one, new or old, could claim to have found more than a part of the answer. We can say that the church accommodated itself to the institutionalized violations of Christianity in the world where it existed, that the American economic system was a game whose rules inhibited the practice of the principles of the Declaration of Independence, that the Soviet system did not create channels of individual freedom and conscience, or checks and balances capable of bringing to light, in time, the most costly crimes of high authority.

This is part of the answer, but does not tell us as much as we want to know. In principle, we can explain how all these things happened in terms of the causes at work in the given time at the given place. The question the new politics really raised is: Does it have to happen that way in the future? Is not another way possible now? The fact that certain results came about in the past is rather powerful evidence that the operative causes that were *then* at work did not permit other results. But the whole point is that even if they did not, that fact is not decisive of the operating causes *now*.

In any case, what we are doing in the present is finding out how much *we* can do, finding out how strong *our* causes are, towards attaining a human solution. History gives no guarantee that we will succeed, but it also makes no fatalistic pronouncement that we must fail. However it turns out in the end, it is better to try than not to try. What one is trying to do politically is, in a sense, to make democracy work now. This effort has, of course, both a substantive and a procedural aspect, and a clear line cannot always be drawn between them. The substantive aspect is usually expressed in terms of human rights, and there is an enormous contemporary literature revolving around this concept. This literature is frequently referred to as the rhetoric of democratic politics, which, while true enough, tends to suggest, because of the flavor of the word "rhetoric," that we are dealing with something not of primary importance. But the suggestion is misleading, for the question of rights, whether acknowledged or not, has been at the heart of all politics, and will remain so until politics has withered away.

Reasoning from the all-destroying consequences of thermonuclear war, we can only conclude that no government has the right to wage such war, and no right to ask or compel anyone to fight in such a war, because human beings have prior rights, which governments were set up to protect, and the primary right is the right to life. This logic is clear, but not self-applying. The new politics understands that human rights are real only to the extent that people really believe in them, and further understands that the only convincing evidence that people believe in them is that they act upon them. In 1776 the statement in the Declaration of Independence that *all* human beings have an inalienable right to liberty was *mere* rhetoric, because nothing was then done about slavery or the slave trade. This does not reflect upon Jefferson, whose original draft of the Declaration contained a concrete condemnation of slavery and the slave trade which would have committed the new government to take action against these practices. But the majority of the "Congress assembled" placed economic interest above principle, and voted that part out, though they left in the reference to the inalienable right to liberty: some, as Jefferson pointed out in his *Autobiography*, because they would not forego the advantage of holding slaves, others because of the profits they were making by engaging in the slave trade. Only as time went on was something done, the hard way, about slavery. However, the part of the Declaration which said that there *are* inalienable human rights, that governments are set up to safeguard them, and that when the people are convinced that any government is repeatedly violating their rights, they have the right and duty to remove the government, by force, if necessary, was clearly not *mere* rhetoric. It became a principle of action—the sovereignty of the people—carried into practice by a revolutionary war.

THE SILENT MAJORITY AND THE SHORT RUN

Political principles are like human rights in that the only convincing evidence that people believe in them is that they act upon them. Conversely, the principles they act upon, stated or unstated, are the ones they really believe in. The majority of American people at the present time do not act on the principle of the sovereignty of the people; in this, they have not caught up with our forefathers. The majority of Americans at present act on the principle of the sovereignty of the government over the people, a much older idea than that of democracy. They do not act on the principle that liberty is an inalienable right. Our contemporary majority did not resist when their civil liberities were alienated during the McCarthy period, without due process of law, in open defiance of law and of a splendid constitutional tradition. The present majority, though in dwindling numbers, still act on the principle that they have a right to just as much liberty as the government will allow them, in the spirit of the English doggerel:

It's because of the Magna Charta
As were signed by the Barons of old,
That in England today we can do as we please
So long as we do what we're told.

The majority at present do not act on the principle that the highest obligation of democratic government is to protect their right to life, the protection of which would mean that the very last thing democratic political leaders would do is take a step which risks the lives ''of the children of this country and all the world'' as Robert Kennedy put it, but took the risk, nonetheless.[4]

The majority at present act on the principle, also much older than democracy, that, when it comes to war, thermonuclear or otherwise, no matter whose life or how many lives are involved, it is a case of ''Theirs not to reason why, theirs but to do and die.'' Can one imagine anything more *stupid,* especially from a democratic standpoint?

The peace problem divides itself into a short run and a long run. The supreme danger is located in the short run and consists in the high possibility of biocide by thermonuclear incineration not only because the biocidal weapons are under control of officials thoroughly conditioned to think and act in terms of the war game, but because these officials can still count on the support of the majority in playing it, whatever the consequences. This means that the problem of highest priority at the present time is political because in our world only governments have the operative power to stock-pile thermonuclear weapons and decide upon their use.

Reduced to its simplest trems, the short-run problem is to prevent the use of these weapons, or any others of like destructiveness, until human forces like reason and love, working at levels in addition to the political, have been able to handle the deeper, bigger, more interesting problems of the long run, through education, philosophy, art, and science. We are not saying that the prevention of the use of these weapons, which is centrally a political problem, does not also need the resources of education, philosophy, art, and science. The need is real and urgent, but it is for something of direct relevance, something that will count politically in the here and now. This is a legitimate demand, as challenging to human creativity as any other, perhaps more than any other.

In the new politics, as in all serious politics since the beginning, two lines of action have manifested themselves: legal and illegal. History witnesses that either can be successful, and morality acknowledges that either can be good. That is, everyone agrees that some laws have been evil, e.g., slavery, and some revolutions good, e.g., ours, thus justifying illegal action against the first and for the second. It is empirically possible that legal and illegal actions may contribute to the same good end, and it is also possible that they might negate each other, preventing a good result. Everything depends upon the end in view and the concrete conditions of time and place. Legal political action, though it move along conventional lines, can have a content and significance far from conventional. In the American tradition the presidency of radicals like Jefferson and Lincoln are classic examples. New parties can be created, and progressive individuals can spring up within old parties.

In addition to the fact that there are legal ways of creating new political entities and establishing new laws, a fact of equal importance to the politics of peace is that the actions of the governments in power which have constituted the most dangerous violations of peace have at the same time been actions that violated the laws of those very same governments. It would be naive to overlook or neglect this aspect of political reality, which can and must be dealt with as a matter of highest priority, not only because of its inherent content, but because it is on a level of consciousness and concern where all people can meet.

PRESIDENTIAL WAR AND CONGRESSIONAL RESPONSIBILITY

The most obvious and massive examples of recent times are the American presidential wars, *initiated* in direct violation of the Constitution of the United States, Article 1, Section 8, Paragraph 11 of which gives to Congress alone the authority to make the decision to enter into systematic war: "The Congress shall have the power . . . to declare war." Article II, Section 2 demarcates the President's authority in this regard: "The President shall be commander in chief of the army and navy of the United States. . . ." The meaning and intent of this constitutional division of authority are unmistakable. Congress must decide *whether* we are to carry on systematic war; the President must decide *how* the war is to be carried on, if Congress decides there is to be systematic war. This would be clear from the language alone, even if we had no other evidence of the explicit intent of the framers of the Constitution. However, in this case we have an abundance of supporting evidence from the debates of the convention which decided the wording of the Constitution, during which this matter was thoroughly ironed out.[5] The distinction between the decision to enter a war and the decision how to conduct it was made plain, and after detailed discussion the consensus was that Congress was too unwieldy a body for the latter, but certainly not for the former.

Recognition of the power of the President, as Commander-in-Chief, to *conduct* the war was in itself a kind of compromise, for the original draft of the Constitution submitted for discussion had given Congress the power to "make" war. It was understood that this wording would have laid upon Congress the burden not only of deciding whether we should enter into systematic war, but of supervising all the details of operation that would be involved. Hence, these were given over to the President. Even then, the Constitution explicitly left to Congress' judgment not only the primary decision whether or not to initiate war, but other broadly important policy decisions involved. Thus, though the President is made Commander-in-Chief, the following powers are not given to him, but to the Congress:

> To grant letters of marque and reprisal [seizure in retaliation] and make rules concerning captures on land and water; to raise and support armies, but no appropriation of money to that use shall be for a longer term than two years; to provide and maintain a navy; to make rules for the government and regulation of the land and naval forces; to provide for calling forth the militia to execute the laws of the Union, suppress insurrection and repel invasions; to provide for organizing, arming and disciplining the militia, and for governing such part of them as may be employed in the service of the United States, reserving to the States respectively the appointment of the officers, and the authority of training the militia according to the discipline prescribed by Congress. (Article I, Section 8, Paragraphs 11-16.)

There is an obvious effort throughout to limit and curb the power of the Executive in the matter of war. It is in no way strange that constitution-makers who would not give to the Commander-in-Chief even the powers listed above, and who would not trust him with the money to carry on war except in two-year installments, would also not give to him the authority to make the most important decision of all, the decision from which all the other consequences flow, that is, to enter war. This plain distrust of the Executive could be clearly inferred from the constitutional provisions themselves, even if we had no direct evidence of the feelings of the framers. But again, we find an abundance of direct evidence in the debates.[6] The consensus, very forcefully expressed, was that no one man, or small group behind closed doors, should make the decision to enter war, as distinguished from the decision to conduct it by this or that strategy, and to supervise its operation, once it is entered upon. The heaviest oppressions that the delegates had all witnessed and suffered had come from the fact that an Executive and his advisers, a King and his cabinet, could plunge a nation into war at their own discretion, for which the people then had to pay with their lives and property. This had been, in Lincoln's words, ''the most kingly of all kingly oppressions,'' and the Constitutional Convention was determined not to place ''our President where kings have always stood.''[7] Congress was closer to the people, elected more frequently, capable of reflecting more accurately the different feelings of people in different parts of the country, and its deliberations were open to the people to see, hear, and judge, *in time.*

In this regard there was agreement from all sides in the Constitutional Convention that the Commander-in-Chief, by definition, always had the power to repel sudden attacks, that is, that there could be occasions and circumstances which did not allow sufficient time for prior approval by Congress if the right of immediate self-defense were to be exercised.[8] But it was also understood that such acts of immediate self-defense in reply to a sudden attack do not yet constitute a war. In diplomacy, they are referred to as incidents. War requires the prolongation and escalation of the physical conflict involved in such an incident, the planning and undertaking of sustained military operations. It is thus obvious that a decision must always be made as to whether any particular incident, any sudden attack and immediate reply to it should be escalated into a war, or whether following the immediate reply other courses should be pursued, diplomatic, economic, or other. It is also obvious that this decision is on a very different level from the kind of decision that represents an immediate exercise of self-defense in response to a sudden attack. It is beyond doubt that the framers of the Constitution, after detailed discussion, by deliberate intent and for weighty reasons, gave the final power to make the decision to enter into *war* only to the Congress and pointedly withheld it from the Executive. Paradoxically, what our subsequent history actually shows is that Presidents who were confronted by sudden attacks (e.g., Woodrow Wilson, Franklin Roosevelt) found it possible to send an immediate message to Congress, setting forth the facts and asking for a declaration of war, even when the attack was as sudden and massive as that at Pearl Harbor. Conversely, Presidents (e.g., Polk, Truman, Johnson, Nixon) have initiated war on their own in the absence of any direct attack upon us when it was quite certain that Congress would not have been convinced the facts called for our entering into systematic war.

There could hardly have been a clearer case than that of the Vietnam conflict. The *Pentagon Papers,* first published by *The New York Times,* confirmed in minute detail by means of official memoranda not only the fact that initiation of large-scale war from the air had been planned and decided upon months in advance, without any thought of asking for the authorization or approval of Congress, but also the fact that every effort was made to conceal from Congress and the people that such a decision would be put into operation.[9] It was taken for granted by the Executive at every step that neither Congress nor the people would have favored such a decision. If this is not evidence of unconstitutional usurpation of authority, clearly acknowledged and documented by signature, what could be? The arguments of government spokesmen, when they are confronted with such facts, sound unbelievably naive and uninformed. They have argued that to let Congress debate the question of escalation into war would have informed the North Vietnamese that we might be about to escalate and make real war against them. By this argument, the decision whether or not it was necessary to enter into war against North Vietnam is blandly assumed to be either a matter of no importance to Congress and the people, or a matter in regard to which our Constitution and laws give to Congress and the people no important role or function except to obey the Executive. Both assumptions are contrary to plain fact. Moreover, what physical risks could a congressional debate about whether to enter into systematic war have entailed, compared to the risks of not having such a debate? For one thing, North Vietnam, a small and distant power, had no means or motive to try to destroy us suddenly had we held such a debate; for another the congressional debate, as everyone knew, would in all probability have resulted in a decision not to initiate systematic war. The danger of not having the debate was that the lives of the youth would be sacrificed in a criminal undertaking.

It is also argued by government spokesmen that the procedures, restraints, and divisions of authority which are laid down in our Constitution are outmoded and do not fit the conditions of the contemporary world. The first answer to this, in any democracy where the officials have taken an oath to uphold and protect the Constitution, is of course, that anyone who thinks this argument is valid should be prepared, by due process of law, to propose amendments to the Constitution. If these spokesmen actually proposed amendments which would take the decision to initiate war entirely away from control by Congress and place it entirely under the control of the Executive, there is hardly any likelihood that the amendments would gain the required approval of Congress or state legislatures. But the staggering thing is that high government spokesmen who have used this argument have not presented it as an argument in favor of possible amendments to the Constitution, but as justification of Executive actions which ignored the existing provisions of the Constitution.[10] Did it escape the attention of these spokesmen that this would make the present government of the United States a self-acknowledged military dictatorship? Or is it precisely to this, as an allegedly already accomplished fact, that they are trying to direct our attention, as gently as possible? This would mean that a quiet political revolution has already taken place from above, a revolution which has nullified the most vital aspects of the Constitution and usurped the most important powers of the Congress.

Another argument offered from the side of the government has been that the various measures voted by Congress in support of the military actions initiated by the Executive in Indochina either amounted to a declaration of war, or transferred to the Executive the legal power to make future war there at his discretion. This reasoning ignores the fact that congressional votes for supplies, reinforcements, and the like did not necessarily indicate a judgment that our war in Vietnam was constitutional, but could have indicated only a judgment that, in the circumstances, this was the best way to protect the lives of those Americans who had already been sent there, legally or illegally. Moreover, the alleged possibility of a transfer, consciously or unconsciously, of constitutional responsibility and power through a measure such as the Tonkin Gulf resolution is so childish that it would be amusing were the issue not so grim. Setting aside the fact that this resolution was later rescinded (without this action having any effect whatsoever on the conduct of the war by the Executive), it is certainly naive to think that any power or responsibility which the Constitution specifically gives to one branch of government could be transferred to another without a constitutional amendment. A specific procedure is of course laid down for amending the Constitution, which requires a two-thirds vote, whereas ordinary resolutions require only a majority vote.

At one time a favorite argument of government spokesmen was that "we made a commitment," presumably to go to war to help South Vietnam, a commitment that allegedly went back to the Eisenhower regime, and was allegedly spelled out in the Seato Treaty. Here again, not only did Eisenhower publicly reject the part of this argument that applied to him, pointing out that his administration had made no commitment to South Vietnam that involved entering into war, but the basic fact must be confronted that no one has the legal or constitutional authority to commit the United States to war except the Congress. Moreover, this very situation is given explicit recognition in the text of the Seato Treaty, which states that any decision by any of the signatories to go to war would have to be made "in accordance with its constitutional processes."[11] In the case of the United States, this would certainly mean that Congress would have to make the final decision as to whether any particular set of circumstances necessitated war, within the meaning of the general obligations set forth in the treaty. Treaties are made by action of the President and the Senate, and nothing in the Constitution gives the President *alone* the power to interpret the treaty's obligations in reference to a particular situation. In fact, when it is a case of interpreting a treaty to mean that we must go to war now, because certain events have now occurred, even the agreement of the President and the Senate would not be sufficient. Congress as a whole would still have to approve. Otherwise, as Professor Francis Wormuth has pointed out, there would be an "assumption that the President and Senate may use the instrumentality of a treaty to make war, depriving the House of Representatives of its voice. If this is true, the President and the Senate might make a treaty with Liberia, let us say, and then embark upon a war with any country in the world. This is to substitute Liberia for our House of Representatives."[12]

The present writer undertook to determine what the members of Congress actually thought about this problem of Executive encroachment upon the powers of the legislative branch. In the spring of 1969, he took a poll of the members of both houses, submitting to them four brief questions. This was done twice in order to give a second opportunity to those who had not replied the first time. Even so, the total replies did not quite reach 10 percent (9.3 percent), which might, in a sense, be the most significant result of all.[13] The first question was: "In view of the fact that the U.S. Constitution gives to Congress alone the power to declare war, do you feel there is a serious constitutional problem in the fact that we have recently found ourselves in two large-scale wars (Korea, Vietnam—more than sixty thousand American dead so far) without any declaration of war by the Congress?" Several brief formulations of possible answers were supplied along with each question; amplified answers were also invited. Ninety-four percent of those responding answered this question with the formulation, "Yes, there is a serious constitutional problem involved." The other two formulations that were provided along with this question were: "There may be a technical constitutional question, but it makes no real difference whether Congress declares war or leaves it to the Executive to decide," and, "There is no constitutional problem." These two alternatives together accounted for only 6 percent. But the federal courts repeatedly refused to rule on the constitutional question.

Question 2 was worded as follows: "If, after the Tonkin Gulf incident, President Johnson had sent a message to Congress asking for a declaration of war against North Vietnam (recognizing it as a state), would you at that time have been inclined to vote for a declaration of war?" The alternatives supplied with this question were: "Probably not," "Probably yes," and "Probably would have abstained." A total of 76.5 percent said "Probably not." If this is representative of Congress, there would be something like mathematical proof that a crime of enormous magnitude was committed in violation of the Constitution. Question 3 was: "Do you feel that the vote for the Tonkin Gulf Resolution can properly be construed as something which handed over to President Johnson Congress' prior approval and consent for him to commit us to large-scale war at his own discretion?" Seventy-three percent flatly answered, "No." Yet that is, of course, exactly what the President did. Question 4 was: "If, in relation to another country, we have signed a treaty which pledges us to go the aid of the country militarily when it is attacked, do you feel that the Executive, without further authorization of the Congress, has the right to decide when such a country has in fact been attacked, and then commit us to large-scale war?" Ninety-one percent answered with the formulation,

"No, Congress must first debate and decide if war is the needed action under the given conditions." Yet this, of course, was never done.

There is increasing evidence that Congress is becoming aware of the gravity of the problem of Executive usurpation of power, and is rousing itself to respond to what could become a mortal challenge to its constitutional powers and vital functions. [14] This is true not only of younger legislators whose political and moral orientation has been formed by the climate which followed upon the rejection and condemnation of "McCarthyism," but of veterans who had to get to the truth the hard way and began to fight for it as part of a tiny and precarious minority in the Congress. That minority now grows steadily, though some of its earliest and most courageous pathfinders, like Senators Morse and Gruening (who cast the only votes against the Tonkin Gulf Resolution, later rescinded by *unanimous* vote of the Senate) lost their seats to opponents more favorable to Administration policies at the time.

These are only a few examples of one aspect of the directly political struggle for peace that is going on within the present legal and constitutional framework of relations between executive powers and legislative powers. While there is evidence that the strengthening of peace measures and the inhibition of war measures are tied up, in the most direct and immediately effective way, with the recapture of constitutional powers usurped by the Executive, and their restoration to the legislative branch, the independent role of the people could become equally effective within the present structure. To cite but one possibility, there is no reason why the people, through a national plebiscite or poll, should not participate directly in the decision whether the country should go to war. Such a poll could be taken at the same time that the matter was being debated in Congress, and could be of great value to Congress in the process of coming to its own decision. In a democracy, what objection could there be to such a poll? Surely not the objection that the question is too technical for the people to decide. *Whether* to go to war is not a technical question; it is primarily a moral question, a question of whether what is at stake is worth the inevitable cost in human and other forms of life. The technical question is how to fight a war, not whether a war is worth fighting. In practically any local election nowadays the voters can find themselves asked to vote yes or no on Propositions concerning bond issues, state constitutional amendments, redistricting projects, and the like which are far more *technical* than the question whether we should enter into war. Since war is a game played by governments with the people's lives, it is the people who must have the right to say whether the game shall be played. If governments do not recognize this, it is also the people's right to say whether such governments shall remain standing.

NOTES

[1] The Pentagon papers, publication of which began in *The New York Times*, though the government wanted them to remain secret, revealed that Walt Rostow, as Chairman of the State Department's Policy Planning Council, had advised Secretary of State Dean Rusk on November 23, 1964, prior to the major escalation into systematic war, as follows: "Our most basic problem is, therefore, how to persuade them (the North Vietnamese) that a continuation of their present policy will risk major destruction in North Vietnam, and that Communist China will not be a sanctuary if it assists North Vietnam in counter-escalation." In other words, Rostow is saying that if, in our judgment, North Vietnam continued to aid the Viet Cong, we (the Executive, without asking the approval of Congress) should make major war against it, and if it should fight back ("counter-escalation"), and China should assist it in fighting back, we (again the Executive, without asking the approval of Congress) should not hesitate to take the same measures against China. Mr. Rostow shortly returns to this point with added emphasis: "Perhaps most important of all [is] the introduction into the Pacific Theatre of massive forces to deal with any escalatory response, including forces evidently aimed at China, as well as at North Vietnam, should the Chinese Communists enter the game." The reader will note that "escalatory response" means we would make the initial escalation. Thus Mr. Rostow was recommending war not only against North Vietnam, but against Communist China, and all this was being recommended less than three weeks after his chief, President Lyndon Johnson, had been elected on a no-war, no-escalation platform. In making these recommendations, Mr. Rostow shows that nuclear weapons played an important role in his thinking. Thus he expresses agreement with the proposition that, "Even if Hanoi and Peiping estimated that the U.S. would not use nuclear weapons against them, they could not be sure of this," and stresses that we must "enter the exercise with the same determination and staying power that we entered the long test on Berlin and the short test on the Cuba missiles." The "determination" in the Cuban missile crisis, as confirmed in Robert Kennedy's

account (see Chap. 1, n. 10), was to open World War III as a thermonuclear conflict, if necessary, in order to remove the Soviet missiles from Cuba. Quotations from "Memorandum from Mr. Rostow to Secretary Rusk, Nov. 23, 1964," which Mr. Rostow entitled, "Some Observations as We Come to the Crunch in Southeast Asia," in *The New York Times,* June 15, 1971, p. 19. *Pentagon Papers* (New York: Bantam Books, 1971), p. 419-423.

  [2]See Chap. 1, n. 10.

  [3]Ibid.

  [4]Ibid.

  [5]See Francis D. Wormuth, *The Vietnam War: The President Versus the Constitution* (Santa Barbara: Center for the Study of Democratic Institutions, 1968), Chap. I.

  [6]Ibid.

  [7]See Chap. 1, n. 2.

  [8]Wormuth, op. cit., Chap. I.

  [9]*The New York Times,* on p. 1 of its issue of June 14, 1971, which began publication of parts of the Pentagon Papers, says in Neil Sheehan's documented summary of the secret Pentagon study: "The Johnson Administration reached a 'general consensus' at a White House strategy meeting on Sept. 7, 1964, that air attacks against North Vietnam would probably have to be launched, a Pentagon study of the Vietnam war states. It was expected that 'these operations would begin early in the new year.' " These views of the top figures, Sheehan reports, quoting from the secret study, " 'were advanced with a sense that such actions were inevitable.' The Administration consensus on bombing came at the height of the Presidential election contest between President Johnson and Senator Barry Goldwater, whose advocacy of full-scale air attacks on North Vietnam had become a major issue. The consensus was reflected, the (Pentagon) analysis says, in the final paragraph of a formal national security action memorandum issued by the President three days later, on Sept. 10. This paragraph spoke of 'larger decisions' that might be 'required at any time.' " (*Pentagon Papers,* op. cit., p. 307). Nevertheless, in statements to the public and Congress, the Executive maintained, up to the time the large-scale air attacks actually took place, which was indeed early in the new year, that no such attacks were contemplated. To argue that this concealment and deception had to be carried out because it was necessary to prevent North Vietnam from having any advance warnings is to forget that North Vietnam had no way of knowing, any more than we ourselves, which of the two candidates would win the Presidency, and was already being thoroughly forewarned, by the explicit campaign platform of one of them, of the fact that they might be bombed. The gain was obviously not military, but political, in that Johnson was elected. But the fact that the people had overwhelm-

ingly rejected Goldwater's policy of escalated bombing, and chosen the opposite, did not deter Johnson from carrying out Goldwater's policy.

The same secrecy and deception were practiced in regard to the decision to enter into offensive ground warfare. Mr. Sheehan, continuing his documented summary of the secret Pentagon study, writes on Page 1 of *The New York Times* of June 15, 1971: "President Johnson decided on April 1, 1965, to use American ground troops for offensive action in South Vietnam because the Administration had discovered that its long-planned bombing of North Vietnam—which had just begun—was not going to stave off collapse in the South, the Pentagon's study of the Vietnam war discloses. He ordered that the decision be kept secret. 'The fact that this departure from a long-held policy had momentous implications was well recognized by the Administration leadership,' the Pentagon analyst writes, alluding to the policy axiom since the Korean conflict that another land war in Asia should be avoided. Although the President's decision was a 'pivotal' change, the study declares, 'Mr. Johnson was greatly concerned that the step should be given as little prominence as possible. The President's desire is that these movements and changes should be understood as being gradual and wholly consistent with existing policy.' " (Ibid., p. 382.) On page 22 of *The New York Times*, June 15, 1971, Sheehan returns to this point: "As a result of the President's wish to keep the shift of mission from defense to offense imperceptible to the public, the April 1 decision received no publicity 'until it crept out almost by accident in a State Department release on 8 June,' in the words of the Pentagon study. The study also says that two of the President's major moves involving the bombing campaign in the spring of 1965 were designed, among other aims, to quiet critics and obtain public support for the air war by striking a position of compromise. But in fact, the account goes on, the moves masked publicly unstated conditions for peace that 'were not "compromise" terms, but more akin to a "cease and desist" order that, from the D.R.V./VC point of view, was tantamount to a demand for their surrender.' D.R.V. denotes the Democratic Republic of Vietnam; VC the Vietcong." (Ibid., pp. 386-388.) The reader will note that these assertions and judgments about publicly unstated conditions which were tantamount to a demand for surrender are here made not by political enemies of the President or by critics of his policy, but by a team of Pentagon analysts directed by Secretary of Defense McNamara to make a detailed chronological record (which would then be "classified"). At this point, Mr. Sheehan reports, the record notes the contradictory aspect of the President's speech at the Johns Hopkins University on April 7 (the very time of the "publicly unstated conditions"), in which speech Johnson asserted to the American public, including the Congress, that his policy was one of offering to negotiate "without posing any preconditions." Sheehan further reports: "In public Administration statements on the air assaults, the study goes on, President Johnson broadened 'the reprisal concept as gradually and imperceptibly as possible' into sustained air raids against the North, in the same fashion that the analyst describes him blurring the shift from defensive to offensive action on the ground during the spring and summer of 1965.'' (Ibid., p. 388.) In regard to the basic motive for our entering into war, which was always presented to the public as our obligation to fulfill a commitment we had made to help South Vietnam, Mr. Sheehan reports in his *New York Times* account of June 14, 1971: ''Another memorandum to Mr. McNamara from Mr. NcNaughton, [Assistant Secretary of Defense] on Jan. 27, [1965] along with Mr. McNamara's penciled comments on it, 'adds perspective,' a Pentagon historian says. Mr. McNaughton stated, and Mr. McNamara agreed, 'that the United States objective in South Vietnam was 'not to ''help friend'' but to contain China,' and both favored initiating strikes against North Vietnam.' '' (Ibid., p. 342.) The reader will note that it was Mr. McNaughton who put the quotation marks around ''help friend.''   1971 © by the New York Times Company. Reprinted by permission.

[10]An official memorandum submitted by the State Department to the Senate Committee on Foreign Relations March 8, 1966, arguing that President Johnson was justified in making the decision for large-scale war against North Vietnam without the approval of Congress, said in part: ''In 1787 the world was a far larger place, and the framers [of the Constitution] probably had in mind attacks upon the United States. In the twentieth century the world has grown much smaller. An attack on a country far from our shores can impinge directly on the nation's security.'' Quoted in Wormuth, op. cit., p. 4.

[11]Ibid., p. 36, 37.

[12]Ibid., p. 37.

[13]John Somerville, ''The Relation of Morality and Law to Contemporary Youth Protests in the United States.'' Paper presented at VIIth World Congress of Sociology, Varna, 1970.

[14]The joint ''war powers'' resolution introduced by Senator Javits and Representative Zablocki which was passed in October 1973, vetoed by President Nixon, and passed over his veto in November 1973, represents a step, though not a strong one, in the right direction. It provides that the President cannot commit American forces to armed action abroad for more than sixty days without obtaining specific authorization from Congress. This does not squarely face either the constitutional issue or the practical problem. It suggests that the President has the right, under the Constitution, to *initiate* systematic war (as distinguished from replying with force to some sudden attack), but the Constitution gives him no right whatever to do this. In practical terms it overlooks the central problem, that is, once systematic war is initiated and escalated by the President (and this could be done within a day or two), everyone then feels an

obligation to ''support our boys who are being shot at,'' and the war which might have been rejected had Congress been given an opportunity to consider it in advance, as the Constitution requires, becomes reluctantly accepted and prolonged. This is exactly what happened in the American involvement in Vietnam. If, on the other hand, hostilities begin with a surprise attack upon us, the question of whether our immediate defensive action should be developed into systematic, large-scale war must, according to the Constitution, be laid before Congress for its decision immediately, rather than after sixty days. If the President is to be allowed to initiate systematic war at all, a respect for law and order demands that the Constitution first be amended. This is no mere procedural formality. What is at issue is life and death, the substantive question of who was given the power, in our system of government, to decide when the nation shall enter into war. Our Constitution deliberately and explicitly gives this power to the Congress. The President can recommend, but the Congress must decide.

3

The New Economics

THE GOOD GUYS AND THE BAD GUYS

Shortly after the U.S. Supreme Court decided that *The New York Times* could proceed with the publication of the Pentagon papers, there was a television interview with Dean Rusk, who had been Secretary of State under Presidents Kennedy and Johnson, and was one of the chief architects of the American government's war policy in Indochina. He was asked what he thought of it all now, as the month of July 1971 was beginning. In part of his answer he said that it was difficult for him to understand much that had happened within this country since he had left office. He expressed the possibility that it might be a new day, that people might have some other way out or that they might be content to live with certain things. But, he said, he was still very much worried about the future. Asked to explain what he meant, he said approximately the following, pieced together from the rough notes I made at the time:

Well, if we don't get peace, we just won't be able to survive. But in order to get peace, the people in certain capitals must be convinced that they can't get away with aggression. They've got to be convinced, when they think of making a move against their neighbors, that there may be certain consequences that they don't like, that something practical will be done about it. Now this doesn't mean that the United States is trying to be a world policeman. We didn't try to play such a role at all. There were hundreds of things happening all around that we didn't get involved in, but somebody's got to take action about some things. The United Nations wouldn't

51

take up this Vietnam problem. We went to the Secretary-General, and the Secretary General said he didn't think it was a problem for the United Nations. Well, then, who's going to convince people in certain capitals that they've got to leave their neighbors alone? It just might be, if they thought the United States was ready to do something about it, that there would be a little more assurance of peace in the future.

Mr. Rusk did not explain what criteria he, as Secretary of State, used in selecting the places in the world where he felt it necessary for the American government to undertake this ad hoc police work, but he stuck to his concept of the United States motive and role in Southeast Asia as those of the upright policeman. (My mind went back to a hearing before the Senate Committee on Foreign Relations in 1964, when Robert McNamara, then Secretary of Defense, and along with Mr. Rusk one of the very top policy-makers throughout the Kennedy and Johnson Administrations, was giving testimony as to why the United States had to be making such large-scale war in Vietnam. The questioning of critics like Senators Fulbright and Morse was very searching and persistent, and at one point Mr. McNamara burst out in an angry tone: *"Somebody's* got to police Southeast Asia."*) Nor did Mr. Rusk in his interview explain why North Vietnam or Communist China could have been expected to accept the jurisdiction of the United Nations in a matter so directly vital to their entire security, when they were not even allowed into membership in the organization. The American Secretary of State should have been the first to anticipate their feelings on this point, as it was mainly by the systematic efforts of the United States, which had never accorded diplomatic recognition to either power, that they were being kept out of the U.N. In any case, the rationale offered by Rusk for the American military intervention, in retrospect as well as at the time, was that of a volunteer policeman doing a public service.

Mr. McNamara often gave the impression of being a rather impatient man, with something of a hot temper. Mr. Rusk, on the other hand, invariably impressed one as being mild, gentle, and pious. Though both were highly educated and disciplined by experience to think in terms of law and world affairs, it apparently did not occur to either one that there was anything incongruous about the idea of a *government* moonlighting as a *volunteer* world policeman, in some sort of selective fashion. It apparently did not occur to them that this was a clear case of taking the law into their own hands, especially in view of the admitted fact that they had gone to the headquarters of the world organization, and had been told that this was not a matter that could be acted upon, especially not in the way of bringing force to bear, in the name of the United Nations. It was as if they, honest citizens, had gone to the Sheriff's office in their efforts to have the bad guys taken in hand, and had for no good reason been turned down by the Sheriff, and then had decided to do the job themselves.

One must not think that it is going too far to bring in the mores and morals of westerns in this connection. It is not impossible that they should play a part, consciously or unconsciously, in the thinking of top officials in the United States. At an especially important meeting of the Senate Committee on Foreign Relations, when General Maxwell Taylor was giving testimony about the increasingly massive American military operations and the mounting American casualties in Vietnam, and was being pressed by critical senators to explain and justify them, Senator Long of Louisiana came to the aid of the witness. ''I want to ask you just one question, General,'' he said. ''Who are the good guys and who are the bad guys out there?'' There was immediate laughter at this in the crowded hearing room, and the witness did not answer. But Senator Long was serious. He wanted to cut through all the technicalities, get right down to the root of the matter, and confront the decisive issue. He therefore persisted, and made his question more direct: ''General, isn't it true that we are the good guys?'' He seemed hurt by the repeated laughter, as Mr. Rusk seemed hurt in his later interview, at the fact that so many people in this country would not confront this most basic of all questions, this clear moral choice that had to be made, this choice from which everything else necessarily flowed.

Of course, as everyone knows, human psychology is very complex, the mind and feelings of the individual very mixed. Sincerity, like all virtues, is a matter of degree, and motives of very different kinds can function, side by side, consciously or unconsciously, in the same person or in a group of persons aiming at the same goal. In his day, President Eisenhower, though he refused to make presidential war, also regarded Southeast Asia as an area of great concern to the American future, an area where the American government should, as a matter of policy, take large-scale measures. On several occasions, he explained the causes and reasons basic to this policy, with much more public candor than was customary in the suceeding Administrations.

For example, in a speech reported in *The New York Times* on May 8, 1953, Eisenhower made a pregnant generalization:

> If we allow any section of the world that is vital to us because of what it provides through trade—the manganese, or uranium, or cobalt or anything that we need—if we allow any of those areas either to become so impoverished it cannot produce the things we need, or if we allow it to fall into a form of government inimical to us, that wants to see freedom abolished from the earth, then we have suffered indeed. It is in such simple facts as these, ladies and gentlemen, that the foreign policy is founded and established and maintained. There is nothing mysterious about it. All of this springs from the enlightened self-interest of the United States of America.

Indeed, there is no mystery in this; it is a very old idea, though very questionable morally and legally, especially if one professes to believe in the equal rights of all nations to sovereignty and self-determination. Something of the kind seems to have occurred to President Eisenhower, for he added, as if by afterthought, "But it does, fortunately for us, lead us into fields in which our whole moral selves are approved for the actions that we take for our collective security, strength and health. And so we have the satisfaction of the approval of our own conscience as we proceed along the cycle in this direction." However, what this afterthought really means does not come through the language with any high degree of clarity. For example, *whose* collective security, strength and health did he have in mind? In the light of the preceding statements it could hardly be *everybody's.* These statements assume a clash of interests: some country perhaps wants to hold on to something it owns but *we* need, or wants to trade with someone else rather than with *us,* or might tend towards a form of government that didn't have *our* kind of freedom. Why, in these circumstances, *our* interest should prevail, even though the resources belong to *their* country, and even though presumably the kind of government they have and their trade policy are *their* business, is not made explicit. Thus a gap is left as to just why our moral selves, our *consciences,* should approve all this. But there is one thing that would fill this gap perfectly, which perhaps is implicitly there already, perhaps considered so self-evident by Eisenhower that it was hardly necessary to spell it out. Is it not just that we *are* the good guys, and those others are either the bad guys or dupes of the bad guys, so that if we take anything away from them, or restrict them in any way, or make our will prevail among them, is that not necessarily good? And since good guys must have good consciences, must not our consciences approve these good things?

Implicit also in Eisenhower's thinking, as in that of Kennedy, Rusk, McNamara, Johnson, and apparently all the top policy-makers, was what might be called the negative identification axiom, again so self-evident as not to need constant mention: that the communists are the bad guys, proper objects of police action. Of course, the difficulty was always to square this with the equally primary axiom on which we claimed to base our foreign policy: that we support the principles of the United Nations (of which we are a founding member), because it is the only organization that brings all nations together, and gives them a framework within which they can negotiate and settle their problems on a basis of equal rights, irrespective of cultural, economic, or ideological differences. This guarantee of equal rights extends, of course, to communist governments, since they also were founding members and made sacrifices and contributions second to none in the victory over facism in World War II, as a consequence of which the United Nations was formed. It is clear that, as ways of gaining peace and a future for the world, one must choose between the United Nations idea and the good guys (capitalists)—bad guys (communists) idea. It is also clear which one our policy-makers really chose.

On August 4, 1953, President Eisenhower addressed the annual Governors' Conference, which was held in Seattle. Here he applied his generalization, with greater concreteness, to the area of Southeast Asia:

You don't know really why we are so concerned with the far-off southeast corner of Asia. Why is it? Now, first of all, the last great population remaining in Asia that has not become dominated by the Kremlin, of course, is the sub-continent of India, the Pakistanian Government.

Here are 150,000,000 people who are still free. Now let us
assume that we lose to Indo-China. If Indo-China goes, several
things happen right away. The peninsula, the last bit of land hanging
on down there, would be scarcely defensible, The tin and tungsten
that we so greatly value from that area would cease coming, but all
India would be outflanked. Burma would be in no position for
defense. All of that position around there is very ominous to the
United States because finally if we lost all that, how would the free
world hold the rich empire of Indonesia?

So you see, somewhere along the line, this must be blocked, and
it must be blocked now, and that's what we are trying to do. So when
the United States votes $400,000,000 to help that war we are not
voting a giveaway program. We are voting for the cheapest way we
can prevent the occurrence of something that would be of most
terrible significance to the United States of America, our security,
our power and ability to get certain things we need from the riches of
the Indonesian territory and from Southeast Asia.[1]

So it is the tin, tungsten, manganese, cobalt, uranium, and other such
resources of the Southeast portion of Asia that we *must* have; it is "the
rich empire of Indonesia" that we *must* hold. At the same time, it is
fortunate for Indochina and Indonesia that this somehow really coincides
with *their* freedom and *their* right of self-determination, equally fortunate
for us that "as we proceed along the cycle in this direction," we have
"the satisfaction of the approval of our own conscience." And the cost is
cheap, only $400 million for the time being, paid by the American
taxpayers to help the French government in its war against the In-
dochinese peoples who had the odd idea that they weren't free under
French control, even though France was part of the "free world."
President Eisenhower himself shrank from adding American lives to the
cost by way of presidential war. That step was taken by succeeding
administrations; to them nevertheless, the cost still seemed "cheap."

This is the very word used by Mr. McGeorge Bundy, one of the chief
policy-planners of the Kennedy and Johnson Administrations, who
served both Presidents as Special Assistant for National Security Affairs.
In a memorandum to President Johnson, February 7, 1965, favoring the

initiation of large-scale, continuous bombing of the North, which was begun shortly thereafter, Mr. Bundy wrote:

> We believe that the best available way of increasing our chance of success in Vietnam is the development and execution of a policy of sustained *reprisal* (Mr. Bundy's emphasis) against North Vietnam. . . . While we believe that the risks of such a policy are acceptable, we emphasize that its costs are real. It implies significant U.S. air losses even if no full air war is joined, and it seems likely that it would eventually require an extensive and costly effort against the whole air defense system of North Vietnam. U.S. casualties would be higher—and more visible to American feelings—than those sustained in the struggle in South Vietnam. Yet measured against the costs of defeat in Vietnam, the program seems cheap.[2]

What would the costs of defeat be? Asian communists might control Asian resources.

Mr. McNamara in his turn, though he did not usually demonstrate in public the degree of candor shown by President Eisenhower, went so far as to say in a speech March 26, 1965, in which he defended the massive escalation recommended by Bundy and undertaken by Johnson: "The third option before the President was initiation of military actions outside of South Vietnam, particularly against North Vietnam." Though this means *initiation* of deliberate acts of war by the President without gaining the prior approval of Congress as required by the Constitution, acts which would be bound to result in serious American casualties, Mr. McNamara made it plain that in his view the cost was justified because of what he called the "strategic danger" of communism in Southeast Asia. That is, Asian communists might control Asian resources. On this occasion Mr. McNamara forgot all about the upright policeman. In private, he even rejected the most frequently used argument of all: that we had made a commitment to our friend, South Vietnam. *The New York Times* of June 14, 1971, p. 32, quotes from the secret Pentagon memorandum of January 27, 1965, written by John McNaughton, Assistant Secretary of Defense, to his chief, Secretary of Defense Robert McNamara, and from the secret analysis and summary prepared by Pentagon personnel at the request of McNamara himself. The Pentagon analyst recorded that Mr. McNamara had made penciled comments on the memorandum. In it, Mr. McNaughton stated, "and Mr. McNamara agreed," that the United States objective in Vietnam was "not to 'help friend' but to contain China." Why must China be "contained," to the extent of not being allowed to have significant influence in a small country at her very doorstep, while we have significant influence and a large military presence in that very region, which is thousands of miles from our border? Because China is communist. What of that? Why, that's a danger to our whole strategy: we might lose control of all the valuable resources in the many smaller countries in that part of the world. Why should *we* have that control in *Asia?* Because we are the good guys who alone should control the good things, like tin, tungsten, manganese, cobalt, and uranium.

What it comes to, then, is an economic issue. In the eyes of our policy-makers, we don't need the territory as such, but we do need to be able to control the disposition of the resources. That is what Eisenhower's generalization, his doctrine of America's "enlightened self-interest," emphasized: that we would suffer ruinous consequences "if we allow any section of the world that is vital to us because of what it provides through trade—the manganese or uranium, or cobalt or anything else that we need—if we allow any of those areas either to become so impoverished that it cannot produce the things we need, *or if we allow it to fall into a form of government inimical to us.*" Eisenhower's candor shows that it would make no difference *how* such an "inimical" government might seem to give signs of coming into being—whether from external pressures or from the desires of the people internally—the grave threat to us would be the same. In fact, in a sense the threat to us would be greater if such a government really represented the will of the people, because it would then be all the stronger in its ability to resist our will.

SPHERES OF INFLUENCE AND EQUAL RIGHTS

To be serious about peace means we must confront the economic realities as they exist in the international arena and in our own country. There is a competition of economic systems now going on in the world at large, socialist-communist vs. capitalist, each side of which possesses state power and thermonuclear weapons, each side of which is made up of a group of states, each of which took part in founding the United Nations. In between there is a third group of states, much weaker militarily and industrially (though not weak in natural resources), trying not to become too closely aligned with either of the giant blocs. In the United States there exists a capitalist system that possesses the most powerful and productive industrial plant the world has ever seen. All this means that for the immediate future the problem of world peace is to find a set of arrangements within which the economic competition of the two giant blocs can go without resort to large-scale war. Under present conditions this objective could not be gained by either bloc trying to force the other to give up its economic system; the very effort to use this method would precipitate the kind of war we are trying to avoid. In the same way, for either side to act in practice as if the other were criminal and had no right to exist, would, if continued, be bound to make global war increasingly likely, and finally inevitable.

What, then, is the answer? What arrangements would simultaneously satisfy these requirements: (1) keep the competition between the two economic systems peaceful; (2) grant equal rights to the two systems to exist, compete, and expand? There are at least two types of arrangement capable of fulfilling these conditions. One is an agreement on what has historically been called ''spheres of influence.'' The other is an agreement that there shall be no spheres of influence, and at the same time no use of military force as an instrument of competition. The second is on a much higher moral level than the first, but much more difficult to practice. In fact, history shows no instance of the second, but affords many examples of the first. The first might stave off global war long enough for other forces to operate towards the adoption of arrangements on a higher level.

The point of most importance to world peace is that one policy or the other must consistently apply to and be applied by both sides. The most dangerous temptation, to which American foreign policy as a whole has yielded since World War II, is to assume the rights of the second policy for itself (freedom to penetrate all spheres), but to deny the same freedom to its giant opponent. In effect, we said to the Soviet Union: ''We have a right to have missile bases in Turkey, or in any other country that invites us, even though it may be very close to you, or, like Turkey, have a land border with you. But you cannot have missile bases in Cuba, even though Cuba invites you. Cuba is only ninety miles from our shores, and your bases there would constitute an intolerable threat to us." We said to China: "You must be contained; you must stay within your own borders. It is all right for us to put half a million ground troops and a continuously operating air force in South Vietnam, bombing and threatening North Vietnam, which has a land border with you. But we do not give you the right to provide similar aid for North Vietnam, even should she invite you; we would feel free to attack you if you tried.[3] We claim the right to put a protective fleet between you and Taiwan, because Taiwan invited us, and we are her friend. But we do not grant you the right to put a protective fleet between us and Cuba, even if Cuba should invite you, and you should be Cuba's friend."

It is clear that if American policy had followed the principle of equal rights among "superpowers" it would have said one of two things to the Soviet Union: either, "Turkey is in your sphere, and Cuba is in ours; we won't put missiles in Turkey, and you won't put missiles in Cuba," or, "Neither of us has a privileged sphere of influence, so neither of us will threaten or use force if the other forms a close alliance with a small power, wherever that power may be located." But we said neither. To the Soviet Union and China we said: "We claim the right to exclude your military presence from territory near us, but we grant you no right to exclude our military presence from territory equally near to you." This is clearly a double standard fraught with great danger, and there is no evidence that our official conception of "détente" recognizes the danger.

As one reads the historical record of American foreign policy since World War II, especially the text of the memoranda that passed between the chief policy-makers, there can be no doubt that one of the major causes of the American government adopting this policy of double standard was the fact that we, as leader of the capitalist bloc, were conscious, over-conscious, of the fact that this bloc had a preponderance of military and industrial power, compared with the communist bloc. That was the practical basis of the original policy of "containment" directed against the Soviet Union. But the Soviet Union would not stay contained, especially after World War II, and her acquisition of thermonuclear weapons, together with the industrial growth of the communist bloc, has progressively narrowed the power gap between the two blocs. No doubt our policy-makers are still convinced there is a preponderance in favor of the capitalist bloc, but it is now clear to everyone that the significance of that preponderance in relation to the issue of thermonuclear war has dwindled to the vanishing point. There is now a situation in which one bloc says to the other something like: "I can destroy you twelve times over," and the other, in reply, says something like, "Don't forget I can destroy you ten times over." Such a situation is no longer a basis for a policy relying on a preponderance of might. As far as the power ratio is concerned, it might as well be counted fifty-fifty, since total mutual destruction is possible. Any policy which relies upon this situation by way of using it as a threat in order to gain one's way over an opponent does not represent a reliance upon one's own superior might, but reliance only upon the superior intelligence and morality of one's opponent.

Spheres of influence, of course, exist as a fact, a very large and important fact, in the world today, and have existed in the world ever since there have been large and small powers along with competitive relations between large powers. Wherever large powers are in competitive relations with one another the small powers that are situated close to a large power inevitably have their freedom of action curtailed in many ways. The big powers always reason that in case of any conflict they have more to lose than their small neighbors have; that, in defending themselves, they must, to a degree, also defend their small neighbors, who represent close stepping stones to themselves, and thus make themselves vulnerable. Hence, the normal attitude of large powers toward neighboring small powers has been paternalistic, not democratic or egalitarian, even when they are joined by the closest ties of religion or ideology. From the point of view of human rights, a small country has as much right as a large country to go its own way and choose its own friends; and this might be the case in practice, if politics had nothing to do with economics. But one thing that all the policy-makers on both sides agree upon is that politics has a great deal to do with economics. To any big power in the world today, regardless of its ideology, a small power in its immediate neighborhood in close alliance with a second big power hostile to the first represents a prime danger. At the same time small countries naturally want to enjoy freedom of choice and independence of judgment, so that they seek ways of resisting or reducing the control exercised by their big neighbor, though they must always reckon with the Damoclean sword under which they live.

The moral problem of creating an international political arrangement which would be more just to small countries, and the moral problem of developing an economic system that would not set big powers in all-out competitive struggle against one another, are long-run problems. When they are solved, spheres of influence of the kind we are discussing will no longer exist. The main problem is to get from the now, when they do exist, to the then, when they will not exist. That is the problem of the short run. If we cannot solve it, there will be no long run at all. In other words, the peace we need for survival, and for getting to a better world, must be sought and found first within the competitive world where spheres of influence already play a major role. To think of solving the problem of spheres of influence first, by some method outside the bounds of peace between big powers (one ''super-power'' subduing the other by military force, thus making it submit economically), and then, after that, solving the peace problem, is to forget there would be no one left to solve the problem or enjoy the solution. What must be insisted upon by all people is that governments, especially those of the major powers, should come to some agreement about spheres of influence in order to keep the competition between the economic systems a peaceful competition. This does not mean that the arrangement would be that the United States, for example, agrees that, as far as she is concerned, the Soviet Union can have a free hand in Turkey in exchange for the United States having a free hand in Cuba. Rather it would mean that neither major power would object to the other having the same kind of relations with small powers that it has, assuming, of course, that the relations in question are acceptable to the small powers concerned.

THE PROFITS OF WAR

The economic factor powerfully influences the peace problem not only in relation to the international competition of opposing economic systems, but in relation to the operation of economic forces within the national community to the extent that war, or preparation for war, can be a source of financial profit to individuals or groups within that community. This is sometimes forgotten by writers who are otherwise most realistic and eloquent in their opposition to war. For example, Risieri Frondizi in one of his papers wrote: ''According to responsible authors, billions of dollars are wasted on Vietnam each month. The figure is higher than all the profits that all the American companies could possibly gain in that area. The war does not have an economic objective; it has an ideological objective. Money is not sought in Vietnam: it is thrown away.''[4] Frondizi is reasoning as if it were simply *money* as such that the American nation was somehow giving to South Vietnam, money which was then wasted in unproductive and destructive ways. The ways are indeed unproductive and destructive in the extreme, but what is given, economically, to be thus wasted and destroyed, leaving lives out of the reckoning for the moment, is mainly products: military weapons and equipment of all varieties, for use on land, sea, and in the air, together with all the civilian equipment necessary to serve the military operations. It is the American government which gave all these things and continued to give them after the ''peace agreements'' were signed. However, the point is that under the present economic arrangements, the government gets these things by using money obtained through taxing the whole nation in order to *buy* them from the industrial concerns which produce them. These concerns are owned by a tiny fraction of the American people, but their profits are truly enormous. From the economic point of view of these owners, the more these products are wasted in Vietnam, the bigger are the profits of the business, just as if some billionaire were wasteful with the private planes and yachts he bought, sinking them or blowing them up by the hundreds. He would be throwing *his* money away, but the producing companies would thereby be making money, in direct proportion. In Vietnam, the government is throwing away the *taxpayers'* money, but the giant companies are thereby making money, in direct proportion. Economically the companies cannot lose, as long as the physical destructiveness does not reach *their* plants and raw materials. Of course, the government has the legal power to take over all military production and put it all on a non-profit basis, but it does not do that. Thus wars have been immensely profitable, economically, to certain groups, and the Vietnam War was no exception. This is an old story, confirmed increasingly in ever-renewed detail.[5]

Indeed, it is not only the owning groups which reap financial benefits from wars and preparation for wars. Wage workers of all kinds have always found lucrative employment in the "defense" sector of the economy. In any case, there can be no doubt about the fact that this sector always has been and now is a very significant part of the economic picture. Not that the profit economy needs *full* employment to operate "normally"; times are considered normal if the rate of unemployment is as high as five percent. As the rate rises between five and ten percent, signs of trouble and danger multiply. If it is not checked, disaster ensues, and if recession becomes depression, who can be sure that he will not "go under"? Thus, the huge "defense contracts" are eagerly welcomed, not only for the unusually high rates of profit, often accompanied by guarantees, which they afford the owners, but for the jobs they afford the workers.

It is not unusual to find labor unions protesting the closing down or relocation of defense plants, navy yards, and other military production centers. Congress itself joins in this kind of protest, not without irony. During the Johnson escalation of the Vietnam War, it happened on some occasions that the Department of Defense, in deciding how best to supply its logistic needs, ceased certain kinds of military production, and closed or relocated certain facilities without consulting the labor unions in advance. The unions brought pressure to bear upon Congress, which took up the matter with the Executive branch, and obtained an understanding that in future, advance notice would be given of projected large-scale changes of this kind, along with the reasons necessitating them, so that they could be discussed beforehand. Thus Congress, which never moved itself sufficiently to obtain from the Executive branch an understanding that that branch would give it advance notice before initiating deliberate acts of war, so that Congress could decide, as the Constitution requires, whether the reasons, as put forward by the Executive, were strong enough to warrant war, nevertheless found the spirit to insist on its role when the continuity of war *production* seemed threatened.

One is not saying that Frondizi was wrong when he asserted the Vietnam War had an ideological objective. What was wrong was to think that the ideological objective excluded the economic objective. In other words, economics is a very important part of ideology, especially so since World War II. The connection of this general fact with our present discussion is well brought out by a speech which Dwight Eisenhower delivered before the jointly assembled houses of Congress in 1951, not long before he was elected to the Presidency. It is worth recalling because it is a perfect reflection of ideas basic not only to the policies of his administration, but to those of all succeeding administrations to date. He said:

> As I start this talk, I think it would be well to establish a certain platform of understanding. Let us make certain assumptions. Now the first I have already made, that the members of Congress here assembled and I have one object in view—the good of the United States. The next thing that I would like to make as an assumption is that we are concerned not only with the protection of territory, of rights, of privileges; we are concerned with the defense of a way of life, and that our own way of life has certain factors that must persist if that way of life is to persist. For example, there is the freedom of the individual, his political freedom, his freedom of worship, and that he will have an economy based upon free enterprise.[6]

Thus the ideological assumptions include, as an integral part, the economic system of capitalism, and calling it "free enterprise" seems to bind it eternally and necessarily to the concepts of individual, political, and religious freedom. I take the liberty of quoting here from what I wrote about this shortly after Eisenhower delivered his speech:

> But is it not clear that the very meaning of this freedom is that we cannot rigidly bind the American nation to any one economic system in perpetuity? I believe that Eisenhower would not fail to admit, were he to address himself specifically to this aspect of the matter, that the principle of the American way of life is that the people as a whole have the right to choose what their economic system shall be; and if, by any chance, their considered desire should be to change from their present economic system to any other, they would be following precisely the American way of life by putting the will of the people into effect. If anyone were to deny such a right to the American people, how could he possibly claim he was giving them freedom of choice as individuals, or as political groups?[7]

Speaking of the Western nations and the NATO treaty, Eisenhower added:

> But far beyond any considerations of sentiment in this job of protecting ourselves, we must look at what are the common factors of fact that bind us in our faith with them, since that is the basic assumption of the NATO Organization. First of all, in Western Europe exists the greatest pool of skilled labor in the world. In Western Europe exists a great industrial capacity, second . . . only to that of the United States. But the significance of that Western European group of nations to us is even greater than that. They have with many areas of the world close blood and political and economic ties. It is scarcely possible to imagine the fall of Western Europe to Communism without the simultaneous fall of certain of these great areas, particularly those and first those areas which have a political dependency upon the European power. We would be cut off, in short, from areas from which we draw the materials that are essential to our existence, our way of life. No matter how strong we would be in keeping open routes of communication, we must always keep open, clearly we must always keep open, the areas, keep them friendly to us when we need their trade. Take such items as manganese, copper, uranium. Could we possibly think of existing without access to them?

Eisenhower answers his own question in this blunt fashion: ". . . standing alone and isolated in a world otherwise completely dominated by Communism, our system would have to wither away. We would suffer economic atrophy and then finally collapse."

Not only economics, but a particular kind of economics is evidently central in these ideas. How could we think of existing without access to manganese, copper, uranium? More precisely, *other people's* manganese, copper, uranium, etc., because, of course, we have a certain amount of such natural resources of our own. If we allowed the people who own them to close their doors to us, we would atrophy and collapse. Hence, we just cannot allow that. In this context it is especially odd to call this system "free" enterprise. Precisely what it is not prepared to grant in the international arena is free competition based upon equal rights for the competitors, and acceptance of the results by all. One sometimes hears the capitalist system described as one in which the competitor who takes part "is not afraid to lose." It would appear that this applies only to the individuals within the system, not to the system itself.

THE ECONOMICS OF PEACE

The capitalist economic system has been classically pictured as one which affords scope for the individual by breaking down traditional restrictions inherited from feudalism, and stimulating his initiative by allowing him to enter, to the extent of his ability and resources, into all forms of economic competition. Historically, there was, of course, validity in this claim in behalf of the individual. Capitalism meant a liberation from the yoke of paternalism and of serfdom, and a great increase in the productivity of human labor. The increased quantity and new quality of the competition which it created were needed, and had socially progressive effects. There is no way to judge human progress save by comparing a later stage with an earlier stage.

But this very relativity, which alone makes possible the concept of progress, equally makes impossible a perpetual retention of the progressive quality originally attaching to any one social concept. To the extent that there were open economic frontiers, and to the extent that opportunities were open to all to enter competitively into them, the competition had positive value. But as the frontiers disappeared, as the technology of production became more massive and complex, the degree of equality of opportunity to compete decreased in proportion, while the pressure to compete continued to increase. The result was that the economic competition became less and less healthy in the life of the individual, less and less progressive in the development of society. The competition increasingly assumed two forms, both of negative import: one in which the victory of the winner meant ruination to the loser, and one in which the means of competition were of such magnitude as to make competition absurd and counter-productive.

What increasingly repels the youth in the economic competition that has developed under capitalism is the fact that it has too much about it that is humanly destructive, that prevents the competitors from treating one another as human beings, within the terms of the competition. If you are competing in the mile run or the high jump, the better you perform, the more you help the others to develop themselves. Of course, all cannot win the first prize, but *all* can be improved. Those who lose are not thereby deprived of any of their athletic resources as the economic losers are of their economic resources. Nor does the victory of those who win place the losers under their control in athletics, as it does in capitalist economics. Thus capitalism tends to make civil life a form of war rather than a mutually beneficial competition.

Looking at their elders, the youth seem increasingly to come to the conclusion that the rules of their inherited economic game have prevented these elders, to a fatal extent, from treating one another with genuine kindness and brotherly love, while at the same time the inherited religion of the elders professes to put the practice of genuine kindness and brotherly love at the very center of human life. If one owns a factory employing a hundred workmen and orders have fallen off 35 percent, it is clear that one could not continue to make a profit if one continued to pay the wages of the hundred workmen while at the same time one could sell only 65 percent of the products they turn out. If one tries to stay in business but continues to lose money, one goes bankrupt. Within the rules of the capitalist game one has no choice but to fire thirty-five workers. Even if there is some provision for unemployment insurance or welfare relief, their lives and those of their families may suffer grievous disruption. If they come to the employer and put the case on human grounds, he can only reply to them: "I feel kindness and love for you, but I must make a profit, or I cannot stay in business." To those of the thirty-five who can no longer keep up the payments on their homes, their cars, their furniture, or anything else, a like reply must be given by the banker, the finance company, the insurance company, utilities concerns, and so on. All this will be done politely, but firmly. Indeed, the church itself may share ownership in these industrial enterprises, on the financial returns from investments in which the church may depend for a considerable portion of its necessary expenses. In this case the church takes part in the decision to disemploy the workers. Thus the economics is not cut to the demands of the religion; the religion is cut to the demands of the economics. When the rules of the two games conflict, it is understood that those of economics will take precedence, especially when the stakes are high. The process has a vast, impersonal fatalism in which human individuality is dissolved and human compassion evaporates.

The consciousness of this situation, either felt directly by the youth in their own lives or candidly observed in the lives of others, together with its effects in the area of international relations, is the reason that a preference for a socialist rather than a capitalist economic order is almost an axiom of the youth in their rebellion. They feel strongly that the inhumanity and hypocrisy at home and the policy of war abroad could be greatly alleviated, if not entirely prevented, by an economic order which did not operate on the basis of the private profit motive, in which the economic security and continuity of employment of the great majority did not depend upon its being economically profitable to a small minority.

Perhaps the most dangerous consequences of the private profit motive for mankind as a whole become manifest when it operates in the international arena. Here, the most precious natural resources to be found in one country can become owned or economically controlled by a small group of people in another country. As legal slavery made individual human beings into objects of sale in the market place, legal capitalism makes the natural resources of whole countries objects of sale in the investment market. As governments in the days of slavery had the duty to protect and enforce the legal rights of slave owners, so capitalist governments today have the duty to protect and enforce the legal rights of their citizens who own big property in foreign countries. Two kinds of wars have repeatedly arisen in connection with these conditions: original wars of conquest waged by the powerful against the weak countries, and trade wars waged by powerful countries against one another for control of the natural resources and markets of the weaker countries. As we have seen, what Eisenhower explained as the basis of American foreign policy in Southeast Asia—the necessity of controlling its rich natural resources—gave rise, in the Kennedy Administration, to a policy of overall military "advisers," and in the Johnson and Nixon Administrations to a policy of large-scale war, escalated and expanded. As the philosophical justification of slavery (e.g., in Plato and Aristotle) could never rise above the level of the principle that we must make sure that the right people are in the slave class (those allegedly without the potential of higher intellectual activity) and that the right people are in the master class (those who have this potential),[8] so also the philosophical justification of capitalist economic imperialism (e.g., in Eisenhower and his successors) could never rise above the level of the principle that the good guys must be in control because allegedly they alone believe in freedom. Moreover, just as Plato and Aristotle considered that the interests of the slave and the master were the same, since the slave was incapable of managing his own life, and therefore his only chance was to live in obedience to a wise master, so also Eisenhower and his successors considered that the interests of Southeast Asia and the USA were the same, since Southeast Asia was incapable of managing its own resources, and therefore its only chance was to live under the guidance of the good guys who believe in freedom and "free enterprise" for themselves.

What can the elders reply to all this? What they usually say is that life has always been like that, and no matter what new system you try to set up, you will get back to the same old problems: in any case, it would be hopeless to try to fight a system as strong as the present one. In increasing numbers, the youth find such arguments unconvincing—lacking in imagination, sensitivity, and historical perspective. Like Ivan in *The Brothers Karamazov*, they feel that if this is the best show that can be put on, they would like to return the ticket. In any case, they mean to find out for themselves, for they understand something that Ivan could not even grapple with, because it did not exist in his time: that the continuation of the old show can only end in the annihilation of the whole human audience.

NOTES

[1] *The New York Times,* August 5, 1953.

[2] *The New York Times,* June 14, 1971, p. 19.

[3] See Chap. 2, n. 1. In announcing his naval-mine blockade of North Vietnam, May 8, 1972, President Nixon explained on national television that it was undertaken to prevent both the Soviet Union and the People's Republic of China from supplying weapons to North Vietnam. He addressed this part of his remarks directly to those two major powers by name.

[4] Robert Ginsberg, ed., *The Critique of War: Contemporary Philosophical Explorations* (Chicago: Regnery, 1969), p. 87-88.

[5] See George Thayer, *The War Business: The International Trade in Armaments* (New York: Simon and Schuster), 1969.

[6]John Somerville, *The Philosophy of Peace,* revised edition (New York: Liberty Press, 1954), p. 258-259.

[7]Ibid., p. 259-260.

[8]Cf. Aristotle, *Politics,* Book I, Chapter 2, and Plato, *Republic,* Book V. *Dialogues of Plato* (New York: Random House, 1937), Vol. 1, p. 732.

4

The New Morality

THEORY AND PRACTICE

In human life there have always been two moralities—the one people dream about and the one they practice. Though the word "moralist" has a negative sound, no one can escape the role. Everyone is a moralist as long as he goes on living, because his actions (and inactions) speak his morality louder than words. These actions and inactions reveal the system of values which the individual is practicing, but they may reveal only dimly or not at all the system of values he would like to practice. Psychologically, all human beings share the ability to feel the emotional attraction of experiences like love, power, sensual pleasure, self-discipline, creativity, honor, prestige, happiness. Historically, people are conditioned by different social systems, different sets of functioning institutions, to place different mental (theoretical) evaluations on these different experiences, and also in actual fact, in their outward behavior, to place them in a certain order of emphasis and priority.

However, this two-pronged historical fact does not mean that the two orders of moral priority conditioned into the individual by the given social system—the order taught in theory, and the order practiced in fact by the system itself—are necessarily the same. If they were, everything would be much simpler for the individual. That is, the massive problem of hypocrisy—the curse of all morality—would be reduced to more manageable proportions if the individual had only his own hypocrisy to contend with. But history shows and contemporary life confirms that the same kind of gap between theory and practice can arise from the side of the system taken as a whole. That is, the social system can be teaching the individual, on the plane of theory, that certain moral principles are obligatory, while it, itself, is systematically, through deliberately constructed institutions, violating those principles in practice. Thus it can teach, by its own deed, the opposite of what it is teaching by word.

This is in fact the situation that so clearly exists throughout the world today. Religions and schools almost everywhere preach and teach the morality of love, while at the same time they cooperate mightily with the state in practicing the morality of power. While verbally teaching the individual to respect the commandment, "Thou shalt not kill," they are at the very same time assisting in the systematic training and preparation of millions of individuals to kill millions of other individuals. With equal intensity and energy, they teach the individual to love his enemy and to destroy him. They condemn the constant pursuit of wealth, yet are themselves constantly pursuing it. They extol honesty but demand conformity, praise humility but practice pride. They preach and teach brotherhood endlessly in racially and economically segregated churches and schools.

The new morality that appeared in the contemporary youth rebellion and peace movement was a rediscovery of the morality of love and humanism. It was also a new consciousness of the fact that the morality that counts is the one that is practiced. For youth to *want* to practice the morality of love is not new. What is new is the degree of awareness of what stands in the way, and the degree of determination to remove the obstacles.

THE MORALITY OF NON-VIOLENCE: GANDHI

One strong tendency in the movement takes its stand on the principle that the morality of love demands a life of complete non-violence. One might think of this stance as Christian, but most of those who take it trace it to Gandhi or Buddhist philosophers, perhaps because they associate Christianity with the practices of the church, and the practices of the church with fatal compromises on the issue of violence. In his turn, Gandhi, who was by upbringing a Hindu, mentions his great debt to a Russian, Tolstoy, while Tolstoy expresses like admiration for an American clergyman, Adin Ballou, unknown and unsung in his own country, while another American clergyman, Martin Luther King, Jr., assassinated in his own country, acknowledged that he was led to this philosophy, not by his Christian teachers, but by Gandhi, likewise assassinated by a fellow-countryman. Verily, a prophet is not without honor save in his own country.

What Gandhi did was to unite the morality of love with revolutionary politics. The result is the strategy of non-violent civil disobedience. This is a form of moral force, not physical coercion; it is not violence because it does not inflict injury or death. It can be used not only against the unjust laws of a state, but against any unjust agency or person, and any form of injustice. Gandhi called this morality "Satyagraha," which, he wrote, "is literally, holding on to truth, and it means, therefore, Truth-force. Truth is soul or spirit. It is, therefore, known as Soul-force. It excludes the use of violence because man is not capable of knowing the absolute truth and, therefore, not competent to punish. . . . I have also called it Love-force. . . ."[1]

Behind this strategy there is a psychological principle. "I discovered in the earliest stages," says Gandhi, "that pursuit of truth did not admit of violence being inflicted on one's opponent but that he must be weaned from error by patience and sympathy. For what appears to be truth to the one may appear to be error to the other. And patience means self-suffering. So the doctrine came to mean vindication of truth not by infliction of suffering on the opponent but on one's self."[2] In relation to the state, this means "inviting the penalty for the breach of the law."[3] Gandhi showed how this could work in India, and Martin Luther King showed how it could work in the American South. It was, in fact, the first strategy that did work in either place. It took many forms, all deriving from the premise that the government wants something from the governed which it cannot obtain without the cooperation of the governed. The different forms are therefore different kinds of non-cooperation; boycotts, sit-ins, sit-downs, non-violent breaking of laws which cannot in conscience be obeyed, followed by voluntary acceptance of the penalty. Voluntary acceptance of suffering cannot fail to influence others, including those inflicting the suffering.

Does this turn people into habitual criminals? Does it destroy respect for law and order? Gandhi answers in the negative, pointing to some important distinctions which are ignored by practically all critics of civil disobedience:

The lawbreaker breaks the law surreptitiously and tries to avoid the penalty, not so the civil resistor. He ever obeys the laws of the state to which he belongs, not out of fear of the sanctions, but because he considers them to be good for the welfare of the society. But there come occasions, generally rare, when he considers certain laws to be so unjust as to render obedience to them a dishonor. He then openly and civilly breaks them and quietly suffers the penalty for their breach.[4]

The civil disobedient is actually respecting and accepting the authority of the law, says Gandhi. But how can that be possible, since by definition he is breaking the law? Doesn't his claim, then, amount to a paradox? It is paradoxical, but valid, because the law itself is paradoxical, in that it provides the penalty for its own breach. He who does not try to evade that penalty, but voluntarily accepts it is thereby accepting and respecting the final authority of the law. This is qualitatively different from the case of the bank robber, with which it is so often compared, and does not constitute *per se* a breakdown of law and order, as is so often charged. It is not the physical authority of the law that is challenged, but its moral content, and that is done non-violently.

Gandhi puts the case in these terms:

A man who has realized his manhood, who fears only God, will fear no one else. Man-made laws are not necessarily binding on him. Even the Government does not expect any such thing from us. They do not say: 'You must do such and such a thing,' but they say: 'If you do not do it, we will punish you.' We are sunk so low that we fancy that it is our duty and our religion to do what the law lays down. If a man will only realize that it is unmanly to obey laws that are unjust, no man's tyranny will enslave him. . . . So long as the superstition that men should obey unjust laws exists, so long will their slavery exist.[5]

This primacy of conscience is what Gandhi shares with Thoreau, who, he remarks, "has left a masterly treatise on the duty of Civil Disobedience,"[6] and whom he credits with coining the term itself. Thoreau put it very bluntly: "Must the citizen ever for a moment, or in the least degree, resign his conscience to the legislator? Why has every man a conscience, then? I think that we should be men first, and subjects afterward. It is not desirable to cultivate a respect for the law, so much as for the right. The only obligation which I have a right to assume, is to do at any time what I think right.'''[7] In other words, for the individual, the only moral absolute is conscience. The law must be respected when it deserves respect, but the individual must not obey it when that would violate his deepest sense of right. When his conscience and the law are in conflict, he should understand that if he chooses his conscience, he will be punished by the law; but he should also understand that if he chooses the law, he is committing moral suicide as a human individual.

Thoreau had the courage to apply his principle to his own conduct, and to the situation which confronted him. In a passage which expresses with uncanny fidelity the attitude and reasoning so evident in the contemporary rebellion, Thoreau wrote:

How does it become a man to behave toward this American government today? I answer that he cannot without disgrace be associated with it. I cannot for an instant recognize that political organization as *my* government which is the *slave's* government also.

All men recognize the right of revolution; that is, the right to refuse allegiance to and to resist the government, when its tyranny or its inefficiency are great and unendurable. But almost all say that such is not the case now. But such was the case, they think, in the Revolution of '75. If one were to tell me that this was a bad government because it taxed certain foreign commodities brought to its ports, it is most probable that I should not make an ado about it, for I can do without them: all machines have their friction; and possibly this does enough good to counterbalance the evil. At any rate it is a great evil to make a stir about it. But when the friction comes to have its machine, and oppression and robbery are organized, I say, let us not have such a machine any longer. In other words, when a sixth of the population of a nation which has undertaken to be the refuge of liberty are slaves, and a whole country is unjustly overrun and conquered by a foreign army, and subjected to military law, I think that it is not too soon for honest men to rebel and revolutionize. What makes this duty the more urgent is the fact, that the country so overrun is not our own, but ours is the invading army.[8]

Thoreau is, of course, here referring to the war of 1846 against Mexico, and what makes the aptness of his point to the present situation even more uncanny is the fact that this conflict, like the American government's war in Vietnam, was a presidential war, deliberately initiated by the Executive (Polk) without gaining the authorization of Congress in advance, then justified before Congress and the people by statements of the Executive which Congress later discovered to have been deceptive. Shortly before the termination of the conflict, the House of Representatives passed a resolution, quoted earlier, that the war had been "unnecessarily and unconstitutionally begun by the President of the United States." [9] Thus Thoreau, on the first page of his essay, wrote: "Witness the present Mexican war, the work of comparatively few individuals using the standing government as their tool; for in the outset, the people would not have consented to this measure." [10]

Although Thoreau's form of protest against slavery and the Mexican war was the non-violent act of refusing to pay his tax, for which he quietly accepted a jail sentence, he also defended violent revolution, as in his statements about the right of revolution, quoted above, and in his "A Plea for Captain John Brown." Referring to Brown, he said: "It was his peculiar doctrine that a man has a perfect right to interfere by force with the slave-holder, in order to rescue the slave. I agree with him. I think that for once the Sharpe's rifles and the revolvers were employed in a righteous cause." [11]

THE AMERICAN TRADITION OF NON-VIOLENCE AND CIVIL DISOBEDIENCE

The most remarkable American expression of the morality of complete non-violence, together with its application to politics, is found in the work of Reverend Adin Ballou, who was "discovered" by Leo Tolstoy, himself in his later period a consistent champion of non-violence. In the years when he was devoting himself to the working out of his ideas on morality, Tolstoy became interested in the views of William Lloyd

Garrison, and entered into correspondence with Garrison's son, who sent Tolstoy a very important document written by the elder Garrison against war: "Declaration of Sentiments Adopted by the Peace Convention Held in Boston, September 18, 19 and 20, 1838."[12] Tolstoy was amazed that this was not known in Europe, or even in America, to any significant extent. He was even more amazed to learn about Ballou. Tolstoy wrote:

> A similar fate befell another American champion of the same doctrine, Adin Ballou. How little is known may be gathered from the fact that the younger Garrison (who has written an excellent biography of his father in four large volumes), in answer to my inquiry . . . wrote me that, so far as he knew, the society had dissolved and its members were no longer interested, while at this very time Adin Ballou, who had shared Garrison's labors, and who had devoted fifty years of his life to the teaching of the doctrine of non-resistance, both by pen and tongue, was still living in Hopedale, Massachusetts. . . . I wrote to him, and he sent me his works.[13]

In one of them Ballou enters into the mind of the average "Christian" and reproduces his manner of thinking:

> Jesus Christ is my Lord and Master. I have convenanted to forsake all and follow Him, through good and evil report, unto death. But I am nevertheless a Democratic Republican citizen of the United States, implicitly sworn to bear true allegiance to my country, and to support its constitution, if need be, with my life. Jesus Christ requires me to do unto others as I would that others should do unto me. The Constitution of the United States requires me to do unto twenty-seven hundred thousand slaves the very contrary of what I would have them do unto me—viz., assist to keep in a grievous bondage. . . . But I am quite easy. I vote on. I help govern on. I am willing to hold any office I may be elected to serve under the Constitution. And I am still a Christian. I profess on. . . . Jesus Christ forbids me to resist evil-doers by taking "eye for eye, tooth for tooth, blood and life for life." My government requires the very reverse, and depends, for its own self-preservation, on the halter,

the musket and the sword, seasonably employed against its domestic and foreign enemies. In the maintenance and use of this expensive, life-destroying apparatus we can exemplify the virtues of *forgiving our injuries, loving our enemies, blessing them that curse us, and doing good to those that hate us.* For this very reason we have regular Christian chaplains to pray for us and call down the smiles of God on our holy murders.[14]

A "Catechism" of Ballou, evidently compiled for the use of his congregation, reads as follows:

Q.   Whence comes the word non-resistance?

A.   From the utterance: "But I say unto you, That ye resist not evil." Matthew v. 39.

Q.   What does this word denote?

A.   It denotes a lofty Christian virtue, commanded by Christ.

Q.   Are we to understand the word non-resistance in its broad sense, that is, as meaning that one should offer no resistance to evil whatsoever?

A.   No; it should be understood literally as Christ taught it—that is, not to return evil for evil. Evil should be resisted by all lawful means, but not by evil.

Q.   From what does it appear that Christ gave that meaning to non-resistance?

A.   From the words which he used on that occasion. He said: "Ye have heard that it hath been said, An eye for an eye and a tooth for a tooth. But I say unto you, That ye resist not evil: but whosoever shall smite thee on thy right cheek, turn to him the other also. And if any man shall sue thee at the law, and take away thy coat, let him have thy cloke also."

Q.   Whom did he mean by the words: "Ye have heard that it hath been said?"

A.   The patriarchs and the prophets, and that which they spoke and is contained in the Old Testament, that the Jews generally call the Law and the Prophets.

Q.   To what laws did Christ allude in the words: "Ye have heard?"

A.   To those in which Noah, Moses and other prophets grant the use of personal violence against those who commit it for the purpose of punishing and destroying evil deeds.

Q.   Mention such commandments.

A.   "Who so sheddeth man's blood, by man shall his blood be shed."—Genesis ix. 6.

"He that smiteth a man, so that he die, shall be surely put to death. And if any mischief follow, then thou shalt give life for life, eye for eye, tooth for tooth, hand for hand, foot for foot, burning for burning, wound for wound, stripe for stripe."—Exodus xxi. 12, 23, 24, 25.

"And he that killeth any man shall surely be put to death. And if a man cause a blemish in his neighbor; as he hath done, so it shall be done to him; breach for breach, eye for eye, tooth for tooth."—Leviticus xxiv. 17, 19, 20.

"And the judges shall make diligent inquisition: and, behold, if the witness be a false witness and hath testified falsely against his brother; then shall ye do unto him, as he had thought to have done unto his brother. And thine eye shall not pity: but life shall go for life, eye for eye, tooth for tooth, hand for hand, foot for foot." Deuteronomy xix. 18, 19, 21.

These are the injunctions of which Jesus speaks.

Noah, Moses and the Prophets taught that he who murders, mutilates or tortures his neighbor doeth evil. In order to combat and destroy this evil, the evil-doer must be chastised by death, mutilation, and some personal torture. Transgressions are to be avenged by transgressions, murder by murder, torture by torture, evil by evil. Thus taught Noah, Moses and the prophets. But Christ forbids all this. The gospel says: "I say unto you, resist ye not evil, avenge not one transgression by another, but rather bear a repetition of the offense from the evil-doer." That which has been allowed is now forbidden. Having understood what resistance we have been taught, we know exactly what Christ meant by non-resistance.[15]

Tolstoy makes a summary comment:

In August of 1890 Ballou died, and his obituary appeared in the

American Religio-Philosophical Journal of August 23. From this obituary we learn that Ballou was the spiritual leader of a community, that he had preached from 8,000 to 9,000 sermons, married 1,000 couples, and written 500 articles, but in regard to the object of his life's devotion not a word is said: the word "non-resistance" is never mentioned. . . . [there is] a wall of silence.[16]

No doubt those who erected "the wall of silence" to which Tolstoy refers felt that this was the best thing to do from motives of "patriotism." From this viewpoint, love of country becomes equated with "my country, right or wrong," which becomes equated with *obeying* the country in whatever it orders. The *country* in turn, becomes equated with the present administration, the present office-holders, whoever they may be. George Bernard Shaw once compared "my country, right or wrong" with "my mother, drunk or sober." Any sensible person understands that he does not show his love for his mother by obeying her every order, especially if he is convinced on a certain occasion that she is drunk. Actually, the case for this purely automatic patriotism is even a degree weaker. Since any given administration is hardly *the country*, but a small group of persons temporarily authorized to act for the country *within certain limits defined by law* (which they might well be tempted to transgress), the formula is really "my country's administration, right or wrong" (my mother's lawyer, drunk or sober). In any case, it is clear that one who really loves his country, if he be convinced that it is entering, or its administration acting in its name is entering, upon some course of action which is illegal or immoral, which will injure or destroy it, must do everything in his power to change that course. Patriotism must not be confused with a blank check given to those who happen to be in power.

MORALITY, WAR, AND FOREIGN POLICY

The publication of the Pentagon Papers—the "classified" documents and the Pentagon analysts' summary of the data in them relating to how the United States government became involved in waging large-scale war in Vietnam—gave rise to a new level of concerned and realistic discussion of morality, government, and war. In *The New York Times* of June 13, 1971, the columnist James Reston wrote: "One of the many extraordinary things in this collection is how seldom anybody in the Kennedy or Johnson Administrations ever seems to have questioned the moral basis of the American war effort." In a reply published in *The New York Times* of June 22, 1971, entitled "Morality and the War," Walt W. Rostow, Chairman of the State Department's Policy Planning Council in both administrations, denied this charge and cited as an example

> the question of whether the defense of American interests runs with or against the interests of those most directly affected. In Asia this has meant, for example, answering the questions: Did the South Koreans in 1950 and the South Vietnamese in 1961 and in 1965 want to fight for an independent destiny, or did they prefer to go with the Communist leadership in Pyongyang and Hanoi? (I can attest that it was this question President Kennedy felt he had to answer above any other before making his critical commitments to South Vietnam in November-December 1961.)

As an alleged example of raising serious questions about the moral basis of the *American* war effort (in Korea as well as Vietnam), this is indeed curious. We are actually being told that the main question, in the eyes of the American government, was whether the South Koreans and the South Vietnamese wanted to fight the North Koreans and the North Vietnamese. The reasoning is that since they did, that fact morally justified the ordering of American forces to join in. In other words, the leaders of the Executive branch of the American government based their war decision on what they thought were the wishes of the people in South Korea and South Vietnam. These leaders construed the main moral problem as finding out if the people of South Korea and South Vietnam really wanted to fight. They did not try to base their decision for wars that would take American lives on the wishes of the *American* people, and did not feel that there was any important moral necessity to find out whether *they* really wanted to fight. Even in 1971 Rostow did not see the moral absurdity of this.

Since the Constitution of the United States requires that, before the people are asked to assume the heavy burdens of protracted war, Congress must have the opportunity to debate and decide whether in its judgment the situation warrants war, the minimal step in seeking a moral answer relative to the American nation would have been to lay the war question before Congress. In addition, or as an alternative, the American people could have been directly consulted in a national referendum. But it is quite evident that neither Mr. Rostow nor President Kennedy had the slightest idea of asking either Congress or the American people *beforehand* whether they wanted to enter into a war in Asia. What was done in both the Kennedy and Johnson administrations, served by Mr. Rostow as head of policy-planning, was, in spite of the Constitution and the whole principle of democracy, to initiate the war measures first, by decision of a few executive officials, and then, when American soldiers began to get killed, to come before Congress and the country and ask that all support be given to our soldiers on grounds of patriotism. That is where the American moral question enters, but apparently it completely and incredibly escaped Mr. Rostow's attention, both at the time and later, when it was raised in the press.

In his reply Rostow goes on to

the broad question of whether the raw power interests of the nation, in general, are decent and morally defensible in at least relative terms. I have for long taken the power interests of the United States to be negative: to prevent the dominance of Europe or Asia by a single potentially hostile power; and to prevent the emplacement of a major power in this hemisphere. These objectives demonstrably accord with the interests of the majority of the peoples and nations of Europe, Asia and Latin America. We could not have conducted our post-1940 foreign policy if this were not so. This convergence of our interests with theirs is reflected in treaties and other agreements which have been approved in accordance with our constitutional arrangements and those of other nations. In the world as it is, I find our power interests, as I would define them, to be morally legitimate.

Can power interests be "negative" if you recommend a policy of sending the youth to die for them? Is this policy really to prevent the dominance of Europe or Asia by some single power? To speak bluntly, is there not a complete lack of moral candor here? Did not President Eisenhower, as we have seen, explain in detail on several occasions, that our raw power interests are interests in certain raw materials found in Asia—he mentioned by name tungsten, tin, manganese, cobalt, and uranium—and that there is nothing "negative" about the nature of our interests in these things? It is simply that *we must* have them. Mr. Rostow knows that we represent a profit economy, and that American control over these raw materials and resources must operate in terms of the profit motive. Surely he would not seriously claim that the profit motive is a negative power interest. Would he differ with Eisenhower, who candidly said: "All of this springs from the enlightened *self-interest* of the United States of America"?[17]

The only difference is Rostow's attempt to give the policy a more elevated moral tone by using the word "negative" to characterize the "power interest" to which he cannot avoid tracing the policy. In the moral context, this word has a vaguely comforting suggestion of things like unselfishness, neutrality, or disinterestedness, especially when placed in juxtaposition to the word "hostile": "the power interest of the United States (is) negative: to prevent the dominance of Europe or Asia by a single potentially hostile power." However, when we reflect upon what this means, we find, exactly as in the case of Eisenhower, the same bland, built-in *assumption* from the start that American power is morally superior to any other power, that it is thus all right for *American* power to dominate Europe or Asia. If we ask why this is all right, the answer is, because it prevents the dominance of Europe or Asia by a single potentially *hostile* power. Hostile to whom? Naturally, to the United States. But does that necessarily mean hostile to Europe and Asia? Necessarily, according to this view, because the U.S. represents what is good and right for everyone. All good people know that communist power is bad for everyone, and that U.S. power is good. So the United States, which is not part of Europe, and not part of Asia, has the right to prevent the dominance of Europe by the (communist) Soviet Union, which is a very large part of Europe, and the right to prevent the dominance of Asia by (communist) China, which is a very large part of Asia. Since the executive branch of the United States government has decided that such bad power dominance can only be prevented by the good dominance of American power, the United States has the moral right to exercise the single-power dominance in Europe and Asia. It also has the right "to prevent the emplacement of a major power in this hemisphere," i.e., North, Central and South America, which means that no major power (besides the U.S.) can place itself in the hemisphere in which we live, but we can place ourselves in any hemisphere we like, and thus prevent any other major power from doing in its hemisphere precisely what we are doing in ours.

But the question will naturally arise: Doesn't this become a form of or attempt at world domination, especially since it does not speak of mutuality in any sense, but seeks to contain other major powers like China and the Soviet Union? Does this accord with our commitment, as a founding member of the United Nations, to the principle of equal rights of nations to exist and to expand? This was the kind of moral questioning the absence of which was noted by Mr. Reston of *The New York Times*. The only answer that can be found in Mr. Rostow's reply is implicit rather than explicit, and is the same answer found in the thinking of President Eisenhower, Dean Rusk, Secretary McNamara, and the other policy-makers: there is a good guy and a bad guy, and the good guy has the right to dominate everywhere because he is the one who believes in freedom, and the people of the rest of the world must, in their hearts, consider themselves lucky that the United States government (at least, the executive branch) is ready to play this role of all-around dominator.

Isn't this last thought about the people of the rest of the world what Mr. Rostow was claiming between the lines when he wrote: "These objectives demonstrably accord with the interests of the majority of the peoples and nations of Europe, Asia and Latin America. We could not have conducted our post-1940 foreign policy if this were not so"? These objectives, as we see, are to prevent the dominance of communist power in Europe, Asia, and Latin America (one wonders why Africa seems to be left on its own; was this an oversight?), and to do this by exercising American capitalist dominance.

It is odd he should add that the proof of the alleged fact that the majority of the rest of the world agrees with this U.S. policy, the policy of containing communism at all costs, is that otherwise, we could not have conducted our "post-1940" foreign policy. The actual fact is that since 1940 the United States has, in sequence, conducted two very different foreign policies, poles apart from each other, morally and politically.

From 1940 to the death of Franklin Roosevelt our policy was one of alliance with the Soviet Union to put down massive military aggression (military aggression, not just political or economic competition) from the side of Nazism, Fascism, and Japanese Imperialism, and, together with the Soviet Union, to set up the United Nations. This meant building upon what the capitalist world and the communist world had in common, first for survival, then for development through peaceful competition. In that part of the "post-1940" period which includes World War II, it could hardly be maintained either that the American government itself, or a majority of governments or nations in Europe, Asia, and Latin America had the objective of weakening Soviet communist power. Without the utmost possible exercise of Soviet power, especially during the war, the majority of them would have gone down to defeat. It was in the course of the Truman Administration that the policy changed from cooperation to containment, from alliance with the Left so that the actual aggression which came from the Right could be counteracted, to alliance with the Right in order to prevent potential expansion of the Left. Conduct of the second policy meant both cold war, which negated the political and moral significance of the United Nations, and hot war by presidential initiative, which negated the legal and moral significance of the Constitution of the United States.

Did the majority of governments and nations of Europe, Asia, and Latin America act as if they agreed with this second policy, the one advised and defended by Professor Rostow? It is plainly absurd to intimate that they did. Seldom has the foreign policy of the leader of a bloc been such a miserable failure in gaining the active support of the bloc. It turned out that even those members of the bloc that were supposed to be closest to the leader in spirit, outlook, and actual power, like Britain and France, were amazed and alarmed at the extent to which, in spite of all our professed commitments to the United Nations idea, and all the evidence that the communist bloc also possesses the most destructive modern weapons, American foreign policy persisted in basing itself on the simplistic morality of cops and robbers, wherein capitalism is the cop and communism the robber. This went so far that France became the openly outspoken opponent of the policy, and adopted a counter-policy of increasingly normal relationships and cooperation with the Soviet Union and China. Britain on her part drew the historic lesson from the failure of the attempt to contain the Soviet Union, and immediately recognized communist China when Mao won his victory on the mainland in 1949, and argued at once that the new government should be given the seat of China in the United Nations. But the United States government refused to recognize the new government of China, and for decades did everything it could to prevent its entrance into the U.N. until it was clear that communist China had enough support to be voted in despite American opposition.

In complete disregard of contemporary historical facts, Professor Rostow went on to make the claim mentioned above: "This convergence of our interest with theirs is reflected in treaties and other agreements which have been approved in accordance with our constitutional arrangements and those of other nations." Entirely in the spirit of the second foreign policy, Rostow remembers the Constitution of the United States only when the plan is to make a treaty, and completely forgets it when the plan is to make a war, completely ignores the fact that if our country is to make war legally and morally, it can do so only by decision of the Congress, not the President, whether the alleged reason for the war is a treaty obligation or anything else. Incredibly, his argument proceeds as if the Constitution makes the President alone the final judge of how to interpret a treaty in relation to war. That is, the final judge of whether some existing set of conditions does or does not fall within the meaning of certain provisions in a given treaty which would oblige us to go to war.

He should have been all the more sensitive to this problem of interpreting treaties, since our principal "allies," with whom our interests are alleged to converge, interpreted the treaty provisions which were used to justify our war involvement in Vietnam very differently from the Johnson and Nixon administrations. It was characteristic of these administrations to place great reliance upon the SEATO treaty as the document that expressed our "commitment" to South Vietnam, which allegedly necessitated and justified the sending of half a million American boys onto the field of battle in Southeast Asia, where more than 50,000 were killed in what became the longest war in all our history. This treaty (which is still in force, and may well be "invoked" again) should be examined as a case study in the incredible lengths to which myth-making can go in the rationalization of presidential war. What does the treaty actually provide? Professor Francis Wormuth sums it up:

The Southeast Asia Collective Defense Treaty was ratified by the Senate in 1955. The other parties were Australia, France, New Zealand, Pakistan, the Phillippines, Thailand, and Great Britain. . . . The purpose of a treaty is to raise an obligation at international law between the signatories. It need hardly be said that the obligations which we incurred in the SEATO treaty run only to the other signatories of the treaty. South Vietnam was not a party; indeed, the treaty does not recognize the existence of a state of South Vietnam, but only of a state of Vietnam, of which, at the Geneva Conference of 1954, the Hanoi government of Ho Chi Minh was accepted as the international spokesman. The treaty therefore imposes no duty upon us toward the so-called state of South Vietnam. Three of the signatories to whom we are obligated under the treaty disapprove of or have refused to support the war in either South or North Vietnam. Four have made token commitment of troops for the war in South Vietnam: Australia and New Zealand, because they believe they are buying American protection in the event of a future war with mainland Asia; and the Philippines and Thailand, which are pensionary states of the United States. But none of these has joined in the attack on North Vietnam. It is not only the case that the war against North Vietnam does not discharge any legal obligation to any party to the SEATO treaty; it is conducted completely outside the framework of the Southeast Asia Collective Defense Organization and without the support of any member of the Organization.[18]

Professor Wormuth adds:

Article IV, Section I of the SEATO treaty provides that each party recognizes that aggression by means of armed attack in the treaty area against any of the Parties or against any state or territory which the Parties by unanimous agreement may hereafter designate, would endanger its own peace and safety, and agrees that it will in that event act to meet the common danger in accordance with its constitutional processes." There was no consultation with the Southeast Asia Treaty Organization before President Johnson attacked North Vietnam on Feburary 7, 1965. . . . Not only did President Johnson not consult SEATO: although the treaty requires that each signatory act "in accordance with its constitutional processes," he did not consult Congress either.[10]

Thus it is very far from being true that the objectives set in the policy which Mr. Rostow defended "demonstrably accord with the interests of the majority of the peoples and nations of Europe, Asia and Latin America." The opposite is demonstrated by the fact that only the tiniest minority of nations anywhere ever actively supported it. We lost friends by it and ended up virtually alone abroad and bitterly divided at home, feeling ashamed and guilty.

Mr. Rostow's overall conclusion on the moral issue exemplifies the spirit and rhetoric of a continuing policy, and thereby sums up a dangerous situation which continues to pose a challenge to the American people and a threat to the peace of the world. He refers to "the moral question of the nation's word, once given," and makes the following solemn-sounding pronouncement: "For a great nation to make the commitments we have to Southeast Asia involves a moral commitment to stay with them. I believe it immoral to walk away from our treaty commitments, which other nations and human beings have taken as the foundations for their lives in the most literal sense." We have already seen, in the light of facts and legal principles, how spurious is the claim that the American nation, by treaty or otherwise, had any commitment to any nation to wage large-scale war in Southeast Asia. We have also seen, in light of the United States Constitution, that the executive branch of the government never has the moral or legal authority to make, by itself, a commitment that the American nation will go to war, or to decide, on its own, that some commitment that has been made in general terms must now be implemented by initiating war.

However, Vietnam was not the first instance, nor will it be the last, in which the emotion-choked argument, "we made a commitment," is used to defend military action by the Executive, especially since our foreign aid program and treaty commitments are world-wide. How can this argument be met in its own terms? For concrete guidance let us make use of the case of Vietnam, and assume for the sake of argument that the American nation did have some kind of *bona fide* commitment to give aid and assistance to Southeast Asia in general or South Vietnam in particular. First of all, the *form* and *amount* of that aid would have to be decided in the light of moral priorities and legal restraints. The aid could be diplomatic, economic, advisory, each in many different degrees. These facts are overlooked by this defense of the war policy, a defense which suggests that if a commitment to give anything exists, it would be immoral for the Executive not to give all, including life itself, or, to speak more precisely, the lives of the youth. Rather, it was the constitutional duty of the Chief Executive to say to the South Vietnamese: "The executive branch of the American government can give you diplomatic, economic and advisory aid; it cannot order American forces to launch a war for you in Southeast Asia because that is forbidden by the terms of the U.S. Constitution, which gives that decision to Congress alone."

What was actually done in Vietnam by the executive branch of our government is a perfect illustration of the reason why the framers of the United States Constitution gave the power to initiate war to the legislative branch, where the question would have to be openly debated. They feared the constant tendency of generals and Executives to plunge into wars on the basis of plans made behind closed doors. The Pentagon papers show that it was not so much a case of the South Vietnamese pressuring our government to fight a war, as a case of the executive branch of our government secretly pressuring the South Vietnamese to continue fighting a war directed by us. Again and again, in the memoranda that passed among the principal figures, and in the account written by the Pentagon analysts, the fear is expressed that the South Vietnamese may want to make peace before *we* feel the proper objectives have been attained, that they might even officially ask us to leave, because they had so little desire to fight a large-scale war. For example, *The New York Times* in its issue of June 14, 1971 (p. 32), sums up the Pentagon account of the situation that existed in January 1965: "Within the Administration in Washington, key policy makers were coming to the same conclusion that Ambassador Taylor and his colleagues had reached in Saigon, that it was desirable to bomb the North regardless of what state of government existed in the South. The political turmoil in Saigon, the [Pentagon] narrative says, 'appears to have been interpreted in Washington as an impending sell-out' to the National Liberation Front. Fear increased that a neutral coalition government would emerge and invite the United States to leave."

Indeed, this feeling was so strong on the part of the President's policy-makers in Washington and his Ambassador in Saigon that, as we have just seen, they all agreed that large-scale war must be initiated against North Vietnam regardless of what might be the opinion of the government of South Vietnam or of the United States Congress. And, in fact, the escalated bombing followed. Was this a case of moral determination to fulfill a legal commitment to South Vietnam or immoral determination to impose an illegal American policy on South Vietnam, regardless of her wishes? Was it a desire to avoid war, or to make war at all costs?

The new moral consciousness, insofar as it applies itself to the problem of war and peace, is first of all a rejection of this sham morality of bogus commitments, carried out by violating the Constitution, and defended by an unstable mixture of economic self-interest and an infantile self-image as the upright policeman who has the determination to use his thermonuclear club in a world game of cops and robbers. The new moral consciousness is a new determination to put love ahead of the power of violence, to solve social problems by social science rather than by military strategy, to approach international relations from premises of equal rights rather than good guys and bad guys, to fit economic practices to human needs rather than human needs to economic practices, to live democracy by letting people themselves decide about their own lives, especially about war and the killing of other people, to learn to live without hypocrisy in relation to oneself or to others, and to rebel if necessary in order to exercise the inalienable right to live in this way.

NOTES

[1]Mohandas K. Gandhi, *Writings on Non-Violent Resistance*. In John Somerville and Ronald E. Santoni, *Social and Political Philosophy: Readings from Plato to Gandhi* (New York: Doubleday, Anchor, 1963), p. 500, 501.

[2]Ibid., p. 502.

[3]Ibid.

[4]Ibid.

[5]Ibid., p. 510.

[6]Ibid., p. 501.

[7]Henry David Thoreau, *On The Duty of Civil Disobedience*. In Somerville and Santoni, op. cit., n. 1, p. 283.

[8]Ibid., p. 285.

[9]See Chap. 1, n. 2.

[10]Thoreau, op. cit., p. 282.

[11]Henry David Thoreau, *A Plea for Captain John Brown*. In Thoreau, *Civil Disobedience* and *A Plea for Captain John Brown* (Chicago: Regnery, 1949), p. 52.

[12]In Leo Tolstoy, *Writings on Civil Disobedience and Non-Violence* (New York: New American Library, Signet, 1968), p. 215-219.

[13]Ibid., p. 220.

[14]See Adin Ballou, *Christian Non-Resistance in All Its Important Bearings* (Philadelphia: Universal Peace Union, 1910), Chap. VII, for Ballou's further analysis of these contradictions and his recommendations.

[15]For Ballou's extended analysis of scriptural passages and refutation of counter-claims, see ibid., Chap. II. It is interesting to note statements of contemporary chaplains interviewed by *The New York Times* in its issue of June 22, 1971: ''In an interview in his office last month, the Army Chief of Chaplains, Maj. Gen. Francis L. Sampson, a Roman Catholic, said violence was an evil 'but the man who doesn't resist the violent man becomes culpable, it seems to me.' He added: 'In the case of nations, innocent friends who are being attacked by aggressive nations, it seems to me if we made a commitment of friendship to a country, we owe it our support.' The commandment against killing, he said, is actually a prohibition against murder and therefore is not applicable to wartime When his designated successor as Chief of Chaplains, Brig. Gen. Gerhardt W. Hyatt, was asked whether he and other chaplains were experiencing doubts about the course of the war, General Hyatt, a Lutheran, replied: 'A man of discernment has to give his government the benefit of the doubt. . . .' 'I believe there is an unjust aggressor keeping them (the South Vietnamese) from their God-given freedom,' said Lieut. Col. Reinard W. Beaver, a Roman Catholic and head chaplain of the Fourth Infantry Division at Fort Carson. . . . A convention of the Military Chaplains Association appeared at times to turn into a rally in support of the United States' effort in Vietnam and against antiwar demonstrators and hippies. The members cheered Senator Sam J. Ervin Jr. Democrat of North Carolina, when he said in a speech, 'I think if you get in a war, you should get in to win.' One Navy Chaplain who said he was embarrassed by his colleagues' stand, but asked not to be named said: 'After a while, a chaplain begins to identify with the military. Off the record, if he wants to survive in the system, he has to repress some things.' ''

[16]Tolstoy, op. cit., p. 227.

[17]*The New York Times*, May 8, 1953. See Chapter 3 for context.

[18]Reprinted with permission from *The Vietnam War: The President Versus the*

Constitution by Francis D. Wormuth, An Occasional Paper published by the Center for the Study of Democratic Institutions, Santa Barbara, California, 1968, p. 36.

[19]Ibid., p. 36-37.

5

The New Education

HOW DOES EDUCATION TAKE PLACE?

Shortly after World War II had ended, an American general who had taken a leading part in it made a public speech in which he said that the United States would never win another war because, with the nuclear weapons now available, both sides would lose. "War," he said, "is now like a fire. You can have a fire, but you cannot win it." The only way to win World War III is to prevent it. If the battle of Waterloo was won on the playing fields of Eton, there is a possibility that World War III could be lost in the classrooms of America.

Of course, classrooms are not the only places where people are educated. If education is a process of imparting information, shaping character, developing habits, forming attitudes, and influencing evaluations, then it takes place through the newspapers, magazines, films, television and radio, on the job, in the church and in the home, quite as much as in the school. The predominant attitude of the American people, or of any other people, towards war in general or any particular war, is as much a matter of what they get from these other sources as from the classroom. It is simply that the school at its various levels has the most obvious and direct responsibility for education.

Why hasn't the school done a better job with the matter of war and peace, with the concept of revolution, with the principle of law and order as applying to the executive branch of the government? Why hasn't the church done a better job with the morality of brotherly love and the commandment "Thou shalt not kill," in relation to actual practice and

94

behavior? Why has the home looked on in relative helplessness? Why have the movie, television, and radio industries assumed so little moral and educational responsibility for what they do? Why did the great majority of newspapers and magazines so quickly and for so long accept the cold war and the hot wars? If one wants better education about war and peace now, one must begin by trying to understand what has stood in the way up to now.

All these sources of education—school, church, home, mass media—are themselves institutions which must struggle for their existence and survival as institutions. This means they need money and must get it from those in a position to give it. In addition, some of these sources of education, such as the mass media, are outright industries which must make a profit in order to stay in business. The home must have a breadwinner, who must hold down a paying job or protect investments. Now, as we have seen, war is a game very frequently played by governments for stakes of tremendous economic value, a game played in terms of policies, strategies, and tactics that are presented as something of urgent necessity to the nation as a whole and as something that should be supported on grounds of patriotism. It requires considerable courage to go against the government and the big economic interests in these matters because this can so easily involve risking one's means of livelihood, and reputation as well.

Yet there are times when not to go against the government and the big economic interests is an even greater risk, the risk of life itself and of self-respect. After all, what one is here speaking about first and foremost is not government as such, or business as such, but the illegality and immorality of certain practices of government and business in relation to war. One is speaking of telling the truth about these practices, and their dangers, the truth about the past, and the truth about the present. This is one of the categorical obligations of education. For the teacher to turn away from it is like the policeman turning his back upon crime. The policeman is hired to do something about crime, no matter who is committing it, even if it is the very official who hired him, or the governor of the state. He therefore has, by definition and by his constituted authority, a relative independence and an absolute responsibility once he is duly hired. This is true of the physician also. He is put in charge of a case not in order to tell the patient's family what they would like to hear, but the truth, as his professional knowledge and equipment enable him to ascertain what the facts are.

All this is no less true of the teacher, and it begins with the choice of curriculum: What shall be studied, and what specific problems shall be selected within the field or the material to be studied? Education, no less than medicine, must keep up, not only with changes in knowledge, but changes in *problems*. In our day, the problem of war has completely changed its character, from something that could be tolerated, like a disease that could be kept within bounds, to a new type of infection so powerful that it could sweep across the world in a matter of days and so deadly that it could wipe out the whole of humanity in a matter of weeks or months.

This means there is more need now than ever before to focus study upon war and peace—to study war in order to identify its causes and what might prevent them, to study peace in order to identify what strengthens and what weakens it, and to clarify the relationship of things central to human life, such as morality, law, religion, economics, to war and peace. As war today calls into question the existence of everything human, so everything human must define its relationship to war, and make its contribution to the prevention of it, in the interest of its own survival.

WHAT IS EDUCATION FOR PEACE?

If education, as the massive social institution it is, had sufficient moral sensitivity, sufficient courage, and sufficient intelligence it would immediately set about reorganizing its entire curriculum around the theme of the need and value of peace in the age of nuclear weapons. The same applies to the church, the home, the mass media, and business, in relation to the functions each performs. What confronts us all is an emergency situation, the greatest emergency that ever confronted the human race. It is a plain and sober fact that the human race stands closer to complete annihilation today than at any other time in all its million-year history. *How* close it actually stands, in the light of all the evidence, might be put in this way: If there were a cosmic insurance company belonging to a superior race of creatures located on some distant planet, and application was made to it for insurance against the complete annihilation of the human race and the planet earth, it would in no way be surprising if the company replied that after feeding all the relevant data into its master computer, it was obliged to reject the application on the ground that the risk was too great. If the company were asked the specific reasons for the rejection, part of its answer might well be that the educational efforts of this race were not centered on those matters that were most important to its survival. The company might add that, insofar as these matters were being dealt with educationally, the efforts seemed mainly directed not at promoting survival, but at its opposite.

The supreme danger is global war, and the supreme danger of global war lies in the relations between capitalist powers and communist powers. Now the United States, the undisputed leader of the capitalist powers, could hardly be expected to have a government or a system of education whose basic orientations were pro-communist, any more than communist powers could be expected to have institutional orientations that were pro-capitalist. A certain anti-communism must be expected from the one side, and a certain anti-capitalism from the other, but if the human race is to have any future, each "anti" orientation must be of the kind that is still compatible with peaceful, cooperative relationships between the two sides, even though there are also irreconcilable differences between them.

But is this possible? Is it realistic to think that peace and cooperation can be developed and maintained between competing systems with irreconcilable ideological differences? It is, if we look candidly at historical experience and the present situation, and act with energy in the light of them, keeping in mind that we have some options not open to computers. Ideologies are very much like secular religions (beliefs intensely held, touching all aspects of life, and related to state power), and the history of religion gives us important leads. For centuries it was taken for granted that because there were irreconcilable differences of faith and practice between religions, it was impossible to think of *peaceful* competition between them, let alone anything like systematic cooperation. Each religion assumed that the other was not only a competitor, but an enemy, and not only an enemy, but a criminal beyond the pale of moral acceptability, one who had forfeited the claim to be treated on a basis of equal right. In effect, it was concluded there was only one possible policy to follow: contain and destroy the other religion, the evil religion; it is we or they.

We are all familiar with the centuries of religious warfare, the "holy wars" between Christians and non-Christians, between Catholics and Protestants, between Orthodox and non-Orthodox. Had there been thermonuclear weapons in those days, it is possible human history would have gone no farther. While we cannot say today that physical strife between religious groups has entirely disappeared, we can say that it has disappeared as a major threat to world peace, and that institutionalized forms of peaceful competition and systematic cooperation have created a qualitatively new set of relationships between religions, even though they continue to have irreconcilable differences.

Consider the implications of the inter-faith council idea, which is carried out not only locally, but on a world scale, at the highest levels of ecclesiastical authority. When Catholic, Protestant, and Jew sit down together in a local body, or when Christian, Hindu, Jew, Moslem, Buddhist, and others sit down together in an international or world body, they do not cease to have irreconcilable differences on matters which each of them considers of the utmost importance. But they acknowledge that they also have agreements on things they all consider important, and that on the common ground of these agreements, they can, in practice, enter into many forms of cooperation valuable to each of them, at the same time recognizing their competition with one another.

Most important of all, they recognize that they can compete with one another peacefully, through arranging, by mutual agreement, the conditions of peaceful competition. The main condition is to begin from the premise of equal rights (not equal truth—no one of them would agree that any of the other religions has as much truth as it has, but no one denies to the others a right to exist and to try to expand). Thus each religion recognizes the right of others to try to convert the unconverted. No one of them proclaims that because it represents the only true religion, it alone has the right to send out missionaries. No one of them says that it has the right to use force to contain the others within their own borders, while it itself acts the part of a world missionary, free to bring its message everywhere. In addition, all recognize that each religion is master in its own house, and that the principle of equal rights applies to the competing activity of religions outside their own houses, not to what goes on within any one of them. The Catholic does not demand equal rights to practice his religion within a Protestant church, nor does the Jew demand equal rights to practice his in a Moslem mosque. It is recognized by all that each religion has the right to decide how much freedom and what degree of dissent it will allow within its own house. In other words, a distinction is observed between internal and external affairs. At the same time, of course, it is possible for them all to come to a common agreement that each within his own house will observe certain agreed upon restrictions or undertake certain agreed upon actions, but this must be by voluntary agreement which recognizes the right of each to enter into such an agreement or not to enter into it. Thus the conditions of peaceful competition are peacefully arrived at, and on the basis of equal rights, even unequal arrangements can be peacefully negotiated to mutual satisfaction.

As a matter of fact, is it not true that we have seen something of the same evolution take place in the economic field *within* our own country and *within* other countries? There was a time when business competition was fought out by physical means, with a blanket hostility that was assumed to preclude even relationships of peace, let alone systematic forms of cooperation. While instances of the older attitudes can still be found, they are not today predominant in business as it takes place *within* the major capitalist countries; however, they *are* predominant today in the international economic rivalry between capitalism and communism, as we have seen, and constitute our central problem, the problem on which everything else depends. In this perspective one can see that what the peace movement demands of the big economic interests and the government policy planners is not something inherently impossible for them to do, not something they have never done. It amounts to this: Stop imagining that the game of economic competition becomes cops and robbers when played internationally. Be content with the ground rules you accept in playing Macy's and Gimbel's, Ford and Buick, Ajax and Dutch Cleanser. Business competition as such is always rough and sometimes dirty, but it can stop short of physical extermination. One must demand at least that, if for no other reason than that the competition may go on, and that people may have a chance to judge among the alternatives that are open to them, including alternative economic systems.

The history of religion and of business also shows that when conditions of peaceful competition were accepted, they led to forms of positive cooperation between the competitors. This, too, is not strange. It begins with the simple realization that if one competes in such a way as to destroy what one is competing for, or to destroy oneself, one is stupid. It goes on to the realization that, in spite of the fact that there are irreconcilable differences between oneself and one's competitors, there are areas of common ground in which friendly cooperation is of positive advantage to all competitors. All or most religions today agree that it is better for children not to die young, that it is better for families not to starve, that it is better to reduce the rate of crime, to increase the rate of literacy, and to enter into cooperation with other religions, the wrong religions, in order better to attain these ends which even the wrong religions believe in. In like manner, all businesses agree that it is better not to have a depression, or run-away inflation, or excessive taxation, and that it is well to enter into cooperation with competitors to achieve these ends.

These forms of conduct lead to the further realization that beyond, beneath, and perhaps deeper than the irreconcilable differences, are truths and values held in common: all religions believe in a supreme being of some kind, in love of some kind for others, in faith of some kind in something felt as good. So, too, a man in business can realize that *both* he and his competitor make a contribution to a larger community. This kind or realization leads, in turn, to two things: (1) the narrowing down, by more precise analysis and better definition, of the irreconcilable differences between oneself and one's competitors; (2) the expansion and enlargement, through the same processes, of the area of agreement and common ground shared by the competitors.

EDUCATIONAL SIGNIFICANCE OF THE UNITED NATIONS

It is a fact of tremendous educational significance, actually and potentially, not only that these processes have already taken place, to one degree or another, in the history of religion and of business, but that, in our own day, a systematic foundation has also been laid for these same processes in the field of international relations and world economic competition across ideological lines. This is, of course, the United Nations, together with its specialized agencies, particularly the United Nations Educational, Scientific and Cultural Organization (UNESCO).

The purpose is nothing more nor less than to prevent war and strengthen world peace by having a world organization to which all the nations of the world can voluntarily adhere in order to engage in those discussions, deliberations, and negotiations, as well as in those projects of practical and theoretical cooperation, which seem to them conducive to the common goal of peace. The organization is by definition pluralistic—politically, economically, ideologically, religiously. Among its founding members were nations representing every religion on earth, as well as outright atheism; socialism and communism as well as capitalism; republics and monarchies of all varieties. Thus a recognition of the fact of international competition in all these fields and on all these levels is built into the very fabric of the organization. The whole effort is to keep this competition peaceful, while recognizing the inevitable implications of the facts of power.

It is in the light of these facts that the organization proper is divided into two main bodies: the General Assembly, in which every nation is represented on a one-nation, one-vote basis, and the Security Council, structured to accord with the implications of power differences in their relationship to peace. The Security Council is composed of the five major powers (USA, USSR, UK, France, China) as permanent members, together with ten other members periodically elected for short terms. The Security Council has the primary responsibility for dealing with threats to peace, and, by the terms of the Charter, is the only organ empowered to make a decision to use military measures in the name of the organization. Moreover, all substantive decisions in the Security Council, including of course any decisions to use force in the name of the organization, require not only a majority vote, but the affirmative vote of all five of the permanent Council members. Behind this provision, usually referred to as "the veto," lies the recognition of the implications of power in the keeping of the peace at this stage of history. That is, the world is now, and for centuries has been, divided up into a number of political entities know as states, each of which possesses legal sovereignty and self-determination. As powers, these states range from very small to very big, and the small ones have always had their actual freedom and self-determination—that is to say, their actual sovereignty—curtailed by the big ones. To put it bluntly, big powers can and do coerce small powers, almost as a matter of course. Small powers sometimes resist by guerilla warfare, sometimes by alliance (or the threat of alliance) with big powers hostile to the big power oppressing them, or by a combination of the two methods. (The American Revolution, together with its immediate aftermath, was an example of such a combination.) If big powers agree, they can always stop wars between small powers, but the converse has rarely if ever been the case.

The arrangement in the Security Council says in effect: ''Let us big powers agree to sit permanently together around the council table (the Security Council is officially always in session) of the world organization to which the member states can bring their disputes and conflicts in order that they may be settled by peaceful means. If, however, armed conflict has already broken out, or threatens to break out, and we big powers can *all* agree on certain measures, including possible measures of force, to suppress it and restore the peace, then these measures may be taken, with the additional agreement of a few other members, in the name of the world body.'' In terms of the implications of power in relation to world peace, this amounts to acknowledging two important premises: (1) Big powers cannot coerce one another, either within the organization or outside of it, save by making the very kind of war that it is the purpose of the organization to prevent. (2) If force were to be used by the organization contrary to the will of a big power, the big power would probably resist, and the result would be prolongation of the war rather than restoration of the peace, with progressive weakening and disintegration of the organization. Underlying these premises is another, as fully justified as the first two: Big powers do not trust one another, and until they do, would not give up their actual sovereignty and self-determination.

In other words, the principle of the big-power veto means that, in the interest of peace, it is better for the organization to take no substantive actions concerning peace, and especially no military actions, save those which have the concurrence of all the big powers; it is better to take no action than an action which is likely to initiate, enlarge, or prolong armed conflict. No big power would be willing to abandon this veto principle, and no big power would have joined the organization if that principle had not been a part of it. This is what is forgotten by those who speak slightingly of the present United Nations, who argue that it should be scrapped, and a full World Government set up in its place, with a world police apparatus powerful enough to enforce all decisions arrived at by simple majorities, even against the will of the big powers. It is clear that the precondition of any such arrangement would have to be that all the big powers would give up control of their armaments and military apparatus to the central World Government, over whose decisions no one of them would have a veto. But what is the precondition of the big powers doing this? Clearly, a vast increase of mutual trust and confidence among them, not an angry break-up of the U.N. because they mistrust one another, and not simply the realization that disputes would be "settled" more quickly if there were no veto. World Government might in the course of time grow out of the United Nations, but could hardly arise as an organization externally opposed to the United Nations. In one world, *two* world organizations politically opposed to each other? But the same nations, represented by the same governments, would have to compose the membership of each.

The problem at the present stage of history is to strengthen the operation of the principles of the United Nations, because those principles, limited as they are in some respects, are nevertheless capable of maintaining world peace if implemented. Moreover, the great majority of powers, big and small, are morally and legally committed to them by membership and would not at this time commit themselves to anything further, even in theory. Thus there are binding standards in relation to maintaining and strengthening peace, and an organizational framework within which to implement these standards and also to point out violations of them. The implementation and strengthening of the principles and standards of the United Nations proceed along two interconnected levels, the political and the educational. As our interest at this point is mainly in the latter level, let us turn our attention once more to UNESCO.

First of all, what educational principles are implied by the very existence of the United Nations, by our country's relation to it as a major founding member, and by the existence of UNESCO as an important specialized agency of the U.N.? Perhaps most directly involved is the question of what is taught in any given country concerning other countries, other ideologies, other economic systems, other forms of government and legal codes, other religious or non-religious faiths. What is important here is not only the *facts* that are communicated about such matters; of equal or even greater importance is the *attitude* towards those facts which is communicated. In one of its Basic Documents connected with its inquiry into "tensions affecting international understanding," UNESCO emphasizes the obligation to study "the distinctive character of the various national cultures, ideals and legal systems, with the aim of stimulating in every country the sympathy and respect of nations for each other's ideals and aspirations, and the appreciation of national problems." This approach, it adds, "implies, moreover, looking upon each culture as a component part of world civilization." In the UNESCO project entitled "Philosophical Analysis of Current Ideological Conflicts," part of its "central aim" is expressed: to clarify "the divergencies of usage and interpretation, to analyze the normative foundations of these divergencies and to search for potential sources of reconciliation."

All this touches directly on the way we teach and learn about subjects like history, philosophy, religions, political science, economics, international relations, comparative law, modern civilization, social studies, art, literature. In fact, it applies to any subject insofar as a socio-historical dimension enters into its study. What this approach is saying is that the education taking place in any one country, insofar as it deals with another country, must, in order to communicate the full truth and lay the most effective foundation for peace in the world, pay as much attention to that which the two countries agree upon as to that in which they differ, to the ideals, goals, and principles they share as to those they do not share in matters of ideology, religion, politics, economics, cultural tradition, and way of life. As to the differences between the countries, an effort must constantly be made to understand the causes of them in terms of the different conditions, needs, and problems confronting different peoples in the course of their national development.

This approach does not imply a suspension of moral judgment, or a blanket endorsement of everything that has taken place in a given foreign country. It does not mean that countries make no mistakes, or that governments commit no crimes, or that nations always behave justly and honorably in their collective actions. What it means is that, in educating about a foreign country—*any* foreign country and *every* foreign country—we must seek to identify its achievements as much as its mistakes, what we can admire as much as what we cannot, what we can respect as much as what we can condemn.

Our education as a whole, past and present, might be described as one in which we have followed this kind of approach in dealing with countries considered by our government to be "friendly," while in regard to those considered "unfriendly" our education has followed the opposite kind of approach, emphasizing differences, ignoring common ground, dwelling on sins, saying nothing about virtues. A contemporary example of the first is our education about Britain, or about West European countries generally. An example of the second is our education about the Soviet Union, or "communist" countries generally, in spite of the fact that our country and the Soviet Union are fellow members of UNESCO and founding members of the United Nations. This double standard in education has had a disastrous impact upon peace, and, though it may sound melodramatic to say so, the sober truth is that it may yet cost the human race its life.

THE EDUCATION OF AMERICAN STATESMEN

Suppose for a moment that Presidents Kennedy and Johnson, policy-planner Rostow, Secretaries Rusk and McNamara, and a few other leaders of similar rank in the executive branch of the government, as well as the members of Congress during these administrations, had been educated in the spirit of the UNESCO approach. Would President Kennedy have thought that he had a duty to risk "the death of the children of this country and all the world" in order to get Soviet missiles out of Cuba while American missiles were in Turkey? Would Rusk have thought that a Chinese sphere of influence among its immediate neighbors in Asia was intolerable expansion and criminal aggression which must be prevented by American military action, as police prevent conspiracies of the underworld? Would the Senate have voted precipitately and almost unanimously for the Tonkin Gulf Resolution, later rescinded by unaminous vote? Would Rostow have advised chang-ing the policy of ''tit for tat'' reprisal against North Vietnam to a policy of ''sustained reprisal''—massive, continuous bombing, thus initiating deliberate large-scale war right up to the Chinese border? Would he have further advised that if China joined North Vietnam in any military actions responding to such escalation on our part, we should direct our armed attack against China as well, even though this could well become World War III? Would Johnson have adopted the policy of sustained reprisal, risking world war, though he had just told the American people he would not? Would Nixon have risked World War III by imposing a mine-blockade on North Vietnam, telling the Soviet Union and China (by name in a television address) that these acts of war were directed against them, in order to prevent their sending weapons to North Vietnam, although we would continue sending weapons to South Vietnam, and continue engag-ing our air force and navy on the side of South Vietnam? Every one of these actions and policies represents a denial of equal rights, moral and legal. How could this be possible on the part of highly educated gov-ernmental leaders thoroughly familiar with the agonizing reality of World War II and the moral and legal implications of the setting up of the United Nations? It was possible because the way in which they were actually educated cancelled out the moral and legal implications of the United Nations, and the significance of the decisive facts of World War II.

These men, like the vast majority of their fellow citizens, were educated to believe that their first duty as citizens and as officials of the United States of America was to fight communism with any and every means, legal and illegal, truthful and deceitful—not to study com-munism, not to understand it historically, philosophically, sociological-ly, but to fight it. In terms of that education, the Soviet Union, North Vietnam, and mainland China did not appear as countries which, while different from our country, were still possessed of equal rights. They appeared more as a series of concentration camps run by gangs of outlaws holding hundreds of millions of innocent victims in virtual slavery. Communism did not appear as an ideology, which, while different from our ideology, was still possessed of equal rights. It appeared more in the nature of a criminal conspiracy committed to destroy us by any and every means—legal and illegal, truthful and deceitful. The impression they received was that communists do not want to compete with us; they simply want to exterminate us. Communists, they became convinced, just do not value life as we do. When, in the summer of 1971, President Nixon took the first American initiative towards bringing mainland China into the U.N., it was clear that such actions were taken because the majority of nations long in favor of them were ready to proceed even against American opposition. There was evidence that Nixon wanted to use his initiatives as bargaining counters to try to "save Taiwan" and to promote his chances of re-election, but no evidence that he had learned anything new about mainland China, or had changed his basic attitude towards it.

These American statesmen were of course fully aware that we and the Soviet Union had jointly with other states founded the United Nations on the explicit basis that all the countries in it, with their respective forms of government and ideologies, had equal rights—legally, politically, and morally. What did they say to themselves about that? Probably something like this: "I know that legally, under the Charter of the United Nations to which we are committed by signature, we are obligated to grant a communist country equal rights, but we don't have to keep that obligation because, communism being communism, the communists probably signed the Charter of the United Nations in bad faith, and would not for a moment consider keeping *their* obligations under it. They would not hesitate to initiate military action against us if they had the margin of superiority over us that we have over them. So why should we hesitate? Their whole aim is to destroy us; it is we or they. Better to have it out now than later. I know we are risking the lives of all the children of the world, and everyone else, but the world will thank us in the future for cleansing it of communism. Either that, or the world will be destroyed in our struggle against communism. If it turns out that it is necessary to destroy the world in order to save it from communism, so be it. Better it should be destroyed by our righteous might than that it should risk falling under the domination of communism. But surely God will help us to exterminate the communists. The communists reject God, and we believe in God.

"I know we are not seeking or gaining the prior authorization of Congress for initiating large-scale war against the communists. I know that the Constitution says that Congress alone has the final power to declare war, and that I took an oath of office to uphold the Constitution. But if we went to Congress first, or to the people as a whole, there would be delays and debates. Congress or the people might not think it necessary to risk World War III, but we know it is necessary. Later on if we win the gamble, Congress and the people will thank us for going ahead and acting on our judgment. They will take into account that we were dealing with communists and everyone knows that communists believe only in force, that communists have no respect for law, order, and the democratic process. Communists believe in the doctrine that the end justifies the means. But we are different. Congress will understand and accept what we are doing because Congress can exist only on the basis of constitutional democracy, and we are protecting that basis. Congress knows that communists believe in the *violent overthrow of governments*, and Congress understands that there can be no compromise with violent revolution. Congress *knows* that violent overthrow of government is the heart and center of the creed of communism, the unbridgeable gulf that separates them from us, the unforgivable sin by which they put themselves outside the bounds of our morality, the self-confessed crime by which they place upon themselves the brand of conspirator and outlaw for all the world to see. Congress and the people know that this has been proved and documented over and over again from the basic teachings of communism. That is what they themselves say about themselves: that they believe in the violent overthrow of government. How, then, could any American, in or out of Congress, who is intelligent, moral, religious, democratic, patriotic, peace-loving, and law-abiding, object to our small but determined group of executive leaders initiating large-scale war against the communists?''

To the degree that this composite summary of the probable mental processes of individuals who played leading roles in the American government's war policy reflects their education as a whole (as indeed it must), numerous questions pose themselves: What were actually the sources of their knowledge about communism in general as a philosophy, ideology, moral system, political system, economic system? What books, if any? What courses of study, if any? Whose lectures, if any? What magazines and newspapers? Whose sermons? What reports? What "briefings"? To what extent did they ever examine basic or original sources, the works of the founders and leaders of communism? To what extent did they ever see, visit, or observe "communism" in operation in any of the countries trying to put it into operation? What is their *background* of knowledge concerning any one of these countries —from the Soviet Union and China, to Albania and Outer

Mongolia? How could one morally or politically judge "what is going on" in a given country today without substantial knowledge of what went on in that country from some time before today? Can one understand and judge Communist China without seeing it in the perspective of its connections with pre-Communist China? Can one understand and judge Soviet Russia without seeing it in the perspective of its connections with Tsarist Russia? Could anyone arrive at such understanding without seriously studying the history, literature, philosophy, and culture of the country in question?

If these American statesmen would respond to these questions they would probably point out that it is impossible for every political leader to be a professional scholar as well, that the statesman is forced to rely on the accounts, reports, and judgments of professional scholars whom he consults. Very well: which professional scholars, and which of their accounts, reports, and judgments did these American statesmen in fact rely upon? In regard to these matters there is a community of professional scholars, national and international, whose standards are open to examination and whose work is known to one another. Did these American statesmen rely on any of these professional scholars whose approach and standards had even a remote connection with the approach and standards implied by the very existence of the United Nations and expressed by UNESCO? Judging from the policies adopted by the American statesmen, they must have relied on scholars of extremely reactionary tendencies, whose approach and standards were quite opposite to those of UNESCO, on scholars the premises of whose approach to everything concerning *communism* were practically identical with those of Adolf Hitler, not with those of the United Nations. Is that what the American people deserve? Is that what the world deserves?

Insofar as such statesmen were church-goers, or felt themselves religious, it would be most instructive if they could be persuaded to set down candidly what impressions or evaluations of communism they received from the side of religion. What attitude towards communists, what way of dealing with communism, were suggested to them by their actual religious training, by their listening to sermons in church and the like? What religious texts were chosen? What arguments were used? What guidelines for action and behavior were set up? For example, were these of the type reported in *The New York Times* of October 17, 1946, and the *Boston Evening American* of the same date, from the public speech of a prominent clergyman who was also the president of a large university? This minister of the Christian Gospel and head of an institution of Christian education is quoted as saying of communist countries: ''The only language that such nations understand is force.'' The United States ''had better pile up armaments sky high'' in order to ''meet the threat of Communism with bigger and better bombs.'' A Cardinal made a public speech in which he said that every individual coming to our shores from a communist country was ''a master of deceit'' and should be treated as a spy. J. Edgar Hoover later wrote a book that became a best seller, entitled *Masters of Deceit.* In *The New York Times* of April 6, 1954, an address of President Eisenhower was reported, in the course of which he said: ''We can be Americans. We can stand up and hold up our heads and say 'America is the greatest force that God has ever allowed to exist on His Footstool.' As such, it is up to us to lead this world to a peaceful and secure existence.'' One assumes Eisenhower had in mind the greatest *physical* force. Surely he was not abandoning his presumed belief that there was once a greater spiritual force, a simple carpenter. Or was Eisenhower saying, and was the clerical university president teaching, in effect, that God has now changed His mind, that He now feels the world must be led to peace not by the spiritual force of the simple carpenter but by this great *physical* force, these bigger and better bombs, this pile of armaments sky high? What is actually taught in the name of Christianity?

It would be equally instructive if those of the statesmen who are still alive would make known the results of candid self-examination as to the sources and content of their education concerning the right of revolution, the Declaration of Independence, the American Revolution, and the relationship of all these to *violent overthrow of government.* For example, in all the references and all the attention given to democracy, in required readings, in classroom lectures and discussions, was the right of revolution ever seriously dealt with, as one of the inalienable rights, one of the self-evident truths central to the Declaration? In the education of the American statesman, was it ever brought home to him that to believe in democracy is to believe in the right of revolution? What *was* brought home to him concerning the Declaration of Independence? Did he read it? What did it mean to him? What did it seem to mean to others? Did he, or they, connect it with revolution? Was it ever discussed by teachers, in their lectures or otherwise? Did it come out that the Declaration of Independence was a serious assertion of belief in the right of revolution? A definitive assertion of belief in the right of *violent* revolution?

In the education of the American statesman, what connection, if any, was set up in his mind between the American Revolution and violent overthrow of government? As a result of his education taken as a whole, did he gain the impression that the American Revolution *was* a violent overthrow of government? If not, what impression of the American Revolution did he gain? Did he gain the impression that it was a breakdown of law and order? Did he gain the impression that it was an example of the democratic process? Were these questions ever discussed? In all the classroom references to and discussions of communism as an ideology that believes in the violent overthrow of government, and gives that belief a basic place in its creed, was it ever brought out that democracy as an ideology believes in the violent overthrow of government, and that the birth of our own country as an independent nation was based upon that belief? If such questions were discussed at all, did anyone maintain that our American belief in the violent overthrow of government is different from the communist belief in the violent overthrow of government? If so, what was presented as the difference? Did anyone point out that the American democratic belief in the right of revolution, the right of violent overthrow of government, was asserted before Marx and Engels were born, that Marx and Engels did not create this concept, but inherited it, largely from our own forefathers? In the education of the American statesman, did it ever seem to occur to anyone to examine what is said about violent overthrow of government—what is meant by it, and under what conditions it is held to be justified—in the Declaration of Independence and the writings of Jefferson, Paine, and our Founding Fathers on the one hand, and in the writings of Marx, Engels, and Lenin on the other hand? If this did occur to anyone, and he examined the writings, did he discover that in these two ideologies—American democratic on the one hand, Marxist communist on the other, the conditions considered to justify violent overthrow of government are the same, i.e., when the government has become a tyranny, denying the rights of the people, and the people are ready to support measures of violence against the government?[1] In the education of the American statesman, was anything of this kind ever done, ever suggested? Was the question even raised as to whether there was anything significant *in common* between the American Revolution of 1776 and the Russian Revolution of 1917? Was the question even raised as to whether there are any significant *agreements* between the basic political principles of what is called democracy and what is called communism?

It was already clear decades ago that the most important matters that any American statesman would have to deal with in the field of international affairs during the balance of the twentieth century were the relations between the superpowers, who were at the same time nuclear powers, capitalist democratic on the one side, Marxist communist on the other. Did the education of the American statesman prepare him to handle these matters intelligently? Was it an education based upon realities that would lead him to strengthen peace, or was it an education based upon myths that would lead him to make war? Was it an education in the spirit of the United Nations, or an education in the spirit of the enemy whom the United Nations had defeated? Was it an education for life, or for death?

The question is sometimes asked: why should *we* educate for peace "unilaterally"? The implication is that it would not be to our advantage to do so unless it were done "universally," or at least by "the other side" as well. It is likely that this line of thought begins with a confusion that equates education for peace with total pacifism or with complete unilateral disarmament. This is a false assumption; no final conclusion, especially no dogmatic panacea is implied. Education for peace begins simply with the recognition that the study of peace has been neglected, in spite of the fact that war is one of the most costly of social evils—now the supreme danger to the life of humanity. To study problems of war and peace systematically, to give them an amount of educational time, effort, facilities, and research commensurate with their importance is by no means to assume beforehand that some one particular program or theory is the right answer.

Study and teaching about peace and war are like study and teaching about health and disease, a process of digging out the facts, trying to identify the most important general truths, examining various theories proposed by different schools of thought within the field, and, above all, encouraging further studies and researches. To say we shouldn't educate for peace unless we are sure our neighbors are doing so is somewhat like saying we shouldn't educate for health unless we are sure our neighbors are doing so. Of course, the greater the number of neighbors who are undertaking such education, the better it is for us, but it does not follow that there is no advantage for us unless our neighbors undertake it also. To think there would be no advantage to us unless they undertake it is to think that all diseases come from the neighbors, or all wars are the fault of our competitors. In other words, it makes the absurd assumption that there couldn't be anything wrong with us. These considerations are especially important in relation to a ''superpower'' both because its educational example is more likely to be followed by others, while its mistakes and faults, especially in the area of decisions and policies that lead to unnecessary warfare, are more costly than the mistakes and faults of others. Thermonuclear responsibility is the heaviest responsibility that has ever entered the affairs of human beings. Albert Einstein saw the problem when he said that the atomic bomb changed everything except our ways of thinking. Education is the name of the solution.

NOTES

[1]For an analysis of the common ground of these conditions in the two ideologies, see John Somerville, *The Communist Trials and the American Tradition* (especially Chap. I) (New York: Cameron, 1956). Also, the same writer's chapter, ''Marxism and War,'' in Robert Ginsberg, ed., *The Critique of War* (Chicago: Regnery, 1969).

6

The New Semantics

THE WEAPONRY OF WORDS

We need to study semantics because words play tricks which cost people's lives. Of course, people need words. Without words, people would not be people, the rational animals. For without words, it would be impossible to think complex thoughts, and to build upon them in action, just as, without a marker and something that can hold a mark, it would be impossible to conceive of complex blueprints and to build structures in accordance with them. But every good thing has its peculiar forms of corruption, and language is certainly no exception. We are familiar with the phrase, "the tyranny of words"; we might also call it the weaponry of words. Some wit said the purpose of language is to conceal thought; a like grain of truth would be expressed by saying, to *prevent* thought. These are special cases, but nonetheless universal threats.

Words and language play an especially important and dangerous part in the problems of war and peace. But fortunately, we can use words to expose words; we can make them give evidence against themselves. We can use language to see through language, just as we use the eye to see through the eye. The word "war" itself is a capital example. As we mentioned earlier, the fact that people go on using the same word makes them think they are dealing with the same thing, even when the thing they are dealing with has obviously changed its nature and become a different thing. We are all familiar with the kind of conjuring trick called the "disappearing act," in which something that was there a moment ago seems magically to have vanished into thin air. What happened to the word "war" involves an opposite kind of trick, which might be called the "staying act," in which something that has really been replaced by something else quite different still seems to be there, its same old self. Semantically the effect is gained by using the same old word to refer to the new thing.

This might seem so simple as to be incredible. Actually, it is neither, as we realize when we reflect on the connection between the use of words and the facts of human psychology and behavior. All sorts of attitudes and habits of evaluation become formed and hardened around a certain name because that name has always stood for a certain thing, and that thing has always had the content and qualities which called for those attitudes and evaluations. The use of the name thus came to trigger off a whole set of psychological or behavioral mechanisms or response patterns within the individual, which is another way of saying it became the habitual cause of a whole set of actions. It is easy to see that this process has its good side, which has helped to preserve and raise people above all other animals. In the life of every human being, certain definite attitudes, certain definite habits of evaluation and consequent action become formed and hardened around a certain word, for example, the word "poison." One can see, in this fact, how marvelous was the invention of words and language—the original computer programming, of which present technological models are only relative refinements. The single word "poison" not only sums up and capsulizes a whole variegated set of data; it also stimulates in the human perceiver, regardless of the avenue of perception (sight, hearing, touch) a whole set of absolutely necessary self-preserving responses. By the single adjective "poisonous" applied to a noun we sum up, as in a formula, a host of interrelated facts about the thing which the noun is the name of: that it contains a chemical which, if taken into the body in certain amounts, will cause biochemical reactions resulting in great damage or death. Then, normally, this same single adjective, written or spoken in an appropriate case, will send signals to the brain that will cause the hand to be withdrawn or to reach for a weapon, depending upon the noun to which the adjective has been applied, will cause the whole body to react quickly in a thousand different ways, depending on a thousand different circumstances, always with a single purpose, dominated by a fixed idea built into the single word "poisonous." All this has saved countless lives and prevented untold suffering and agony.

However, like so many other examples of the processes and powers that enter into human life, this linguistic-behavioral complex can operate destructively as well as constructively, can be the bearer of as much evil as good to people. From the time written language was invented (about 4000 B.C., according to present evidence) until 1945, when the first atomic bomb was exploded, the word "war" stood for something that, even in its strongest form, could be waged with advantage, sometimes extremely great advantage, to at least one of the sides in a given conflict. Whatever be the moral judgment of it in a given case, the fact is that individuals have become national heroes because they won wars or battles, as a result of which they have risen to power and glory within the nation and on the world scene—Eisenhower, Theodore Roosevelt, Grant, Napoleon, Washington, Genghis Khan, Julius Caesar, to name only a few. Small states have acquired immense territories and empires by force of arms, and have become dominant powers in the affairs of the world: our own country's history, through World War II, as a result of which the United States became the world's leading power, is a prime example.

The Roman Empire, the British Empire, the French Empire, every empire in the history of the world, is a tribute to what can be accomplished by war. And the tribute is by no means unspoken, unwritten, unsung, unpainted, unsculpted, or undramatized. All the fine arts and popular arts the world has ever produced are filled with expressions, depictions and celebrations of the power and glory of wars of conquest and of liberation. In all human history so far war has been the honorable occupation of the upper classes as well as of the lower orders, regarded as a sacred duty and a high art, blessed by the church and rewarded by the state. Of course, at the same time, there have been protests, negative depictions and judgments, dissenting voices and movements. But they have been of little avail, possibly because of the fact, however dubious morally, that war *was* usually won by one of the sides, that one side *did* emerge stronger, richer, more powerful, that most of the human race *was* still alive after the war was over, that the planet earth *was* still intact and habitable. These were undeniable facts, and they prevailed over the relatively rare and scattered currents of moral condemnation set in motion by brave souls who often suffered heavy penalty for their courage.

In other words, for thousands of years "war" was experienced as something which, while dangerous, was also the source of extremely great advantage, profit, power, and fame, something which gave individuals a chance to escape from the deadly monotonies and suffocating inhibitions of ordinary life and national states a chance to attain the dominion and splendor of world powers. For thousands of years the predominant educative forces within state, church, school, home, arts, and society drove into the brain and nervous system of the vast majority of people all these compressed summations of data, all these attitudes of acceptance, all these positive evaluations, which grew into strong habits and mighty response patterns ready to spring into action at the sight or sound of the word "war." Then, after thousands of years of these repeated processes and behavioral responses, in the year 1945, the thing that had been called war, to which all these facts, evaluations, and behavioral responses had been connected, suddenly became an objectively different thing. Why? Because it could now be fought with new weapons which in objective fact contradicted all the old positive evaluations and attitudes of acceptance because, in objective fact, these new weapons eliminated the possibility of the advantages, profit, power, and fame upon which the old attitudes and positive evaluations had depended. The new weapons were capable of destroying *everything*.

However, in spite of the qualitative change which had objectively taken place in the thing called "war," the new thing into which it had changed continued to be called "war," so that subjectively, all the old attitudes, evaluations, and behavioral responses remained predominantly operative in the great majority of people. A small proportion of people immediately felt the force of the new objective situation strongly enough to change their subjective situation in accordance with it. This proportion has steadily increased since 1945, but has not yet become predominant. This is the history behind the fact that statesmen today can talk and write about "war" between the United States and China, "war" between the United States and the Soviet Union, "war" to contain communism, without being immediately committed to asylums for the insane by the people who hear and read their words.

NEW THINGS AND OLD WORDS

Though of course it would not solve the whole problem, it would obviously help greatly to have a new word for the new thing. I have proposed ''biocide.'' We are already familiar with terms like ''homicide,'' ''suicide,'' ''patricide,'' ''matricide,'' ''regicide,'' ''genocide,'' and (recently) ''ecocide,'' as words meaning the act of killing a particular person, group, or area within the totality of living things. The word we now need is one that stands for the act of killing all existing life—plant, animal, and human—for this is what thermonuclear weapons can do, on a planetary scale. Then, if someone spoke of ''war'' between the United States and the Soviet Union, he would be interrupted with the question, ''But isn't that biocide?'' just as a physician advising his patient to starve himself to death in order to contain obesity would be interrupted with the question, ''But isn't that suicide?''

To take an actual example: When Walt W. Rostow was Chairman of the Policy Planning Council of the U.S. Department of State, he wrote a leading article for the magazine section of *The New York Times* of June 7, 1964, concerning the Cuban missile crisis, in which he had played a certain part. Speaking of the fact that the Soviet Union had accepted Cuba's invitation to set up Soviet missile bases on its territory, and without attempting to question the legal right of these two countries to enter into this arrangement, or its similarity to the arrangement between the U.S. and Turkey concerning the American missile bases in Turkey, Rostow wrote: ''From the Soviet point of view this was a limited thrust whose success depended on . . . the likelihood that the United States, in the face of these dangers and schisms, would not be prepared to initiate—I repeat, to initiate—military action. We were determined to eliminate Soviet offensive weapons from this hemisphere, and prepared to do whatever was necessary to achieve that end.''

The accuracy of Rostow's account of the government's intentions was never questioned by any other member of the executive branch of the United States government, nor, so far as the present writer is aware, did anyone save himself comment upon this point in print.[1] Yet if the word ''biocide'' had been in currency it would without doubt have facilitated serious questioning and discussion, especially since the chief negotiator with the Soviets during the crisis, Mr. Robert Kennedy, was eager to testify, as his later account showed, that ''military action'' meant bombing and that it was thoroughly accepted by the American officials that any such bombing would begin a war which would become a thermonuclear holocaust resulting in the death of all humanity, and literally the end of the world.[2] (The original subtitle of Robert Kennedy's posthumously published *Thirteen Days* in *McCall's* was: "The Story about How the World Almost Ended.") Mr. Rostow could then have been asked: Is it not true that your statement, translated into more precise language, would read as follows? "From the Soviet point of view this legal action of accepting Cuba's invitation was a limited thrust whose success depended on . . . the likelihood that the United States, in the face of these dangers and schisms, would not be prepared to initiate—I repeat, to initiate—biocide, that is, the extinction of all life and the end of the world. We were determined to eliminate Soviet offensive weapons from this hemisphere, and prepared to do whatever was necessary, including the initiation of biocide, to achieve that end."

If the annihilation of all existing life is worse than the killing of one person, this kind of policy statement is infinitely worse than the medical advice of a physician who would say to his obese patient: "When people invite you to dinner, I must consider it a limited thrust at your welfare, a thrust whose success depends on the likelihood that I would not be prepared to initiate—I repeat, to initiate—a prescription of suicide for you. I am determined to eliminate the excess weight from your body, and prepared to do whatever is necessary to achieve that end."

If this statement had appeared under the by-line of the physician in an explanation printed in *The New York Times* there can be no doubt that immediate action would have been taken by the medical authorities, by the other patients of the physician, and by his family. Why, then, was not similar action taken upon the publication of Rostow's article? The answer might be put in this way: There is a word which unmistakably means killing oneself; it is "suicide." When a physician writes that he was so determined to save his patient from the dangers of disease that he was prepared to initiate a prescription of "suicide," the reader is forced to recognize the actual meaning of his statement. His nervous system has no way out, and sustains a shock, in consequence of which he immediately thinks: "Either this is a joke, or this man is mad. Something must be done at once if he is actually a practicing physician."

If the physician had not used the word "suicide," either because the word had not yet been invented, or because he did not want to face the consequences of a completely candid statement and had used instead some ambiguous expression, such as "progressive food reduction action," or "prolonged cessation of food intake," the reader's nervous system, which shrinks from shocks, would have utilized the margin of ambiguity as a kind of anesthetic. He would have thought: "This physician probably doesn't mean he would actually advise the patient to kill himself. After all, he's a doctor, and would certainly stop short of that." Everyone tries to avoid believing something that he does not want to believe, with a force proportional to his desire not to believe it.

In the case of one superpower possessed of an abundance of thermonuclear weapons adopting the policy of "initiating—repeat, initiating"—military action against another superpower possessed of an abundance of thermonuclear weapons, in order to prevent the second superpower from doing something within its legal rights, something which the first superpower, on its part, has already done and is doing, it is all the more difficult for the American reader to *believe* it, because the force of his desire not to believe that *his* government has adopted such a policy is so great. Moreover, if there is no one word in currency which directly expresses the enormity of what is objectively involved in the policy, things are made much easier both for those who wish to pursue it and for those who wish to avoid the truth that it is being pursued. In this case there is an additional factor on which the policy-planner can count when he uses and repeats the word "initiate," emphasizing the fact that our side would be the one to shoot first. That is, the great majority of his American readers have been thoroughly conditioned to believe that communists are evil incarnate—*all* communists, in *everthing* they do, so it is only common sense to shoot first. One doesn't wait for a rattlesnake to strike first when it appears in his garden. The policy-planner can further rely on the operation of all the outmoded attitudes, evaluations, and behavior-responses connected with the outmoded facts which the old term *military action* stands for. Thus the nervous system of the reader is, by these various semantic conditions, anesthetized against the shock that would otherwise have been received and have sent signals to the brain, which would have resulted in the taking of some kind of immediate inhibitory or preventive action.

In these matters there is a stage, psychologically and semantically most complex and interesting, in which an individual sees both the outmoded situation, with its outmoded evaluations and responses, and the new situation, calling for new evaluations and respones, realizes wherein the new responses ought to differ from the old, even states this difference in the most powerful language, and yet in practice follows the old responses. This is the stage that was reached by John Kennedy, when he made the statement that is often quoted: "Either man must put an end to war, or war will put an end to man." This was the same John Kennedy, who, according to his brother Robert, was fully prepared to follow out to the end the policy described and advocated by Mr. Rostow, even if the end were the end of the world. In other words, John Kennedy felt that if it was necessary to end the world in order to eliminate Soviet missiles from this hemisphere, then it was sad but true that the world would have to be ended. We are told by Robert Kennedy that this troubled John Kennedy very, very deeply, but not deeply enough to cause him to refrain from delivering the ultimatum to the Soviets. We are told by Robert, as we have seen, that his brother's anguish took the poignant form of dwelling upon "the death of the children of this country and all the world," innocent as they were and unaware of what was happening. But even this supremely anguished and poignant realization did not have force enough to cause him to refrain from delivering the ultimatum, or even to share with Congress or the people this infinitely fateful, historically un-precedented decision, which no one man was ever given the moral or legal right to make for all mankind. Yet he made it, and the incredible moral horror of it is equalled by its psychological and semantic com-plexity.

For, to cause this in a man of exceptional education and background, of more than average intelligence, there had to be present in his nervous system tremendous psychological forces with their own moral color of justification working in terms of words that presented themselves as compressed summations of "undeniable" facts so often repeated as to seem unquestionable, which were implacably connected with attitudes, evaluations, and behavioral responses that had reached a level of com-pulsive habit that could not be overcome, whatever the consequences would be. What words could possibly be capable of combining all these forces, pitched to such magnitudes? If the time had been the Middle Ages, one would have said that this man must have been "fighting the Devil." That alone could have justified destroying the world and all its innocent children. But that would have justified it, by the standards of the

Middle Ages. However, John Kennedy didn't live in the Middle Ages. The only thing that would justify it in his world was that he was "fighting communism." The word "communism" must have had about the same impact on his nervous system, and that of Rostow, Johnson, Rusk, McNamara, and the other high policy-makers, as the word "devil" had on the nervous systems of the high policy-makers for the church-state complex of the Middle Ages. The "facts" it summed up and the attitudes, evaluations, and behavioral responses connected with these "facts" took precedence over everything else, including the life of the entire world.

Actually, the phenomenon by which we are confronted in our time is of more amazing magnitude than the medieval phenomenon. To make the medieval psychological-semantic complex equal to the contemporary phenomenon in its dimensions, we would have to imagine first of all that the Christian church had been engaged for six years in a global war against some mortal enemy, an enemy which was also the mortal enemy of the Devil, and which had attacked the Devil as well as Christianity, so that Christianity and the Devil had formed an alliance. Together they finally managed to conquer their common enemy, a goal which, as everyone agreed, neither of them alone could have attained. After their victory, and especially in view of the new weapons of unlimited destructiveness which had been invented in the closing stages of the war, Christianity and the Devil decided that henceforth war itself was their common enemy, the enemy of everything in the world, so together they established a world organization to which each would belong, with equal rights and privileges, in which they would not cease to compete with each other, but would not compete by means of military war. In addition, we would have to imagine that the church, as the administrator of Christianity on earth, had a Constitution in which the power to initiate war was not given to the Pope, but was explicitly and deliberately given instead to a Congress of Clergy, and that all within the church had taken a solemn oath to uphold this Constitution.

Then we would have to imagine that, in spite of all this, the Pope, with a small group of Cardinals as his trusted advisors and policy-makers, saw that the Devil had presumed to accept an invitation to set up a few missile bases on an island some ninety miles from the Christian mainland, which island had a government sympathetic to the Devil. They gave this matter very serious consideration, and sent secret messages of protest and inquiry to the Devil, the contents of which later became known. The Devil, in reply, pointed out that the Pope maintained Christian missile bases in Turkey, closer to the Devil's domain than Cuba was to the Christian mainland, and proposed the simultaneous removal of both sets of missile bases. However, the Pope and his advisors decided not to accept this proposal, but instead delivered to the Devil an ultimatum to remove his missile bases, or they would be bombed, even though this meant war in which each side could be expected to use its most destructive weapons, capable of ending all life and the world. They also decided not to allow the Congress of Clergy to have a voice in the decision to initiate war, even though the Constitution gave this power to the Congress of Clergy alone.

If all *this* had happened in the Middle Ages and had been confirmed and documented over the signatures of the principal parties, how could we explain it? We could only conclude that the Pope and his advisors believed more strongly in the evil of the Devil than in anything else, more than in the facts that they had lived through during the war, more than in the solemn commitments they had signed after the war, when the world organization was established, more than in their own Constitution, which they had taken a special oath to obey. We could only stare in amazement at the force of that belief, which was capable of overcoming the evidence of the senses, the testimony of reason and logic, the restraints of morality and law, the feelings of tenderness and love for the innocent children of the world, who must *all* be incinerated in order to save them from the Devil.

This is not an overstatement of the case, for if fact, reason, and logic had played their normal roles, various questions would have inhibited the decision. If the Devil was a necessary ally in overcoming our mortal enemy who would otherwise have been able to destroy us, how could he be all bad? If we, the embodiment of the true and good, *needed* the Devil in order to survive, how could the Devil be all bad? If *we*, the true and the good, freely signed a Charter to grant equal rights and privileges to the Devil, how could *we* maintain that the Devil is all bad? Would we really be the true and the good, if, in initiating war on the Devil, we not only violate the compact we made with him, but the Constitution we made for ourselves? Would we really be the true and the good if, in initiating this war on the Devil, we initiate a conflict in which all life is destroyed, including the lives of all the innocent children? It is perfectly clear that all these questions had to be answered and that, given the facts, they were all answered the same way: we still have to initiate—repeat, initiate—war on the Devil. But why? And then comes the answer of absolute finality, the semantic triumph which acquires the psychological force to sweep everything else aside, the irresistible force which cancels the claim of fact, silences the voice of reason, cuts the bond of morality, and anesthetizes the feeling of love: *The Devil is all bad by definition.* Voilà! The thing is done.

If the Devil is all bad *by definition,* is the supreme, all-inclusive evil *by definition,* then it follows that anything else is better than the Devil, even universal death. No matter what sins *we* commit, we are still better than the Devil, and if we commit these sins in initiating war against the Devil, they will be forgiven. It will be seen that they are not really sins. In this situation, the detailed facts are immaterial. If the Devil is all bad *by definition,* no *facts* could possibly alter the final judgment. Thus there is no point in knowing the Devil, observing the Devil, studying the Devil, except for the purpose of making war on the Devil. All else is subordinate to that *by definition.*

But how does such a definition become accepted? How is it made to prevail? That is the job of education—in the school, the church, the state, the law, the home, the arts, the mass media, the businesses, and professions. The school teaches it directly. The church declares it orthodox doctrine. The state rewards it when it is carried into practice. The law punishes dissent from it and disobedience to it. The home echoes it. The arts depict it. The mass media spread it. The businesses and professions make profit out of it. How, then, is it possible to get an accepted definition rejected? By making changes in the school, the church, the law, the home, the arts, the mass media, the businesses, and professions.

That these things change is clear; otherwise, there would be no history. For example, our medieval ancestors, including those of Kennedy, Johnson, Rusk, Rostow, McNamara, and the other high policy-makers, actually and literally believed in the Devil, but it is very unlikely that the contemporary high policy-makers share that belief, in the actual and literal sense in which it was held by their medieval ancestors. It is probable that, at most, only vestiges, half unconscious, remain. That definition (of the Devil) lost its original force because of changes that took place in science, the economic system, religious interpretations, forms of government, criminal and civil laws, the atmosphere of the home, the content of the arts, the messages of the mass media. In the course of time, something came to take its unique place, perhaps given all the more force by its similarity to the older concept: *Communism* is all bad by definition.

In our American world, the world in which the makers of the contemporary war policy were educated, this is the definition which was taught in the school (''we must learn about communism in order to expose its evils''), preached in the church (''communists are all masters of deceit, who understand only the language of force; we need bigger and better bombs''), rewarded by the state (billions for anti-communism), enforced by the law (the Smith Act, and the many others like it), echoed in the home (''communism abolishes the family; look at what it says in the paper''), depicted in the arts (*Animal Farm, Brave New World, 1984*), spread by the mass media (''Secret Agent,'' ''Man from Uncle,'' ''Spy for the F.B.I.,'' etc.), and promoted by business (''defense'' contracts sky high). It is not surprising that the high policy-makers accepted the definition that communism is that which is all bad, the supreme evil, the destruction of which must take precedence over everything else, as a duty above all other duties, by any means necessary, legal or illegal, and no matter whose death is entailed.

Looked at from the point of view of logic, the fallacy involved in this incredible semantic triumph is not difficult to identify. What one is dealing with is an empirical definition, that is, the definition of something that can only be verified by the data of observation, sense perception, and experience, together with reason capable of analyzing these data. Communism is, of course, something that can be examined in this way, in regard to actual facts of practice in the various countries that are called communist (the Soviet Union, China, Poland, Bulgaria, Romania, Czechoslovakia, East Germany, Albania, Mongolia, Yugoslavia, Cuba, North Korea, North Vietnam), and in regard to its theory and doctrines in the works of its founders, principally Marx, Engels, and Lenin. Whether communism is or is not all bad must depend, first of all, on what is found by thorough and responsible examination of the facts of practice and the doctrines of theory. Second, it must depend upon accepting some particular standard of "bad", which must be brought out in the open and clearly expressed in order for the judgment to have any meaning.

This is the method of reason. Any American, or anyone else, who is of normal intelligence and willing to use this method would quickly find, if he began to examine the facts of practice in any of the given countries and the doctrines of theory in any of the given works, that it is impossible to sustain the judgment that communism is all bad. For example, one of the first things he would find is that the standard of living of the masses (the majority) had been raised by the communist regimes—educationally, in terms of literacy and opportunities for higher education and professional training; economically in terms of purchasing power and continuity of employment at the level of qualifications; health-wise, in terms of longevity, infant mortality, industrial mortality, and the incidence of disease. Raised in comparison to what? Naturally, in comparison to the conditions before the communist regime took power in the given country. Anyone using the method of reason would also quickly find that these things were stressed in the theory of communism and deliberately planned for. Logically speaking, he would already be forced to reject the definition that communism is that which is *all* bad. This would not be easy, in view of all his previous conditioning, but let us suppose that he does arrive at this rejection. How, then, should he define communism? If it is not *all* bad, *how* bad is it? How much good is there in it? He would probably find various things that he considered bad, and further things he considered good. The more he used this method in relation to capitalist as well as communist countries, the less he would be disposed "to initiate—repeat, initiate—military action" which he himself would have to admit carried the *calculated* risk of destroying the world. The less he would be disposed to accept *everything* done in the name of anti-communism. The more weight he would give to the moral and political premises of the United Nations and to the methods recommended by UNESCO. The more wisdom he would see in the provisions and safeguards contained in the Constitution of the United States in regard to initiating war.

WITCHCRAFT WORDS: WHAT IS FREEDOM?

Bound up with the semantics of war in contemporary American life is a whole host of tricky words, a whole language of working magic. Outstanding examples playing central roles are terms like "freedom," "the free world," "un-American activity," "subversion." In each case, in different ways, the word becomes perverted into a lethal weapon. "Freedom" is the oldest, antedating America, working its potent magic already in the ancient world. "We are a free city," said Pericles of Athens in his famous oration, and generations of scholars have sung the praises of the *freedom* of Athens, forgetting that in Athens the largest single class of human beings was made up of *slaves* who could be bought and sold in the open market.

The peculiar magic of the word "freedom" is that the beautiful sound of it prevents people from using their common sense. It is truly a bewitching word. In fact, it is so bewitching that people by the millions use it correctly every day, in accordance with its actual, plain, prosaic, even negative, meaning, and at the same time retain in their consciousness a shining, romantic, seductive image of it which is in absolute contradiction to the reality with which they are daily on the most familiar terms. This is pure witchcraft, but it works.

Perhaps the best means by which to see this process in action is to call to mind the ways in which we daily use the word "free," or "freedom." Five random examples will suffice.

(1) We ask whether we have to pay for something, and someone says, "It's free."

(2) We have allergy troubles, and the physician says, "You must work in a room free of dust."

(3) We read in a newspaper: "The maniac gained freedom from his doctors by leaping out of the window of the prison hospital."

(4) We attend a funeral, at which the preacher says, "Our brother is free from the cares of life."

(5) We switch on television and hear a voice: "At last Mr. Hyde was free from Dr. Jekyll, free to commit the crimes devised by his demonic brain. But this freedom was fortunately short-lived."

These are all obviously correct usages of "free," "freedom," "freedom from," and "freedom to." In each case, the meaning is obviously that something is absent from something. In (1) the need for payment is absent from the situation. In (2) dust must be absent from the work room. In (3) the doctors' control is now absent from the maniac. In (4) the cares of life are absent from the deceased. In (5) Jekyll's influence and the restraints of morality and reason are absent from Hyde's actions. It is equally obvious from these examples of correct usage that freedom is not always a good thing. It is good to get something free of charge, and good to have a room free of dust, especially when we are allergic to dust. But it is not good to have freedom from doctors, especially when we are suffering from grave mental illness. It is even worse to have freedom from the cares of life if that means we have freedom from life itself. It was certainly not good that Hyde had freedom from Jekyll, reason, and morality, but it was good that this freedom did not last long. So, freedom is plainly sometimes good and sometimes bad. It all depends on what it is freedom *from*, and what it is freedom *to*. If the language is such as to convey what the freedom is *from* or *to*, then we know what is meant, and we can make up our minds about whether the freedom spoken of is good or bad. But if the language is such as not to clarify or specify what the freedom is *from* or *to,* it would be impossible to ascertain the meaning of it, and equally impossible, therefore, to say whether it would be good or bad. If a man said to a group of people, "Excuse me a minute; I want to bring you something that is free," and left the room, but never returned, who could say what he meant to convey by the word "free," or whether it was good or bad? The most we could say was that he must have had in mind some kind of instance of something that was absent from something else, essentially a condition of negativity. Had he said "round," or "blue," instead of "free," everyone would know specifically what to look for on his return, for these terms connote the *presence* of a specific quality, not the *absence* of anything you please from anything else you please.

This means, of course, that it wouldn't make any sense for anyone to say that he loves freedom in general, all freedom, just freedom, or that he wants to be free in general, all free, just free. Unless he specifies free from what or free to what, he is saying nothing, for there is no such thing as being free from *everything,* and if there were, it is extremely doubtful that anyone would desire it. Freedom is always specific, relative to "from" and "to."

With these considerations in mind, let us examine five more examples.

(1) President Eisenhower says that we must not "allow any section of the world that is vital to us" to fall into a form of government "that wants to see freedom abolished from the earth."[3]

(2) The Secretary of State says that we must defend "the free world."

(3) "The land of the free and the home of the brave."

(4) "Unlike the communist world, we have a free press."

(5) "Donate to Radio Free Europe."

What does it mean to talk of a government that wants to see *freedom* abolished from the earth—not freedom *from this* or freedom *to that,* but freedom itself, just freedom, all freedom? Plainly, is not this pure nonsense? We know that President Eisenhower had in mind *communist* governments when he spoke of a form of government that "wants to see freedom abolished from the earth." But it is perfectly clear that no communist government would want to see freedom from capitalism abolished from the earth, or freedom to build socialism and communism abolished from the earth. It is equally clear that President Eisenhower, on his part, would have liked to see freedom *from* capitalism abolished from the earth, and freedom *to* build communism reduced to zero. What he had in mind, therefore, would be better conveyed by saying: "We capitalists must not allow any section of the world that is vital to capitalism to fall under a communist government." But that would take all the magic and seeming moral beauty out of it. When he uses the word "freedom," presenting our government as its champion and advocate, and another government as its enemy and destroyer, it sounds as if our government is standing up for a precious value which it is eager to share equally with all the world, whereas some other government is out to destroy all forms of that value, so that not a soul on earth would have any of it any more. When we realize, however, that each government is offering freedom from the other, and each would like to have *its* kind of freedom prevail, we then see more possibility of peaceful competition on a basis of equal rights and less need to call for holy war.

These same considerations apply to "the free world." Free from what, free to what? There are obviously many bad things this free world is not free from: war, crime, poverty, to name only three. Some wit said that very few things are free in the free world. Actually, health care, higher education, food, and books cost more in the free world than in the world that is not supposed to be free. But, in any case, it is pure moonshine to think there is a world that is "free" in general, just *free*, and another world that has *no* freedom, that is just unfree. There is a capitalist world and a communist world, each of which is free from some things the other is not free from, each of which is not free from some things the other is free from. When we look for these specifics and relativities, without which the word "freedom" has no meaning (only a beautiful sound), we find that what is meant by "the free world" is the non-communist world (even fascist Spain is counted part of the free world), and that what is meant by calling it "free" is that the individual in most parts of it has a greater degree of freedom from direct government action, and from the dominant political party than he or she has in the communist world. That is what it gets back to, if we approach it rationally, non-mystically.

But it would be ridiculous to think that in the communist world the individual has less freedom from prostitution, veneral disease, drug addiction, pornography, involuntary unemployment, illness, industrial accident, premature death, infant mortality, poverty, discrimination based on race, sex, or family background, and economic barriers to higher education and professional training. From most of such things, if not from all, the individual in the communist world has more freedom than the individual in the non-communist world. Whatever the exact reckoning may be, the important point is that we are not faced with an absolute contrast between two worlds, one free and the other unfree. We are faced by different degrees of freedom from different things, different degrees of freedom to do different things. In the capitalist world generally, there is more individual freedom to dissent from and oppose the government and political party in power; in the communist world generally, less freedom to do these things, but more freedom to get higher education and professional training irrespective of sex, race, family, or wealth, more freedom to stay healthy, and to remain employed at the level of qualifications. In the capitalist world there is less freedom of the from the power of big money and the influence of the church; in the communist world there is less freedom from the influence of politics and power of the state. It is safe to say that both worlds need more freedom, but not necessarily the same kind at the same time. Countries have different needs at different times, because they are at different stages of their development and faced by different conditions. Thus at a given time, one kind of freedom may be far more important to a given country than another kind of freedom. However, the most important point of all is that the supreme danger is reached when the magical myth of an absolute freedom, with its power to generate the psychology of the holy war, is accompanied by the scientific reality of an absolute weaponry. How far the myth can go and how potent can be its magic is demonstrated by the fact that our country, at a time when it had legal slavery on a massive scale (more slaves than in any other country), could use as a national anthem a song which referred to itself not only as "the home of the brave," but as "the land of the free," and the contradiction could pass almost unnoticed.

What is a "free press" free from? Our press is certainly freer than is the communist press from control by the government and pressure by the dominant political party. The press in communist countries is certainly freer than ours is from control by commercial advertisers and the power of private money. Our press is freer from censorship; their press is freer from pornography. One can have a meaningful debate if one poses the issue of what it is better for a press to be free from as a general condition, or what it is better for some given press to be free from at some given time, but if one poses the issue as that of a free press vs. a press that is not free, a meaningful debate is impossible, because the issue as posed has no cognitive meaning. It is not a rational call to a meeting of minds. It is a bugle call to a clash of arms.

"Radio Free Europe" is exactly the same thing. In this case, after years of posing as a private and independent organization that was not subsidized by any government, soliciting and collecting funds from the public on that basis, it was revealed that "Radio Free Europe" was secretly subsidized by agencies of the American government. The same sad fate befell the fanatically anti-communist Committee for Cultural Freedom, after years of self-righteous posturing. Radio Free Europe was not free from State Department foreign policy, and the Committee for Cultural Freedom was not free from CIA money.

WHAT IS UN-AMERICAN?

Just as, in the wonderland of semantic magic, one doesn't call upon people to fight for capitalism or defend private profit, but to fight for freedom and defend the free world, so also one doesn't call for laws to punish and persecute one's political opponents. That would look bad enough, after all the fine talk about freedom. Rather, one calls for laws to punish and persecute "un-American activity," or "subversive activity." When, by linguistic levitation, the matter is raised to this higher plane, one can even see how especially un-American and especially subversive are those who oppose the fight for "freedom," and the defense of "the free world." Miracles, like more prosaic events, have their own logic and hang together in their own way.

History does not record who invented the term "un-American activity," but early in the decade of the 1930s, there appeared a new committee in the United States House of Representatives, the Committee on Un-American Activities. It became extremely powerful and still is, though early in the 1970s it changed its name to Committee on Internal Security, without, however, changing the nature of its business. Dozens of similar committees have been created at the state and local as well as the national level. Numerous individuals and organizations suspected of "un-American activities" have been subpoenaed to appear before the Committee, in the full glare of national publicity, to answer questions about their "activities" (associations, relations with friends and relatives, the books, magazines, and newspapers that they read, the meetings and gatherings that they attended, conversations they had, letters they wrote, trips they took, clubs they joined as students, etc.) not because any of these activities might be criminal, but because they might be "un-American." Merely being called before such a Committee is enough to cause loss of job, to ruin the careers of many individuals and to break up the functioning of whole organizations. If one did not answer the questions (which might be about one's associates, friends, or relatives, whereupon *they* might be called before the Committee), one could be cited for contempt of Congress and serve a jail sentence. Many who thus went to jail were "blacklisted" in their professions. Some were artists of international fame who remained honored in the rest of the world. Some suffered nervous breakdown, and some committed suicide.

A nation became intimidated by a word, a word that was a weapon pointed at its head: "un-American." A special kind of fear spread throughout the country, similar to what must have spread throughout Salem at the time of the witchcraft trials, or throughout Europe in the time of the Inquisition, similar to what Kafka depicted in his prophetic play, *The Trial*. What is an un-American activity? That was, in itself, half the semantic triumph—the vagueness, the uncertainty, the lack of any justifiable standard, the unshared, unconfirmable arbitrariness of the whole thing—except the punishment, which was plain and fearful enough. Half the anguish of the victim in Kafka's play was that he could not find out what exactly he was being accused of, what it was he was supposed to be guilty of. But he knew he was under a heavy cloud of suspicion, and might pay a heavy penalty. He became obsessed and unnerved.

In 1948 *The New York Times* decided to send a reporter to Washington to interview the then Chairman of the House Committee on Un-American Activities, Congressman J. Parnell Thomas of New Jersey. In the course of the interview he was asked what was the Committee's standard of Americanism. His answer was: "Americanism is conservative. We've got to stop the radicals and stop them now."[4] This at least was candid and expressed what the Committee had actually been doing for more than a decade, and is still doing (under another name). When the effects of the mighty "un-American" shot administered by the semantic witchcraft of what came to be known as the McCarthy period have really worn off, have really been eliminated from the blood stream of the nation, the logical import of Chairman Thomas' statement will be realized in all its grotesque enormity. But at the time, and even now (save for the youth, and scattered cases of stubbornly self-arrested development) the nervous system had been too heavily anesthetized to feel the shock. The necromantic shot had done its work so well that the public, Congress, the educational system, the church, the home, the press, the mass media, were as under one hypnotic spell, which made it all seem natural: "Americanism is conservative. We've got to stop the radicals and stop them now."

Americanism=conservative. Un-Americanism=radical. What does this do to the American claim of freedom, political freedom, the freedom of the individual? Freedom for the Right, but no freedom for the Left. The radicals must be stopped. America, the land of the free, is for conservatives only. The free world is just the world of conservatives. The greatest enemy of America could never have delivered a more trenchant blow, a more shattering indictment: the meaning of America is not democracy, not civil liberty, not progress, but just conservatism. What does this do to the signers of the Declaration of Independence, who, by their act, created America as an independent country? It makes them all un-American, for they were, to a man, revolutionary radicals, declaring the theory and practicing the fact of forcible overthrow of government. What does it do to Lincoln, who wrote a sympathetic letter to Karl Marx? It exposes him as un-American. What does it do to Franklin Roosevelt, who pronounced himself to be "left of center," and who was throughout the world the most honored American President since Lincoln? It signs his own confession of un-Americanism. What does it do to the whole of American history? It purges it of the subversive influence of progress.

These are but a few examples of what happens to the egregious myth of "un-American activity" at the slightest touch of logic. But the myth works, and goes on working, though it is rapidly losing power among the youth, who now increasingly insist that the meaning of words be rooted in reality, and it is slowly losing effectiveness among the older generation. The first force that arose in American life to confront this moral and political monstrosity with a mass challenge of sufficient strength to sweep it into the dust bin of history was the youth rebellion and peace movement that may yet become the second American Revolution.

NOTES

[1] In John Somerville, "World Authority: Realities and Illusions," in *Ethics, An International Journal of Social, Political and Legal Philosophy* (Chicago: University of Chicago, October 1965), p. 42-43.

[2] See Chap. 1, n. 10.

[3] *The New York Times*, May 8, 1953.

[4] *The New York Times Magazine*, August 1, 1948.

7

The New Science
of Peace

WHAT IS A SCIENCE OF PEACE?

Is a science of peace possible? To answer this question a prior question must be raised: what does one mean by a "science"? It is quite obvious that *study* of peace is possible, and *knowledge* about peace is possible. What does "science" add? It adds the kind of understanding, the particular kind of knowledge, that leads to greater and greater predictability, which in turn leads to greater and greater control. This is what Francis Bacon, the philosopher who showed how philosophy becomes science, meant by saying, "Knowledge is power." The father of social science, Auguste Comte, put it neatly: "To see is to know; to know is to foresee; to foresee is to control." In French it rhymes and chimes, like a bell: "Voir, c'est savoir; savoir, c'est prévoir; prévoir, c'est pouvoir." This is the same thought Friedrich Engels had in mind when he pronounced the apparent paradox which has puzzled so many: "Freedom is the appreciation of necessity."[1] Actually and literally, what Engels said was, "Freedom is insight into necessity." ("Ist die Freiheit die Einsicht in die Notwendigkeit."[2]) The fact that "Einsicht" was strangely translated as "appreciation," also as "recognition," both of which are too weak to do justice to the idea, added to the suggestion of paradox. Engels' thought was that freedom from or to anything is gained by insight into the patterns of necessity (causality) that govern the situation of the given thing. In other words, the more you understand of the causes and laws operating in yourself, and in the situation in which you find yourself, the more freedom you will be able to gain in that situation because understanding

135

of laws and causes is the kind of understanding that increases predictability, which in turn increases control. In the third Aphorism of his *Novum Organum* Bacon expressed the thought: "Human knowledge and human power meet in one, for where the cause is not known, the effect cannot be produced. Nature, to be commanded, must be obeyed."[3]

But does this apply to *human* nature? It would *not* apply if, and only if, human nature had neither causes nor laws, if the needs, wants, acts, and practices of human nature had no governing or necessary relationships. But to think that needs, wants, acts, and practices are possible without cause or law is to think children possible without father or mother. When one says people are not predictable, one has in mind all sorts of instances in which one did not know all of the causes operative in the situation. It is safe to say that this will always be the case, since the causes extend back in infinite regression, and it is impossible to reach the end of an infinite series. This is a mathematical guarantee that there will always be surprises, happy and unhappy, in human life.

But even if we admit the possibility that some human actions, some parts of human behavior will forever remain unpredictable, so that it will be forever impossible to understand and explain them completely in terms of the operation of laws, regularities, or patterns of necessity, that does not preclude the possibility of a science about human behavior. For science and scientific knowledge are matters of degree. They are not in the nature of absolutes which are either all there or not there at all. A science begins in a small way, and grows by deliberately seeking the kind of knowledge that increases predictability, that relates to possible causes and laws, that judges its own validity by the test of new prediction. This is the difference between knowledge in general and scientific knowledge in particular. To the degree that a given field develops *this* kind of knowledge, it begins to be called a science. Recent cases are cybernetics and ecology: somewhat earlier ones are psychology and sociology. In almost all cases (ecology is an exception), the science was an outgrowth of philosophy, brought into being by thinkers who called themselves philosophers, and their work philosophy, but were called scientists by later ages, e.g., Archimedes, Copernicus, Galileo, Newton, Dalton, Comte.

Everyone knows that science is a problem-solving activity, but what most do not learn, because of the disgracefully mechanical way most of the sciences have been traditionally taught, is that it is a highly creative activity. That is, there is nothing pre-ordained or automatic about how many sciences there should be, what fields should be sciences, or what problems should be studied. The most challenging, important, and difficult task in the history of any science is to discover the *problems*. This is a necessarily creative process, in which the difficulties to be overcome are as much psychological as logical, and call as much for moral courage as for logical ability. The psychological and moral aspects of this process in science are very similar to what they are in painting, music, sculpture, poetry, or the novel. Degas once said that the painter must approach his work in the same frame of mind as that in which the criminal commits his crime. That is, he must not feel bound by the rules, the tradition, the prevailing canons. Of course, a man or an artist can break the wrong law, or break a law for the wrong reason, but a man or an artist incapable of breaking the law is something less than a man or an artist. Most of our teaching of science takes place in what might be called a postmortem atmosphere, whereas the atmosphere that is needed is a prenatal one.

A science of peace—let us call it paxology—is thus as *possible* as any other social science, and today perhaps more needed than a good many others. Not that one can create a full-fledged science simply because it is needed. One's need for a grandchild may be very great, but to have a grandchild one needs first to have a child. There are similarly necessary relationships among sciences. In many respects, the ones that developed later are, logically and methodologically, children and grandchildren of the ones that developed earlier. Astronomy would have been impossible without mathematics; physics would have been impossible without astronomy; chemistry needed both mathematics and physics, and so on. Comte's concept of the possibility of social science rested consciously and systematically upon the previous development of physical and natural sciences, culminating in modern biology. Marx and Engels, younger contemporaries of Comte, shared this idea, but differed with Comte about how it should be worked out and what aspect of it needed primary emphasis at the time.

Paxology is a social science which can now be built up on the basis of previously developed social and behavioral sciences like sociology, psychology, economics, political science, as well as from the rich mother-lode of philosophy and literature. Much work done within it will for some time be indistinguishable from work done in one or another of the related disciplines, and people will continue to argue about whether there is actually a separate science of paxology, or, in any case, whether it had not better be called a "study," and so on, until so much work has been done in its name that such disputes begin to appear more and more pointless. This is the kind of process which all previously developed sciences have gone through.

At the present time, an increasing abundance and variety of research work, articles, journals, books, courses, centers, institutes, and organizations devoted to the study of problems of peace are appearing. Some of this work is aimlessly descriptive and merely academic, in the bad sense of that word. Such work is always "safe," but could only *accidentally* turn out to have *scientific* relevance, which is determined by contribution to increased predictability, something which is in turn determined by selection of problem. (One knows in advance that the solution of certain problems will add to predictability.) Some of the work being done at present is of direct practical and political relevance, but not cast in scientific form. This does not mean that it is lacking in value, for there are diverse means to a good end. Peace is more important than the scientific truth about peace, as health is more important than the scientific truth about health. But, as those truths about health which give us increasing power of prediction and control are thereby means of strengthening health, so those truths about peace which give us similar power become means of strengthening peace. While in neither case is scientific knowledge the only means necessary (art, love, and other human wellsprings that are not mainly intellectual are also powerful means of strengthening peace and health, and must play their part), scientific knowledge is a very important means, as natively human and creative as the others, and must not be overlooked.

IS A SCIENCE OF PEACE "VALUE-FREE"?

One of the issues confronting paxology, an issue which has already made its presence felt, is that of "value-free" science, the claim that science, to be science, must be free from value judgments, that science, as science, is neutral in the struggle of values, and since peace is a value preferred in opposition to war, a science of peace would not be value-free, and therefore would not be a genuine science. The answer is that on these terms a genuine science of health would be impossible, since health is a value preferred in opposition to disease, so that a science of health would not be value-free. Another way of putting the answer, which disposes of this objection in its own terms, is to point out that all one wants is a science of peace *as value-free* as the science of health is. When paxology arrives at an understanding of the social causes and laws governing peace and war, to an extent approximating that which biological science has attained of the physical causes and laws governing health and disease, the main problems will be solved. They might possibly be solved sooner some other way, though there is very little evidence to support this hope. Clearly, what has greatest claim on our attention is the fact that each passing day they remain unsolved in a world of steadily augmented thermonuclear arsenals increases the possibility that man will annihilate himself.

In any case, the claim of "value-free" science is grossly exaggerated, as are most claims for the moral "neutrality" of important concepts. If power is a value, preferred in opposition to powerlessness, as it obviously is, then science is by definition value-oriented at its very roots, for, as we have seen, the specific difference of science is that it is the kind of knowledge which increases man's power to predict and control. Science is not neutral about people and their struggle against the forces of nature which would injure or destroy them. The kind of truth that science gives people is, by deliberate intent, the kind that puts into their hands weapons which they use every day against their natural enemies. There is an infinity of undiscovered, complex *truth* which would add nothing to people's power to predict and control. Although it is real truth, it is humanly and scientifically unimportant, and no one thinks seriously of pursuing it.

For example, all would dismiss as absurd such a project as a million researchers, living in different parts of the world, each starting out from his house every morning of one year for the purpose of cataloguing, each day, every detached, inanimate, unowned object weighing between one ounce and one pound encountered on his research walks through the city, setting down its name and exact weight, in order to obtain the average weight of the objects and the average number of letters in their names.

Everyone will admit that this would be new knowledge, the truth of which would be far more certain than that of the major propositions of nuclear physics or urban sociology. This truth would really be neutral and value-free. Isn't that exactly the reason science would turn away from it? "Pure" truth, in the sense of truth that doesn't have any potential of practical application, immediately or eventually, that is, doesn't have any power-potential to increase man's ability to predict and control, is the last thing in the world science is interested in, not only because this kind of truth is useless, but equally because it gives no depth of *validated* understanding, proof confirmed by prediction. One may be fascinated by something that is purely useless, whose power potential in relation to oneself is zero (if that is really possible), but fascination is different from understanding, though the two can be united, as in science. To be fascinated by the purely or relatively useless is nonetheless a delightful process as long as it lasts, though it could hardly be expected to last very long, unless the fascination begins to project a message or meaning that carries over into other parts of life, in which case we would have to say that the purely useless thing has ceased to be purely useless and has taken on functional importance. This kind of experience, moral or esthetic, gains depth, I would argue, in proportion to the extent that it adds to the individual's power to deal with his further and ongoing experience, his other situations and problems. This way of adding to human power does not contradict the scientific way, but supplements it and is sometimes united with it. There can be moral grandeur and artistic beauty in a scientific truth, as there can be scientific skill and depth embodied in a work of art or a moral principle. Man needs all these strands of being, and at a certain level needs to join and interweave them for his greater enrichment. That this is possible is shown in the work of a man like Leonardo da Vinci.

There is only one sense, rather narrow and obvious, in which science could be said to be "value-free." This is the sense in which it is true that the scientist must avoid thinking that something is so because it fits in with his moral preconceptions, or that something is not so because it would offend his moral preferences. He must recognize that a fact is a fact, whether it disappoints him morally or not, and in giving an account of the facts, he must avoid both the temptation to give too much weight to those he morally approves, and the temptation to deny or suppress those he morally disapproves. Value preferences have no place when it comes to deciding what the *facts* of existence *are* in a particular case. The moral bias of the scientist must not interfere with the *accuracy* of his observations. Value judgments cannot be *substituted* for factual data.

These are truisms, and it must be noticed that what they apply to is only that part of the scientist's work which has to do with the relation between any factual conclusion to which he comes and the evidence at his disposal. These truisms do not apply to the scientist's selection of a problem to work upon. They do not apply to the *kind* of truth (predictive) that science chooses to seek, and the kind of truth it chooses not to seek. They do not apply to *why* the scientist is a scientist. All *these* central elements and aspects of science are, as we have seen, saturated with value judgments.

We said above that science, because of the kind of knowledge it deliberately chooses to seek, places in people's hands weapons they can use to overcome their natural enemies. If science were only physical and natural, we could leave the statement at that. But our history has long since reached the point where we have felt the need and demonstrated the possibility of social science. However, when we look at human society nothing is clearer than the fact that man does not have, and never has had, just one society, but many, and many antagonistic to one another and within any one, mutually antagonistic groups and classes. Thus the power which science gives does not simply become a weapon used by humanity as a whole against a common enemy, but becomes equally a weapon that can be used by one human group against another human group. It follows from these facts that the scientist, because of the kind of knowledge he produces as a scientist, is prevented from being neutral, not only in the struggles between man as a whole and forces of nature that threaten man as a whole, but also in relation to the struggles among human groups that threaten one another, as groups. This becomes especially clear in social science.

Thus the social scientist, because he produces the kind of knowledge that has a power-potential which becomes a weapon in social struggles, is prevented from playing an objectively neutral role in these struggles. He either consciously chooses a side, or unconsciously takes one. He cannot avoid this involvement, even if he would like to, because he cannot avoid choosing problems to work on, or, what comes to the same thing, choosing to let someone else make the choice for him. It is clear that every society, every human group, and every social class has problems, which, if solved, will help it in its struggles against its social antagonists. Conversely, the solution of any particular ''social problem'' is unlikely to give the same amount of additional power to all contending parties on the given social scene, but is likely to place more weapons in the hands of one than of another. In short, to be a scientist is to make a commitment, not only to the general value of adding to human power, but also, willy nilly, to the specific value of adding to the social power of a specific social group. Some scientists have realized, only when it was too late, that the kind of work they did added to the power of a social group whose values they abhorred.

Paxology neither claims nor wishes to be neutral between peace and war, any more than microbiology claims or wishes to be neutral between people and microbes. But just as, in order to implement the value judgment that lies at the basis of microbiology, it is necessary to struggle against the actual behavior and policies of people who promote the life of pathogenic microbes rather than the life of human beings, so also, to implement the value judgment that lies at the basis of paxology it is necessary to struggle against the actual behavior and policies of people who promote war rather than peace. This is exactly the kind of situation faced by the new science of ecology today. It is not neutral between a living environment and a dead one, between rivers in which fish cannot live and those in which they can, between a polluted and an unpolluted atmosphere. It does not approach the study of the environment in a disinterested, value-free spirit. (The fanciful example we used earlier, of a research project aimed at a worldwide cataloguing of unowned, in-animate objects, simply with the aim of discovering the average of their weights and of the number of letters in their names, would be part of a *value-free* ecology.) The ecology that is actually developing as a science chooses and formulates its problems with the deliberate aim of finding knowledge that meets the criteria of increased prediction and control not only in relation to the environment as such, but in relation to *strengthening* its *life-sustaining* properties.

To a certain extent, but only to a certain extent, such knowledge can also be used to the opposite effect of polluting the environment and weakening its life-sustaining properties. It is true that there is a good deal of knowledge, found especially in the physical and natural sciences, which has the character of power that could be used equally effectively for constructive or destructive ends, to protect life or hasten death, to add to the social power of a group that would place the long-run life of the environment above the short-run making of profit or a group with the opposite priority. But most knowledge in most sciences (military science is an exception) is by design weighted on the constructive side.

This weighting is determined by the choice of problems, but probably could never be made to fall entirely on one side. For example, while military science is aimed mainly at destruction, the solution of the problem of the most effective way to destroy a bridge could, at least in part, be utilized in peace-time construction, for instance, in situations where it was necessary to remove an old bridge in order to build a new one. One must say ''in part'' because the purpose of military destruction is the weakening of the enemy, so that military science sets before itself not just the problem of destroying a bridge, but the problem of destroying a bridge in such a way that the enemy will be put to the expenditure of maximum time and trouble to replace it. The optimum point is that at which the enemy is forced to do the greatest amount of further work of destruction before the work of constructing the new bridge can begin. Biochemical warfare goes further than toxicology as such: the former, unlike the latter, deliberately poses the problem of finding the *least detectable* way of spreading the *most effective* poison for which there is *least available* antidote or protection. It also poses such a problem as the most effective way to cause forest fires and ruin crops, while ecology, for example, poses exactly the opposite problem—the most effective way to prevent forest fires and strengthen crops. In this case, neither kind of knowledge could be used *equally* for the opposite purpose. If a sociologist makes a contribution to the problem of raising literacy or reducing crime, it is not likely that his contribution would prove equally effective to the end of lowering literacy or increasing crime. Paxology is like ecology in that the solution of its problems would have a very direct and obvious relation to the increase of power and strength on the constructive side, the side of life, so long as they were genuinely scientific problems, i.e., problems whose solutions would contribute to further predictability and control.

THE PROBLEMATICS OF A SCIENCE OF PEACE

But does paxology actually have such problems? What are they, concretely speaking? If paxology is the science of peace, how should its specific problems be formulated? In trying to answer these questions, the present writer would argue that the point of departure should be a recognition of the fact that the specific components of the general problem of peace are drawn from a number of areas, each of which is the subject matter of an existing social science or discipline, e.g., such fields as sociology, economics, psychology, philosophy, political science. This is true also of ecology, whose specific components are dealt with separately in geology, chemistry, biology, botany, zoology, sociology, and related fields. The same situation is seen in cybernetics, made up of components which were, and still are, dealt with separately in fields like logical theory, neurology, language structure, and information theory. There is nothing historically new about creating a new science in order to deal better with an important problem which cuts across the areas of a number of older sciences.

If, within paxology, we raise at once so broad and fundamental a question as the cause of war, we realize that we must reformulate it in the plural, the causes of war. General knowledge is enough to indicate that the causes are diverse in nature—economic, political, sociological, psychological, ideological. These facts suggest numerous specific problems whose solutions would contribute to predictability, thence to the possibility of control: What were the economic, the political, the sociological, the psychological, the ideological, or other causes of specific wars? In each case, which causes were major and which minor? The difficulty of answering such questions becomes a concrete stimulus and challenge to the development of better means of measurement and comparison, more precise methods of collecting data, more strategic programs of observation, more sophisticated concepts of causation.

Work of this kind would no doubt yield different conclusions relative to different types of war, e.g., small-scale, large-scale, short, long, colonial, guerrilla, national liberation, civil, world, and the like, which would in turn lead to problems of better typology, perhaps new types, new terms, and better definitions. It would also lead to the problem of historical changes over the centuries, and to the possibility of formulating a law of such change. In other words, what does the *history* of warfare show, with respect to the causes of war? Was one type of cause stronger at one time than another? What do the facts of history show with respect to the question of whether any one type of economic system or political system or social or cultural system has any special influence on the frequency or duration of wars? What do the facts of history show with respect to the relation between the practice of religion and the practice of war, in general, and in regard to specific religions?

The problems of paxology might be divided into two large groupings—the prevention of war and the strengthening of peace. Though these groupings overlap, their problems are in many ways different, as problems of preventing disease have certain differences from those of strengthening health. More knowledge of the causes of war, because it would enable us better to predict the occurrence of war, would give us more power to prevent war, since an effect can be prevented by forestalling or eliminating any one of its necessary causal conditions. However, the causes that enter into the strengthening of peace go far beyond countering the specific causes of war, and their pursuit opens up a very wide range of problems involving many different areas.

In one sense the strengthening of peace is attained by increasing the use of methods other than war for the settling of disputes between governments or between people and governments. What are these other methods? Under what conditions has each worked successfully? Under what conditions has each failed? Investigation of these "conditions" again takes us into many different fields: economics, politics, sociology, psychology, and others. Is it possible to correlate certain conditions in each of these fields with the successful functioning of methods other than war? Is it possible to correlate certain conditions in each of these fields with the unsuccessful functioning of methods other than war?

As work is done on such questions the need inevitably arises for more precise definitions of "peace" and "war." William James, no doubt speaking from his experience as a successful pioneer in the shaping of psychology as a separate science, once remarked that in the beginning stages of a new field a certain degree of vagueness is what best consists with fertility. In other words, let different conceptual demarcations and definitions be tried. These are not matters of logical correctness, so much as matters of methodological fruitfulness, and the standard by which they must be judged is not truth—many different variants could be consistent with truth—but the degree to which each facilitates the attainment of solutions (truths) that increase predictability.

In ordinary language the word "peace" has, of course, very broad connotations—peace of mind, a peaceful scene, at peace with oneself, and the like, in addition to international peace. The word "war" has similarly broad connotations—war against ignorance, at war with oneself, a price war, and the like, in addition to military war among nations. Our main focus of interest is war among nations fought with modern weapons because this threatens mankind with more dangerous consequences than any other kind of "war." However, it might turn out in actual scientific experience that the solution of problems involved in preventing this kind of war is facilitated by treating them in terms of what they have in common with problems involved in the other kinds of war. In this case the concepts "war" and "peace" themselves would be defined very broadly, and paxology would be said to include them all. Alternatively, it might turn out that narrow definitions of war and peace best facilitate the gaining of predictive knowledge. In that case the definition of war would be restricted to conflicts between large groups of people fought out with physical weapons in relation to political goals, and paxology would be defined in correspondingly strict terms. The same considerations apply to the scientific definition of "peace." These are not matters that are determined on purely logical grounds or purely factual grounds, but on grounds of methodological strategy. The logical and factual requirements could be met by either type of definition, broad or narrow.

The general danger of very broad definitions is that they tempt the problem-solver to try to solve too much at once. If paxology is the science of peace, and we define peace very broadly as the absence of any conflict, or the absence of any destructive conflict, or the presence of harmonious relations among the components within any given situation, the problem, for example, of "strengthening peace" would take on a multiplicity of aspects hard to handle in one package. If war were defined in correspondingly broad terms, confusion might also be increased at the value level, since the general presumption is that it would be well to eliminate or prevent *physical* warfare, whereas the general presumption also is that it would not be well either to eliminate or prevent conflicts of many other kinds—intellectual, artistic, political, and the like, since such conflicts can be very beneficial. This broad terminology also carries the danger of suggesting that a debating contest is, after all, a small war, so that a war between the United States and the Soviet Union could be likened to a big debate. When we give two things that have differences as well as similarities the same name, as we do, and must do in our language systems, it is on the implied basis that the similarities factually outweigh the differences, and that the similarities are morally more important than the differences. A new science needs new words, but in its beginning stages has nothing to work with but the old words, which are like lights that shine on not all the right places. The main point to remember is that we must try to fit language to specific realities, not the realities to a language, and the realities to which we want to fit language are singled out in terms of different human needs. Words are beautiful by psychological association, logical by consistency within a system of rules, scientific by predictive power. The need determines the choice, including the choice to create new words and new language systems.

Very broad definitions also sometimes stand in the way of scientific development by making problems seem too difficult. This form of discouragement manifests itself in statements to the effect that war is conflict, and conflict is an inherent part of human nature; or that war is a manifestation of aggressiveness, and we don't want to eliminate aggressiveness from man. While such statements are not difficult to refute logically (they are equivalent to saying that, since eating is a necessary part of human life, it is impossible or unwise to try to stop man from eating too much, or from eating poisonous food), they play a negative role in that they discourage the use and application of scientific method to any part of the matter in question. What is of primary concern is whether the *particular form* of conflict or aggressiveness that is called war between nations, and that is fought out with modern weapons, can be prevented, whether *that specific form* of collective behavior is an ineradicable part of human life.

A whole set of methodological problems revolves around the question to what extent war between nations can be explained by the causes and laws that determine the behavior of individuals as individuals. Do the same causes and laws and the same consequent possibilities of prediction, prevention, and control apply to war and peace between nations as apply to conflict and harmony between next-door neighbors? One must take account of the fact that the decision to enter into international warfare is not made by individuals as individuals but by individuals acting as agents or leaders of *governments*. Of course it could also be said that relations between next-door neighbors are not relations between individuals as individuals, but are usually between individuals acting as members or heads of *families*. This is true, but changes only the terms in which the question must be put: to what extent can war between nations be explained by the causes and laws that determine conflicts between families? To what extent can methods which are successful in peacefully resolving conflicts between families, or other small social groups, be applied to the relations between governments? They might or might not be equally applicable. In fact, it is not altogether inconceivable that it might prove easier to find ways of preventing massive violence between nations than the small-scale violence between smaller social units.

To raise a somewhat fanciful aspect of this whole question: If human violence be defined as the use of force with the intent or knowledge of its inflicting injury, would it be inconceivable that a specific chemical agent might be found which had the effect of eliminating the desire of human beings to use violence in any of their relations with other human beings? Would it be desirable, or under what conditions would it be desirable, for human beings to make use of such a causal agent? Would it be justifiable for one group of human beings to apply it to all human beings, whether the others consented or not? This question would arise in its pure form, so to speak, if there were satisfactory evidence that the chemical agent in question had no dangerous side-effects. If there were dangerous or inconvenient side-effects, then these would have to be balanced against the main effect.

In either case, certain relevant existing facts would have to be taken into consideration. We already have compulsory vaccination and compulsory quarantine against certain communicable diseases. Why not against violence, the infliction of injury? In the public sale of food-stuffs and in the manufacture and use of all sorts of industrial products, including various stimulants and narcotics, we are in fact allowing commercial motives a great deal of latitude in deciding questions concerning contacts between chemical agents and human beings. Why not allow social motives to decide in this case? The present writer would argue that it would be a very good thing if the United Nations could sponsor an international research project to investigate the contribution which chemistry might make to paxology, and that the member states would be well advised to provide a budget for such research similar in scale to the budget that was provided by the United States in order to produce the first atomic bomb. While most people might regard this whole idea as something to associate with alchemy rather than with the science of chemistry, it must always be remembered that the actual development of the genuine science of chemistry, as a result of the building up of predictive knowledge and consequent control, has attained a degree of power over natural forces which makes the wildest dreams of the medieval alchemists seem like the pale productions of a weak imagination. Contributions to a new science could conceivably come from any of the older sciences; old and new sources would by no means be mutually exclusive or contradictory, but would supplement one another.

RELATIONS OF A SCIENCE OF PEACE TO SOCIOLOGY, ECONOMICS, AND POLITICAL SCIENCE

In any case, most attention at present is naturally directed to channels which have already been used to some extent for dealing with peace problems, channels provided by sciences like sociology, economics, political science, psychology, as well as the still fertile mother of sciences, philosophy, which may yet see another of her progeny grow to independent stature, and play an important part in the world. In each instance a wide range of problems is involved. When one speaks of "the sociology of war and peace," one has in mind the systematic examination of the relation between sociological conditions almost limitless in number, extent, and variety on the one side, and the occurence of war or strengthening of peace on the other. Sociological conditions subdivide themselves geographically and regionally, ethnically, occupationally, by age, education, socio-economic class, religious outlook, political preference, marital and family status, and in many other ways. In each of these subdivisions problems may be posed concerning the relation of elements or factors within it to war and peace, which, if solved, would add to predictive knowledge.

The economics of peace involves like perspectives and possibilities.

Economic factors as a cause of wars have already received considerable investigation and confirmation; yet, in relation to the magnitude of the subject, all that has been done is no more than a beginning. In relation to many well-known wars, economic factors have been little examined, either as causes or consequences. In relation to some types of warfare, such as the long drawn out invasion and occupation of North, Central, and South American Indian lands by the white man, the facts are known, but the implications of the facts are little developed. It would be of great value to have studies of wars which would compare and contrast the officially declared motives, reasons, and causes for entering into the war, on the one hand, with the economic results, consequences, and actions, particularly of the victorious side, on the other hand. Series of such studies should be carefully examined with the aim of finding recurrent patterns which would facilitate prediction and lead to the possibility of establishing a social law. This point applies to any group of studies which lend themselves to comparison and contrast with one another.

Valuable studies combining economic and political factors could be made by taking instances of wars wherein officially declared reasons for entering were in contradiction to subsequent actions, and then examining different forms of public reaction or protest, with a view to determining the degree of effectiveness of the different forms of protest. Detailed studies of the profits of war could likewise be combined with psychological and public opinion studies of reactions of various groups to the economic facts. What actual efforts have been made ''to take the profits out of war''? What is the state of general public opinion, labor opinion, management opinion, and the opinion of other social groups concerning the desirability of taking the profits out of war? What causes account for the public's so long accepting the fact that in war the lives of the youth are disrupted and drafted into national service while the property of the rich remains in private hands, and often increases enormously? What would be the probable effect of a law which provided that whenever the government waged war, and drafted the youth, all industry and capital would become public property for the duration, that private profit and private dividends would cease (be socialized), and all salaries would be limited to the scale of military pay? What proportion of the public would accept the moral principle that, if lives are drafted, property should also be drafted?

The activities of munitions makers in relation to the promotion of wars in which they stand to make great profit should be further researched. How does the "military-industrial complex" against which President Eisenhower himself warned the nation actually operate? How did it grow so strong that so conservative a president, with a lifetime background of professional military experience, culminating at the highest level, should feel compelled to put the country on guard against the dangerous magnitude of its power? What were the points, in this process of growth of the military-industrial complex, at which something could have been done—by agencies of government, by education, by the press and other mass media, by political parties and the pressures of public opinion—to curb it in the public interest? What causes can be identified as the main ones which would account for the fact that such things were not done?

Work of this kind touches not only to the economic, but also to the political area, the area that stands in closest relationship to the actual decision to enter into warfare. This decision is always preceded by conferences, debates, and discussions among those leading governmental figures who operatively have most power to make the decision. Although such conferences, debates, and discussions for the most part take place in private, they require that a good deal be put in writing in order to carry on the governmental business, and a good deal finds its way into print or writing in the memoirs and correspondence of the leading figures. The records which thus exist, or can be found, yield important data capable of adding to our knowledge of causes and patterns of behavior, to our ability to predict. For example, in making the decision for entering into war, what do the records reveal concerning the extent to which the leading figures feel themselves bound by existing legal obligations, in relation to international law on one hand, and in relation to their own national law on the other?

What constitutional or legal provisions exist in different countries in regard to the question of who makes the decision to enter war? What legal machinery exists in different countries to deal with violations of these provisions on the part of officers of government? To what extent has such machinery been used? To the extent not used, can we identify the causes? In making the decision to enter into warfare, to what extent do the leading figures feel themselves bound by moral, as distinct from legal, obligations? To the extent they do, what moral obligations play a role in their consciousness? To the extent that they do not feel bound by ordinary moral obligations, what causes can be identified? In what ways, and to what extent, have governments ever consulted the people beforehand about whether the people wish to enter into a specific war? What ways would seem physically feasible? What are the opinions of present officers of government—legislative, executive, and judicial—about utilizing ways that are physically feasible?

What are the actual opinions of persons still living who were members of either the legislative or judicial branch of the American government when it entered into large-scale war in Vietnam, as to why they did not take action, within their own constitutional powers and responsibilities, to pass judgment on the legality or constitutionality of the Executive's making the decision for war? Why actually did such a constituent part of the Congress as the House Committee on the Judiciary never even hold preliminary hearings on the citizens' petitions duly sent it for a proceeding of impeachment to decide whether President Johnson had exceeded his constitutional authority in making war, after his systematic escalation of the bombing of North Vietnam? Why were hearings never held after similar petitions were sent following President Nixon's secret bombing and subsequent invasion of Cambodia? What were the feelings and reasonings of the Chairman and members of that Committee at each of these times? Are they willing to share their thoughts and feelings with the American people? If not, why not? What were the feelings and reasonings of the various federal judges, including the members of the Supreme Court, who refused to rule one way or the other on the constitutionality of the war while giving no substantive reasons for their refusal to rule? Most of these persons, too, are still alive. Are they willing now to share their thoughts and feelings with the American people, and possibly make a contribution to history and science? If not, why not? What has been the actual role of *international* law and international courts? Why has it been a limited role? How could it be widened?

RELATIONS OF A SCIENCE OF PEACE TO PSYCHOLOGY, RELIGION, AND PHILOSOPHY

The psychology of war and peace, interacting with all these other aspects of the problem, likewise involves a multitude of questions, some of which have had some attention, though none has had anything like sufficient attention. For example, what actual images, impressions, and evaluations of war do the people of different countries have in their consciousness? How do these images, impressions, and evaluations differ from country to country? How do they differ within each country, according to groupings by age, occupation, sex, marital status, or other standards? Do the images, impressions, and evaluations possessed by men who have taken part in actual wars differ markedly from those who have not? Among those who have participated, is there a marked difference between troops and officers? What actual impressions and evaluations do people in these different groupings have of conscientious objection to war? What causes can be identified for the differences between groups, either in regard to war or to conscientious objection?

In what ways and to what extent does participation in war in general, particularly the experience of killing people and seeing them die, change the character of the participant? Studies might be made of groups of young men before and after participation, and comparative studies of groups of the same age who did and did not participate. In the case of the American armed forces in the Vietnam war, many studies will no doubt be made and have been made of unusual special problems that arose, such as the killing of officers by their own troops, the widespread use of drugs, and the atrocities. It is of the utmost importance that the results of such psychological studies made within the armed services, on the spot in the combat areas, and immediately after release from combat, should become available to scientists not attached to the military services. They must be looked upon not in the way we look upon military secrets, to be kept from the public, but in the way we look upon medical data that become the basis of scientific progress in the public interest.

In this connection, the psychological orientation and impact of the training programs operative in the American armed services during the period of the Vietnam war should be studied in terms of short-time and long-time effects on those involved, in relation to changes in their attitudes towards the value of human life, the torture of human beings, the question of whether Asian peasants should be regarded as human beings, and like matters. Of equal value would be comparative studies of the state of mind, before and after combat service, of those who participated in the

Vietnam war (or any war) as to the reasons why it was fought, comparative studies of why individuals enlisted, and, having served, whether they thought it was worthwhile, and what changes it produced in their own self-image and in their image of others. Everyone who has taken part in a war is a potential source of valuable data, not only in relation to the specific questions and problems mentioned, but in relation to many other aspects of what is called war. It would be mutually beneficial to the individual and society to tap this source, not only immediately after completion of his service, but also at later times, to bring out possible changes in his evaluations.

Conflict resolution has been a subject of increasing study in contemporary psychology. Much of it has been focused on the behavior of individuals in relation to one another in small groups. Much more attention is needed to the area of conflicts between governments. Studies could be undertaken of sets of instances in which serious disputes between governments, which, if not settled peacefully, would have been likely to involve armed conflict, but which were settled peacefully; the aim would be to try to identify the causes that brought about a peaceful resolution in each case, and to locate causal factors common to many cases.

As an ounce of prevention is worth a pound of cure, conflict incitement must be researched as carefully as conflict resolution. General knowledge suggests that practically any national government at practically any time has relations of special tension, characterized by fear of the possibility of war, with some other national government. These tensions and fears are accompanied by widespread feelings of hostility, which appear partly as effects and partly as causes of the tensions and fears. It would be valuable to make studies, on as wide a scale as possible, of these feelings of hostility towards the presumptive "enemy." What impressions do people have of the moral character of this "enemy" nation or group? How, and from what sources, did they gain these impressions? What impressions do the people in each country have of the way of life of the other country? What are the specific sources of these impressions? What impressions do the governing officials in each country have of the moral character and way of life of the other country, and what are the specific sources of their impressions? In particular, what impressions do the people and the governing officials have of the specific intentions, declarations and attitudes of the people and government of the other country towards their own? What are the sources of these impressions? What is taught in the educational system of each country concerning the other? How is each country portrayed in the mass media of the other country? Such studies would include, of course, comparison and contrast between what was taught, said, or portrayed about the presumptive enemy and actual confirmable facts. In our own country, since World War I, "the enemy" has been communism and communist governments. What are the impressions of different sections of the population, and of the governing officials, concerning the theory of communism, the way of life in communist countries, concerning what is taught in communist countries and presented in their mass media about capitalist countries? What are the specific sources of these impressions? Most important, what are the causes of distortions, and how can they be counteracted or prevented?

Many studies of this kind would be as much in the field of education as in that of psychology. Our previous discussion has had occasion to indicate the important relation to war and peace of what goes on in the educational system and the mass media. Studies should be made not only about what is presented concerning the presumptive "enemy," but what is presented concerning the subject of war in general and about specific wars. What is conveyed concerning the *causes* of war in general and the causes of specific wars? What aspects of war are mainly singled out for treatment? Causes? Effects? The political aspect? The moral aspect? The economic aspect? The casualties? The sufferings of the civilian population? The atrocities? The decisions of the governmental leaders? The relation of those decisions to law, and to morality? The question of war crimes? What is the relative emphasis given to these different aspects? What is consistently avoided, if anything? What can be determined as to the causes of the relative degrees of emphasis? In the case of a given war, comparative studies could be made of the different accounts of it presented in the different countries.

These types of questions would be equally relevant to the field of religion. To what extent do problems of war and peace form a part of sermons, of religious instruction and training? Insofar as such problems are dealt with, what are the predominant attitudes taken towards them? To what extent do clergymen deal with the principle of conscientious objection? Insofar as it is dealt with, what is the predominant attitude taken towards it? Advocacy? Neutrality? Opposition? What is conveyed about the presumptive "enemy" in peace time, e.g., during the cold war in America, about communism? What is conveyed about the actual enemy in war time? In each case, what sources or authorities were relied upon for the validity of what was taught or conveyed? The activities of chaplains form a special branch of this subject-area. To what extent do soldiers seek out chaplains? What types of question or problem do soldiers actually bring to chaplains? What kinds of advice do chaplains actually give? To what extent are there similarities and differences from sect to sect, age group to age group, war to war, certain conditions of combat to other conditions of combat?

Similar questions should be researched in relation to the field of philosophy, a traditional part of which is the study of morals, ethics, values, and social principles. To what extent do problems of war and peace enter? What kind of treatment is given them? What net conclusions do students come away with? What works are mainly studied in relation to war and peace? What authorities are mainly relied upon? What are the attitudes of administrative officials towards the inclusion of such study in the curriculum? What are the attitudes of professors of philosophy generally towards doing work on problems of peace and war? What kinds of research have professors of philosophy actually done on them?

All the problems here mentioned represent, of course, but a few of those that enter into paxology. In any case, perhaps the most fertile source of problems in any science is its own actual, ongoing work as, so long as the problems one begins with are of the kind whose solutions would add to predictability, whatever results are gained will suggest related problems of high predictive value—problems perhaps impossible to formulate concretely until the first set of results is in hand. Specific problems concerning the motion of the stars in relation to one another could not be formulated until there was evidence that there was such motion, that the stars were not really "fixed," as everyone had assumed. The central problems that Einstein solved not only could not have been *solved* by him before Newton had done *his* work on gravitation; they could not even have been *formulated* before that, any more than problems about the action of different vitamins could have been formulated prior to the discovery and conceptualization of vitamins. Part of what we are here saying is that a science progresses by raising problems not only about its subject matter, but about itself, its own methods, because it finds that in order to answer the questions it raises about the subject matter, it must create new concepts, coin new terms, invent new instruments, devise new techniques of measurement, develop new systems of observation. It creates as well as discovers.

However, all this must apply, especially in a social science, not only to problems about the subject matter and methods of the science, but also to the problem of getting its results implemented in practice, in actual social life. The main obstacles are social inertia, fear, superstition, and, perhaps most formidable of all, the fact that changes of social practice, in proportion to their depth and range, can threaten the economic, political, and moral power of established authority. But the method of science has a built-in reflexive potential: it can be applied to the problems it itself creates as a result of its own progress. This is reflexive, but not automatic. Science—any science—needs people in order for it to do anything. But has the very progress of science made automata of people, or could it make automata of people, so that peace would either be impossible, or only purchaseable at too high a price? Let us consider these questions in the chapter that follows.

NOTES

¹Friedrich Engels, *Anti-Dühring*, Burns' translation (New York: International Publishers, n.d.), p. 130.

²Friedrich Engels, *Herrn Eugen Dühring's Umwälzung der Wissenschaft* (Stuttgart: Dietz, n.d.), p. 112.

³Francis Bacon, *Novum Organum,* Book I, Aphorism 3. In Edwin A. Burtt, ed., *The English Philosophers from Bacon to Mill* (New York: The Modern Library, 1939), p. 28.

8

The New Relation
to Technology

TECHNOLOGY AND HUMAN HISTORY

On the question of the interrelations of the individual, technology, and society, Karl Marx is not only the most challenging thinker of modern times, but the one whose basic influence on the peace movement has been greatest, in terms of secular social philosophy. Early in his career he developed a distinction which became central in his thought, between what he called "the material powers of production" and "the relations of production."[1] The material powers are the tools, forces, sources, and techniques of production, instruments, power sources, raw materials, methods, know-how. This is what we call technology, and without some form of it people would of course perish of starvation and exposure.

Thus technology always plays a central role in human life. But the role it plays is far from being merely physical or automatic, like the role played by oxygen or solar energy, without which man would perish also. While man depends for his very existence as much upon oxygen or solar energy, or gravitation, or numberless other physical, chemical, and biological processes and components as he does upon technology, the difference is that man does not consciously enter into a process of creation of these other things. Since his need for them can be satisfied automatically or unconsciously, they do something *for* him, but they do not necessarily *engage* him. What they do is the same for each individual. They are important in regard to what every human being has in common with every other living thing and what every society has in common with every other society. However, technology is important not only in regard to the common factors, but in regard to the differences among individuals and among societies. This means that people, in creating what they create at the technological level, are making themselves different, are creating themselves, as individuals and society.

This process of self-differentiation and self-creation takes place not only because tools and techniques do not make themselves, but also because they cannot use themselves. They are created and used by people, and the process of their creation and use is the primary historical process through which people develop their rationality and become social, human. The "transition from ape to man" is the gaining of greater rationality and more complex sociality, and both were gained first of all through making and using more and more effective tools. The use of tools, and more effective tools, in order to supply the food, shelter, and protection without which people would perish, implies coordinated, cooperative activities of individuals and groups. Such activities in turn imply a structure of authority relationships. In any productive activity involving coordination and cooperation of a number of persons, all sorts of decisions must be made concerning when, where, how much, who does what, who gets what, and so on. This is what Marx referred to as "the relations of production"—not the *technical* relationships between different parts of work processes (those are included in "the material powers of production"), but the authority relationships, that is, the accepted or enforced relationships in which individuals and groups stand to one another in the social process of production, in the making of the kind of decisions just referred to. In actual historical sequence, the predominant authority relationships have been those between tribal members and chiefs, slaves and masters, serfs and lords, wage workers and private capitalists, state employees and socialist state employers.

It is obvious that any given system of such relationships, which Marx calls also "the economic structure of society,"[2] is a very important aspect of the life of any individual and any society, a very important aspect of the sense in which people create themselves, make themselves collectively different, group from group, and individually different, person from person. It is obvious, in other words, that the accepted or enforced relations of production have a direct and fundamental bearing on the whole quality of life of the individual as individual and the society as society. In regard to them, neither the individual nor the society has any neutral ground to stand upon. In a certain society, the individual is either slave or free, in another he either lives in poverty or he does not, and such facts will in many important ways limit and condition what he can and cannot do in the course of his life. The same is true of the quality of life of the society as a whole. The existence and enforcement of the master-slave relation, or the propertied-unpropertied relation will in many important ways limit and condition what the society as a whole can and cannot do, can and cannot be, morally, politically, culturally.

Marx wanted first of all to account for history, and what he saw as fundamental was the interrelation between the two broad factors we have been talking about—the material powers of production, or technology, on the one hand, and the relations of production on the other hand. The point, as Marx put it, was that people's "relations of production correspond to a definite stage of development of their material powers of production."[3] The kind of authority relations of production which exists at a given time in a given society is not arbitrary, is not and cannot be made out of whole cloth, because these relations must satisfy certain functional requirements set by the character of the material powers of production that are available. There will always be a certain minimal degree of correspondence that must exist between the socially accepted authority relations of production and the material powers of production, if production is to perform its necessary function.

So far, this is to say no more than that if a boat containing more than one person is to complete a journey across dangerous waters, some authority relationships will have to be accepted by the voyagers, and these relationships must have a functional correspondence with the purpose and mechanisms of the boat. To follow the rule that the amount of authority must be directly proportional to weight, or inversely proportional to height, might easily prove fatal, as would many other rules that we can imagine. However, this does not mean that the authority relationships which actually prevail in a society at any given time are the best, the most rational, or the most ethical (this would be to make the picture too static); it means only that they must meet the minimal requirement of functionality. To claim more than that would be to forget the facts of history, not only in their ethical aspect, but in their root empirical aspect. History itself is here in question, for there would hardly be any such thing as human history if man's material powers of production, his technology, did not undergo qualitative changes, and if man's relations of production did not also undergo qualitative changes, considering the centrality and pervasiveness of these things in the life of man. If such qualitative changes had not taken place man would still be living in primitive tribal society, only in larger tribes, or, more likely, the transition from apes to humans would not yet have occurred; there would only be a greater variety of apes.

In other words, technology is never static, nor is the system of relations of production. In examining the degree of correspondence between the technology and the authority structure, one is examining a correspondence between two sets of phenomena, each of which is in process of change. Precisely what interested Marx, what became, as he put it, "the leading thread in my studies,"[4] was not simply the idea that there must be a certain degree of functional correspondence between the technology and the relations of production (that was only the beginning of the story), but the search for the major causes of the qualitative changes that took place in the relations of production. This search became centered on how the changes that took place in the technology became the cause of changes taking place in the system of relations. "How" means through what *social* mechanisms, institutions, media, functions, and struggles this process is carried out.

The essence of Marx's thesis became the conception that qualitative changes in the authority relations of production, from tribesman-chief to slave-master, slave-master to serf-lord, serf-lord to proletarian-capitalist, were caused mainly by the fact that changes in the existing technology, that is, new tools, methods, sources of energy and raw materials, had accumulated to the point where the old relations of production no longer could satisfy the requirements of functional correspondence to the new, more productive technology. More productive technology is, of course, technology with a greater capability of supplying human needs for food, clothing, shelter, education, travel, health care, and the like—in other words, of supplying the material facilities necessary to survival and development.

However, the more productive technology does not come to prevail simply because it is more productive. The process by which it comes to prevail is neither simple nor moralistic, though moral values are very much involved. One must remember that the *old* technology is socially dominant in terms of a system of authority relations which gives dominant social, political, and moral power to a certain stratum of the population—tribal chiefs, slave owners, feudal lords, capitalists, as the case may be in different historical periods. To become dominant in practice, to be actually put into use, the *new* technology requires a new system of authority relations, one which will have at least a minimal degree of functional correspondence with *it*. Speaking in the barest empirical terms, this means that tribal chiefs are to be replaced by slave-owners and tribal brothers by slaves, and later, that slave-owners are to be replaced by feudal lords, and slaves by serfs; still later, that feudal lords are to be replaced by capitalists and serfs by proletarians.

But this could not have been done without a great deal of struggle, because in each case it meant challenging the existing ruling class, which had, of course, firmly established its rule—physically through the armed forces, politically through the form of government, ideologically through the content of the educational system, morally through the prescriptions of the religion. But all these institutions are made up of people and only function to the extent that the population as a whole cooperates with them, obeys their edicts, and accepts their judgments. Put bluntly, when enough people have suffered enough from the incapacities of the old system, but not until then, they will turn against it and risk an outright struggle to get rid of it, that is, risk taking up a revolutionary stance. The revolutionary struggle is always piecemeal and non-violent in the beginning. Under certain conditions it can win, and has won, a non-violent victory, but usually a bloody civil war of one kind or another takes place before the new system can become established.

As pointed out in the first chapter of this book, revolutions are significant, either positively or negatively, to the extent that they bring about qualitative changes, measured by range and depth, in the principles and practices of established authority and social institutions. The victory of a revolution, therefore, must manifest itself by the degree to which it brings about a new kind of politics, law, economics, morality, education, art, science, technology, and the like. Marx's point was that the most significant revolutions are those that include and base themselves upon economic changes, those changes in the authority relations of production which are made increasingly feasible and necessary by new developments in technology, and which are increasingly demanded by increasing numbers of people because the old relations of production, which reflect the old technology, have become increasingly unsuccessful in meeting the life needs of people. Such a movement against the established relations of production will be articulated in politics, law, morality, education, religious interpretation, art, science, and life-style, because the authority relations of production are like the blood stream of social life, flowing everywhere, energizing everything, and giving everything a special quality, good or bad. Think how much effort it must have taken to make tribal brothers into slaves. To make people who were your tribal brothers into your slaves in a way that would stick, and become a norm of respectability, you need a whole new system of laws and government (the state, as a permanently organized police enforcement apparatus, was thus born), a new system of religious interpretation, a new morality, a new educational system, a new kind of art and science. This was at once the price, the expression, and the fruit of civilization, the only way actually found to establish the technology and economy that made possible the transition from "savagery to civilization."

One is not saying this was the only possible way of doing it. Morally, much better ways could easily be conceived. But the fact that something happened in the way it did, and not in some other way, has an undeniable claim on our attention, not only empirically, but morally. "Insight into necessity" is the basis not only of freedom but of compassion: *Tout comprendre, c'est tout pardonner.* But compassion is an act, not just a feeling. In socio-historical terms, this means that in order to raise the moral level of society—of its operative institutions, laws, principles, its accepted standards and their rationalizations—we must understand how it happened that the operative institutions, standards, and rationalizations got onto their low moral level in the first place. We must understand the causes, for without that empirical understanding it will be impossible to follow through with the action which compassion demands. To avoid effects as well as to produce effects, we must locate causes. Marx was pointing out that slavery became institutionalized because it became functionally advantageous when division of labor began to develop, along with possibilities of accumulating surpluses and of trading. Forms of conduct and authority relationships that violated the rules and the norms of a given social system could grow into a new system eventually replacing the first because they were capable of increasing the production of those things the society and the individuals as individuals increasingly needed for their survival and development. Once this has happened, the new system of authority relations does not give way until the point is once again reached where technological developments have rendered the then existing authority relations disfunctional. In a word, slavery was not abolished until it, in its turn, became economically unproductive. More precisely, the moral struggle against slavery did not succeed until the slave system was no longer the most productive economic system.

SCIENCE, TECHNOLOGY, AND HUMANISM

Facts of this kind convinced Marx and Engels that the hope of implementing the politics and morality of humanism depended primarily upon economic factors. This dependence had three very important aspects: (1) liberation from inhuman exploitation would not in fact come about until there was in existence a technology that did not functionally need inhuman exploitation and at the same time was significantly more productive than the technology that did functionally need inhuman exploitation, a condition now met by modern industrial technology; (2) the struggle for human liberation must therefore focus primarily upon the economic roots of human misery and exploitation, their real causes, forming its strategy and tactics, and educating the exploited masses, in the light of these root facts; (3) when the revolutionary struggle against capitalist exploitation is victorious, its first and most important task must be to set up a system of authority relations of production which radically reduces or no longer provides the opportunity or incentive for human beings to exploit one another economically. Then it will become possible to work out ways of living in which people would cease or begin to cease to exploit one another non-economically. Put bluntly, Marx felt that new economic relations, corresponding to a technology capable of increased abundance of productivity, would create the opportunity for moral forces to get rid of the old social injustice and immorality quicker than moral forces operating within the conditions of the old economic relations. This applies to war and to all other social evils.

But Marx, as I understand him, was not a dogmatist, though dogmatists spring up in every school and movement. Marx was trying to read history aright in order to lay a basis for man to liberate himself from oppressive social conditions. He felt his conclusions were right in the way a scientist does, i.e., that his evidence can be confirmed by observation, and that his solution works in practice. If evidence were found that the major causes of the major historical changes in human society had not been economic, or that there was some quicker way to eliminate the major forms of exploitation and misery than to organize a mass political movement pointed towards the feasibility of a new economic system on the basis of advances that have been made in technology (in addition to the inalienable right of revolution), I believe he would have accepted the situation and rejoiced. In any case, if there is agreement on the need for radical changes, the efforts of different groups or individuals who start from different premises, use different approaches, and make different emphases need not frustrate and exclude one another, but can supplement one another, and make it possible to learn from one another.

For example, whether one agrees with Marx's theses or not, they embody a distinction which is incontrovertible and can be useful to any social thinker, perhaps especially to contemporary ones—the distinction between the technological powers of production and the property (authority) relations of production. This is especially relevant today, because a good deal of our contemporary social thought is characterized by a kind of blanket hostility towards technology. Thus the question needs to be raised: Is the right target, is the enemy technology itself, or is it the present system of authority relations still clinging to that technology? If the distinction between these two quite different things is not recognized, or if it is assumed that some particular state of their interrelationship is unchangeable, self-frustration is invited. A good example of the dangers involved, or so I would argue, is found in Theodore Roszak's *The Making of a Counter Culture,* at the beginning of which he lays down his central definitions and theses in these terms:

> By the technocracy, I mean that social form in which an industrial society reaches the peak of its organizational integration. It is the ideal men usually have in mind when they speak of modernizing, up-dating, rationalizing, planning. Drawing upon such unquestionable imperatives as the demand for efficiency, for social security, for large-scale coordination of men and resources, for ever

higher levels of affluence and ever more impressive manifestations
of collective human power, the technocracy works to knit together
the anachronistic gaps and fissures of the industrial society . . .
Politics, education, leisure, entertainment, culture as a whole, the
unconscious drives, and even, as we shall see, protest against the
technocracy itself: all these become the subjects of purely technical
scrutiny and of purely technical manipulation.[5]

Roszak sees merit in the ideas of Jacques Ellul on the relation between
scientific prediction and human autonomy. Ellul's thesis is:

Technique requires predictability and, no less, exactness of prediction. It is necessary, then, that technique prevail over the human
being. For technique, this is a matter of life and death. Technique
must reduce man to a technical animal, the king of the slaves of
technique. Human caprice crumbles before this necessity; there can
be no human autonomy in the face of technical autonomy. The
individual must be fashioned by techniques, either negatively (by
the techniques of understanding man) or positively (by the adapta-
tion of man to the technical framework), in order to wipe out the
blots his personal determination introduces into the perfect design of
the organization.[6]

Roszak quotes also from one of the manifestoes put up in the Sorbonne
in May, 1968: "The revolution which is beginning will call in question
not only capitalist society but industrial society. The consumer's society
must perish of a violent death. The society of alienation must disappear
from history. We are inventing a new and original world. Imagination is
seizing power."[7]

But there is nothing new or original about the world that is being
envisaged and invoked behind these complaints, if that world is one
without complex industry, without advanced technology, as well as
without modern capitalism. We have already had that world, and we
cannot go backward. The adolescent cannot return to infancy. Once the
new powers, new needs, and new drives that constitute adolescence have
come into existence, they cannot be exorcised by an effort of will. Such

an attempt only makes the situation worse. Either they are acknowledged and handled, or they make human happiness impossible. This does not mean that a given adolescent must accept the authority relations which control or try to control the powers of adolescence in his society. He may have any number of legitimate complaints against such authorities. But if he directs these complaints against the powers of adolescence themselves, and longs for a world where these powers do not exist, he is deceiving himself. He is too late.

As it is physiologically impossible, even if it were desirable, to invent a human world from which the complicating powers of adolescence would be expunged, it is historically impossible, even if it were desirable, to invent a human world from which the complicating powers of industrial technology would be expunged. Industrial technology is the application of science to economic production. It is the invention and use of bigger, more complex, and more efficient tools. How does one expunge science? How does one do without tools? If we still need some science and some tools, where and how does one draw a line? Would not this require a massive censorship, a totalitarian control for which indeed a most powerful imagination would be required? In sheer empirical terms, quite apart from all questions of human freedom, human rights, and morality, could this ever really be done?

If one decided that we needed only simple tools, simple technology, and the basic sciences, and therefore tried to draw the line, let us say, at the end of the fourteenth century, so that all scientific books, all technological processes, all tools and instruments brought into being after that point were utterly destroyed, and declared unthinkable on pain of death, would that do it? Imagine even that by these means, post-fourteenth century science, and its technological offspring, came to be forgotten, and new generations were brought up in ignorance of the fact that they had ever existed. Could that be expected to prevent the re-discovery of heliocentric astronomy, Newtonian physics, and modern chemistry, in the very same way that Copernicus, Newton, and Lavoisier arrived at them—by building further on the old foundations? The same applies to whatever cut-off point one would choose, for science represents a process of growth which can be delayed but hardly prevented. If the mighty and concerted efforts actually made by the church-state complex for centuries failed to prevent this process in the first place, how could its repetition be prevented after the spreading plant had once borne fruit? It can be cut away only at the surface. The roots are too deep and widespread in the soil to be removed.

But it is hard to believe that what is being complained of is science itself: nuclear physics, Einsteinian relativity, Darwinian evolution, genetics, industrial chemistry, cybernetics, ecology, etc. The human being is both a truth-seeking and a power-seeking animal, and these are wondrous combinations of the two. It is equally hard to believe that it is technology itself that is being complained of: the automobile, electrical power, automated machinery, atomic energy, space ships, giant computers. All these things are obviously capable of benefiting people, of easing their toil, expanding their knowledge, lengthening their lives, increasing their enjoyments, facilitating their development. Is it not true that what is being complained of is rather the way these things have been turned against people, beginning with the way they are produced, and used to produce other things, dehumanizing people, stultifying them with the endless repetition of mechanical motions, making them mere appendages to the machine, robots, ending with the production of thermonuclear weapons which may at any moment annihilate them and all their works? Cannot this very same technology work just as effectively *for* people? Nobody complains when an automobile is utilized to save a life or see an ocean, when electrical power makes it possible to do the wash in an easy hour rather than a long day of drudgery, when automated machinery, making products by the use of mechanical robots, replaces older forms of machinery which, in turning out the same products, made human robots of the people who operated them, when atomic energy is used in medicine, when space ships, guided by giant computers, open up other planets to human beings. In essence, this is a very old story: the simplest tool, such as a hammer or a file, can be used constructively or destructively, and it can be produced by slave labor or freely chosen work. When it is misused, or produced by exploitation of people, one does not blame the hammer or the file, and call for a world without tools.

Rather, one raises questions: Why was the tool misused? How did it come to be produced in a way that dehumanizes the producer? What causes the producers to use the same machines and energy-sources to produce devices that save and prolong life, and also devices that destroy and shorten life? These questions, by the way, are not peculiar to contemporary science, technology, and industry. The same questions were posed by every preceding system of production because every preceding system also had some kind of technology which could be, and was, used both constructively and destructively. The only difference is that contemporary science and technology have placed in our hands immeasurably more power that can be used *either constructively or destructively.* But why are any technological powers used destructively? Since the powers do not use themselves, we must examine the authority relations in terms of which they are produced and used. Who in fact decides upon their production and use? What are the major motives that come into play in these decisions? In accordance with what system of rules and laws are these decisions made? How is this system of rules and laws kept going? In other words, the destructive use of technology must be, or must be thought to be, of advantage and profit to some segment of the human community, some segment that is capable of effective thought, organization, administration, and systematization.

In the United States it is obvious that the system of authority relations of production is what is called capitalist. It is equally obvious that the capitalist system operates on the profit motive, and that the major reason destructive things have been produced, and that things have been produced in a destructive way, is that there has been a profit in it. There were and are, no doubt, other reasons and motives, but this is the major one.

Another way of expressing the same economic fact is to say that a relatively small number of persons own most of the technology as their private property. This private ownership, protected by law, justified by ideology, moralized by religious interpretation, indoctrinated by education, and dramatized by the mass media, is the socio-economic mechanism, the basic authority relation of production which allows, encourages, and even (within the system) necessitates that the owning group use the technological apparatus in such a way that it brings a private profit. In the capitalist system of private ownership of the means of production, private profit must come first, else the system breaks down.

Of course, if there were no means of production, no technology of any kind, there would be nothing to make a private profit out of, but there would also be nothing with which to supply the needs of survival and development. This would be the hard way to solve the problem, akin to starving the patient to death in order to cure his ulcers. The other possibility is to change the authority relations of production, so that the technology is not privately owned by a relatively small group, not used in such a way as to make a private profit, but collectively owned by the society as a whole, and used in a way that involves least alienation and most happiness, least sickness and most health, least death and most life. This possibility must be thoroughly tested before pronouncing a medieval anathema upon science and technology, which comes close to anathematizing the human being as such, *homo sapiens* and *homo faber,* close to the original concept of original sin, the original inner alienation. Does it seem likely, after all that has happened, that this anathema could be made the basis of human happiness and development?

It seems more likely that it reflects a failure of nerve, induced by a lack of understanding. It is as if one were hypnotized and paralyzed by the size and power of the opponent, so that one feels hopeless about struggling against him, can think only of avoiding him, and makes this effort on the philosophical ground that bigness and power are sins in themselves. Roszak spoke of the opponent as "that form in which an industrial society reaches the peak of its organizational integration," in which it "works to knit together the anachronistic gaps and fissures of industrial society." He seems so surprised that it should do this, and so confused by the degree of its apparent success, that he does not seriously pose the question of accounting for the degree of its failure, or raise the question of how such a system ever got defeated in the past. He makes no distinction between the technology itself and the authority relations which determine the uses to which it is put, and proceeds to argue as if the very existence of the machine, though it was created by people, compels them to use it against themselves. He attaches no importance to the fact, or else it has escaped his notice, that the machines he complains against are not under the control of those who actually created them, and that they are not used against people as people, but by a relatively small group of people against the majority. He blames science, technology in general, and organizational integration itself, as if modern hospitals, large libraries, international postal systems, and other such helpful institutions which utilize modern technology either did not exist or must be reckoned as harmful in principle.

How, in fact, does a big and powerful social order begin to fail? How, in historical fact, has such a system ever been defeated? To throw light on these questions is the point of much social science upon which Roszak has impulsively pronounced his anathema. As a part of this scientific work we have already seen one line of answer, which, without being taken dogmatically, opens up certain credible perspectives. This answer is that the increasing contradiction and disfunctionality between the authority relations of production on the one side and the technological powers of production on the other increasingly obstructs the fulfillment of human needs, increasingly thwarts the obvious possibilities of human development, and thus increasingly generates human misery and alienation. This result becomes the effective cause of a political movement, an educational movement, a moral movement, a religious movement, an artistic movement which can become powerful enough to overthrow the outmoded system of authority relations in question. As we have seen, this kind of process has already been gone through a number of times in human history.

Just as, in the social struggles and revolutions of the past, both sides made as much use as they could of the cultural resources that existed—the arts, the sciences, the educational facilities, the religions, the political and legal forms, the concepts of morals and human rights, including the right of revolution—so also in the social struggles and revolutions of the present the same is seen and is to be expected. Roszak was bedazzled by what he quoted from Jacques Ellul: "Technique requires predictability and, no less, exactness of prediction. It is necessary, then, that technique prevail over the human being." But he forgot to ask from whose point of view it is necessary that technique prevail over the human being. After all, technique as such has no point of view. The hammer does not jump out of the tool box by itself and clout people on the head. Dehumanizing assembly lines do not make themselves and then force the workers to work them. It is necessary for technique to prevail over the human being only from the point of view of someone or some group to whom this is profitable. But the others can resist and fight back in which process not the least of their weapons will be scientific predictability.

Roszak and Ellul forget that for every way in which the powers given by science have been used to repress man, there are ten ways these powers can be used to liberate man; for every scientific study carried out for the purpose of finding more effective ways to exploit man for profit, ten can be made to find more effective ways to resist and abolish the system of exploitation. As we have seen, all this depends on the type of problem one poses, and the degree of success one attains in solving the problem. Roszak and Ellul might as well complain that the Establishment cunningly uses all the subtle and powerful resources of the English language, applying it to every kind of situation, sending it into every nook and cranny of the social structure, in every form of printed matter, distributed through a whole network of commercial transactions, all for the purpose of strengthening the Establishment, and therefore we should condemn the English language as an example of repressive communication and condemn books, irrespective of their contents, as instruments of exploitative cooptation.

Instead, as we see, they write books, have them published in English, and sold on the commercial market. This is what they should do, all the more so because it is inconsistent with the weak part of their theory. They realize they are dealing with a sick society whose death agonies might become the death agonies of all mankind, and they have the courage to say so, and to try to do something about it. What they do in a positive way has merit, but unfortunately they discourage and condemn other kinds of effort which have equal merit and are equally necessary to attain the goal. Roszak feels drawn to mysticism, poetry, art, religious mythology, and skillfully and movingly brings them to bear against the contemporary social pathology. But he does not yet understand science, either in its creative dynamics, its actual methodology, or its relation to moral values, and thus berates a powerful ally as if it were the enemy incarnate.

The historical record since 1945, when examined against the background of Marx's theory of revolutionary social change, shows significant ways in which the actual course of history both followed and diverged from his theory. Marx had said that cumulative changes in the technology of production always sooner or later reach a point where the existing relations of production, with their socio-cultural superstructure, become so disfunctional, relative to human needs and new possibilities, that revolutionary change in these relations of production becomes necessary for survival and development. The most dramatic and significant advance of contemporary technological power was made in 1945 with the splitting of the atom, which opened up a whole new world of possibilities in the utilization of atomic energy. It is only a question of time, and development of safeguards before atomic energy becomes the basis of a system of production in which it will be possible to produce all that is now produced in a fraction of the human labor time now necessary. Or, to put it differently, it will be possible to produce many times as much with the same expenditure of human labor time.

This is the happy side of the picture, possible beyond a reasonable doubt, but not yet actual. It is happy because this could mean, for the first time in the history of human civilization, the literal end of poverty, deprivation, and shortage, the literal end of the sicknesses, diseases, sufferings, agonies, and premature deaths caused by poverty, deprivation, and shortage. It would mean that for the first time, the human race would possess enough physical and technical facilities to educate everyone to the limit of his or her abilities, to provide the highest level of physical and mental health care for everyone, and decent housing for everyone, to increase the range and freedom of work-choices for everyone, to provide abundant leisure for everyone to develop his or her interests, talents, creativity. For the first time the physical basis, the technical prerequisites of all this would be brought into existence, so that we could really begin to learn the truth about what mankind as a whole can do when mankind as a whole is given a fair chance. The ancient owners said, "We *need* slaves; there is no other sufficient source of energy available," and philosophers explained that slavery was rational and natural. The medieval owners, including the church, said: "We *need* serfs; there is no other sufficient source of labor to work the land," and theologians attested that serfdom was agreeable in the sight of God. Capitalist owners said: "We *need* cheap labor; there is no other way to meet the demands of production, and to keep the costs of production within competitive bounds," and many an economist proved it. There was no capitalist way to run the productive system and at the same time meet fluctuating economic demands without masses of cheap labor. In a private property system, this of course meant that the masses could not count on economic security and often were unable to buy what was necessary to a decent standard of living. In terms of the system of property and profit relations, there was never enough to go around.

Poverty, deprivation, and shortages were both causes and effects of the system, and became institutionalized aspects of it.

As the history of technology, from ancient times to the present, is a history of increasing capability of production, so also is it a history of closer and closer approximation to the physical capability of producing a sufficiency for everyone, closer and closer approximation to the physical capability of eliminating poverty, deprivation, and shortage not simply by taking away from the rich and powerful, and giving to the poor and weak, but by rationally utilizing the new technology so as to render obsolete the distinction between rich and poor. This would become possible not only physically, not only because there would be a physical sufficiency available to all, as a sufficiency of water or air is available to all in an unpolluted and naturally fertile environment, but psychologically and legally, just as no one in such an environment can build up prestige or status by drinking more water or breathing in more air than others, or profit by collecting and storing up water or air. No doubt there would be prestige and status in making use of the things abundantly available to everyone in ways that gained unusual admiration and respect. This is competition, but it would not be based upon exploitation. Our argument is, of course, assuming that necessary population controls and ecological safeguards can be developed, that there is no reason to regard such problems as unsolvable in principle.

Nevertheless, say some, there would be inevitable sources of envy, jealousy, hostility, spite, boredom, violence, crime, and suicide, as Dostoevsky insisted. But to the same degree? Do these things have nothing to do with people's environment, with the natural and social conditions under which they live? This is hardly the case, but the only way we can find out is to try whatever is possible in an environment without man-made poverty—different methods of education, ways of communal living, systems of physical and mental health development, programs of research in behavioral and social science. We should hardly be inclined to go back to an environment of poverty in the midst of plenty, as we already have ample knowledge and long experience of what people do in such an environment, of what happens to the majority of people. It is not likely that in the midst of a rationally organized sufficiency the great majority of people would follow the advice of the bored gentleman with the "reactionary and ironical" countenance, whom Dostoevsky pictures in his *Notes from the Underground,* who some fine day would urge us to kick this whole damned thing to hell. Today, this gentleman might have at his disposal thermonuclear means to lend an edge of practicality to his advice, and we have evidence of more than enough willingness to take the risk and the plunge. But I would argue that these tendencies are not an inherent part of human nature. They are the result of centuries of conditioning by an environment of deprivation which placed a premium on exploitation and cut-throat competition. Not until an environment of rationally available abundance has been given as long an opportunity as the other to mold and condition people would we have the right to say that human beings as human beings, the vast majority of people, are irredeemably destructive and self-destructive. It is significant that Dostoevsky, so realistic as a novelist and so poor as a philosopher, pitched the underground man's *argument* on ''freedom,'' but had him begin the *narrative* by saying, ''I am a sick man.'' It is sickness speaking in the argument.

TECHNOLOGY AND REVOLUTION

In any case, the atomic technology we now have the possibility of developing made its first appearance in the form of a weapon of destruction, a weapon which puts humanity under a threat which, in a sense, is infinitely greater in scope than the promise of beneficence which it also holds out. This is the unhappy side of the picture, which, even more urgently than the happy side, demonstrates Marx's thesis that the accumulation of technological powers in each historical system of production eventually reaches a point of grievous contradiction to the prevailing authority relations of production, a disfunctionality with these relations that is adverse to the fulfillment of people's needs of survival and development, that increases people's miseries and sufferings beyond the point of endurance. In this case the disfunctionality is charged with a threat to man's survival and development so ominous and fateful that it has no precedent in all previous history. One must again emphasize that this threat is not posed by the thermonuclear weapons themselves. They did not make themselves, and they cannot select their own targets. Only persons, groups of persons, can do these things, and they can do them only within a system of authority relations of a certain kind. You cannot really expunge the science and technology which produced the weapons, nor would it be wise to do so even if it were possible. You can destroy present stockpiles, but if you leave standing and operative the system of authority relations and its associated motives which made possible, and seemed to make necessary, the production of the original stockpiles, they will be produced again when like crises again arise. But the system of authority relations can be replaced, all the more so because it is no longer functional.

Although this loss of functionality manifests itself most sharply, clearly and urgently in the fact that small groups of persons have been allowed to retain and exercise the legal authority, under established governments, to order the production of biocidal weapons, using for this purpose vast sums of money taken as taxes from the people, and to order their use in warfare which can become biocide, the psychological truth is that this fact is so monstrous that it is difficult for people to believe it, as distinguished from *understanding* that it is a fact. It is correspondingly difficult to react to, all at once. Perhaps the disfunctionality appears more credible in the piecemeal, daily form in which it must also manifest itself in the ordinary economic processes associated with peace rather than with war.

That is, to the extent that the atomic technology which was not brought about by private investment or risk, but by the government making use of money taken from the whole people, is placed in the hands of private owners who put it into peacetime production under ''competitive'' conditions in order to make private, ''free enterprise'' profit, it would obviously disemploy a constantly increasing proportion of the labor force. From the point of view of profit-making, this is a happy prospect: as labor costs go down, the rate of profit can go up. But what of the disemployed labor force? When technological improvements disemploy only between five and ten per cent of the labor force, the profit system can remain functional, and even prosper. The process may be referred to as technological ''displacement.'' Some of the ''displaced'' are retrainable; some go on welfare; some sink into hopeless and chronic poverty, a certain degree of which can be contained by the system, and has been around so long that its presence seems normal. But it is easy to see that if the technologically disemployed should reach a level like 25 percent, and it became clear to all that the technology was such that in the not distant future, the level reached could be 35 percent, 45 percent, and so on, that would be a qualitatively different situation.

This is the kind of situation on which Marx put his finger, which he identified as the genesis of the most significant revolutions, when, referring to the property relations of production, he said: "From forms of development of the forces of production these relations turn into their fetters. Then comes the period of social revolution."[8] In the contemporary case the attempt to *own* the new technology privately and make its increased productivity the source of increased *private* profit will have economically disastrous effects. It will progressively decrease the ability of greater and greater masses of people to buy the products which are now technically produceable in greater and greater abundance. Production will thus be inhibited (the "fetters") because, under capitalist relationships, there is no point in producing things that cannot be bought at a price that brings a *private* profit, for the continued attempt to do so would soon plunge the firms which tried it, from whatever motives, into bankruptcy. Since they would have to continue to pay all their expenses of production, but would not be bringing in a profit, their capital would soon be drained away to the point where they would be unable to pay their bills.

This is what happens in a depression, and is the reason producers would rather destroy the foodstuffs or other products than give them away to the unemployed who cannot buy them, though the prices are lower than ever, because their purchasing power is gone. The prices are lower than ever because of the relative abundance on the market for those who still have normal purchasing power. *They* are the potential buyers to whom the capitalist producers must turn, or perish as capitalist producers, and the quickest way to force prices up in relation to those who *can* buy is to create a relative scarcity. In times of acute crisis, this is done by deliberate destruction of part of what has been produced, in "normal" times by deliberate sequestration of goods from the market and prevention of further production. This process has reached a point where large landowners in the United States are paid huge annual subsidies for *not* planting certain crops, not because the resultant products could not be used by people who need them, but because they could not be *bought* by such people. These people who need them cannot buy them because they haven't the purchasing power to pay a price that would yield a profit, and they lack this purchasing power because their labor is either "not needed" in the capitalist process of production, or is worth too little in competitive profit terms in that process. Thus, the more productive the technology becomes, the more the capitalist relations of production become its fetters.

The capitalist property relations, in these circumstances, not only act as self-obstructive mechanisms, inevitably preventing fulfillment of the productive potentials of the technology; they become the cause of external opposition and obstruction from the side of the disemployed workers. At first this opposition takes the desperate form of physical destruction of the improved machines which have displaced the workers. This is put down with relative ease by police measures and then the opposition passes into phases of trade union collective bargaining, characterized by strikes, lockouts, terror, violence, and varying degrees of interruption of normal life and production. The aim of the workers is to force the employers to continue to employ more personnel than the technology actually calls for in a "normal" working day in the production of what can be sold *profitably* on the *private profit* market. Related goals of their bargaining are to force the employer to lower the hours of work for the given wage, or raise the wage for the same hours of work, methods of making him share with the workers at least a portion of the higher rate of profit made possible by the more advanced technology.

These measures are half-way houses, steps towards the realization that the technology could be used more rationally, more fully, and more justly if it were not *owned* privately, and not restricted in its operation by the necessity of making a *private* profit. In other words, if a transition were made to collective ownership of the means of production, ownership by the whole people, this would allow production to be planned, not for making a private profit under conditions of private competition, but in relation to the actual needs and wants of the people involved. Under these conditions, improved technology, no matter how much improved, would be no threat. Since there would be no private competition for a private profit, such improvements would be automatically translated into a lowering of the hours of work for all, at the given wage, or an increase of wages and products for the given hours of work, or both, in varying proportions as needs of all rather than profits for owners, may motivate. Full employment could be maintained, as hours of work were decreased in proportion to improvement of technology. These measures would be made possible by socialist collective ownership, by socialist relations of production, and, as the technology of production, cybernation, and automation progressed in association with such relations of production, it is conceivable that a point would be reached where money would no longer be necessary, because the sufficiency of products would be such that they could be had for the taking.

The transition from capitalism to socialism, from private property relations of production to socialist relations of production is, of course, a revolution. What Marx's view amounted to (disregarding his time table and place schedule) is that this revolution takes place successfully when enough people have suffered enough from the denial of their survival-needs and development-needs, have been able to identify the major causes, and have been able to organize themselves politically in order to come to power and remove these causes. Having replaced the restrictive, capitalist relations of production with developmental, socialist relations, they can then offer every baby born alive a fair chance. In itself the revolution creates the possibility, but not the guarantee, of a better quality of life for all. The degree to which the possibility is actualized depends upon the human resources of intelligence, feeling, and creativity that are brought to bear.

REVOLUTION, FREEDOM, AND PEACE

What has happened in the Soviet Union since 1917, and even more, what is thought to have happened, is much discussed in this connection, and widely considered to cast doubt on the value of conceiving of revolution in terms of economics and politics. It is even considered by some to be proof positive that attempts at political organization based on economic class struggles are inherently detrimental to the prospects of a humanistic revolution and should be rejected on principle. The present writer happens to have had unusual opportunities to pursue independent observation and research in the Soviet Union, over some three years, both before World War II and after Stalin's death, with a knowledge of the language and without ties to any party, government, or historically embattled nationality. What I found was a party and government adapting the concepts and theses of Marxism to the doubly difficult task of replacing capitalist with socialist relations of production in an economically and politically backward country, which in 1917 was more agricultural than industrial, and at the same time building up in that country the advanced modern technology which it had never had. Surprisingly, they succeeded in this double task, but at the cost of a lack of civil liberties and a heavy, pervasive power wielded by bureaucracies.

One must say a lack, not a *loss* of civil liberties, because pre-revolutionary Russia had never built up a tradition of civil liberties and parliamentary government such as Western countries like the United States, Britain, and France had done over the preceding centuries.[9] Likewise, the pervasive power of bureaucracies was nothing new in the life of this country. In these two matters, some progress has been made, but certainly not as much as should have been made. But of course we must keep in mind, at the risk of departing from reality, that these particular matters are, in the nature of the case, felt much more by outsiders than by the Soviet people themselves. This does not mean that these matters are not important to the Soviet people, but it helps to explain priorities: poverty, starvation, unemployment, illiteracy, perilous infant mortality, unchecked communicable disease, are more important than bureaucracy or lack of civil liberties. *They* had to be dealt with first, and in the quickest possible way, which is exactly what was done, not without mistakes, but with unprecedented historical success. Taking into account the size of the country and the population (one-sixth of the land surface of the globe, one-tenth of the human family), the social, economic, and technological conditions at the time the new regime came to power (among the very worst in Europe), the time that has passed since (fifty-eight years, eight of them in civil war and World War II), and the levels reached socially, economically, technologically, in relation to solving the basic human problems mentioned (levels among the highest in the contemporary world), the amount of social progress made has indeed no precedent in past human history.

Looked at in this perspective, those who made the Soviet revolution were struggling with the problems of a vast human alienation caused directly by economic insecurity, chronic poverty and intolerable deprivation. Almost everyone there felt this alienation without any special effort, on his own skin and in his own guts. Those who are trying to make a contemporary revolution in advanced western countries are struggling with the problems of a no less real and vast human alienation which is actually charged with an even greater threat to survival. But this alienation is one which presents itself in immediate perception as a frustration of development-needs rather than survival-needs, as a robotization of the human individual confronted by a technology of potential abundance which, however, seems to be controlling him rather than he controlling the technology. Actually, most of the human race in the "third world" is starving, suffering, and dying prematurely for the want of the products which that technology is capable of producing, but which are not produced because *those* unfortunate people are not capable of paying a price which would make it profitable for the owners of the technology to produce for *them,* and *they* cannot produce for themselves because they haven't yet got the necessary technology. *Their* alienation problem is like the Soviet problem of 1917, but exists in the same world, and has the same roots as the more "advanced" alienation found today in big Western countries and, though in different forms, in the Soviet Union.

In this perspective, the problem of big Western countries is to replace capitalist relations of production with socialist relations, so that their technology can be used by and for people, so that the tradition of humanistic morality and civil liberties can be revitalized in consciousness and fully implemented in practice. The Soviet problem is to create a socialist tradition of civil liberties, which means scope for individual conscience and the operative possibility of dissent, and to carry it out in practice in terms of institutions which will replace the old bureaucracies. This is also the problem of China, as a giant socialist power. Both socialist giants have solved a gigantic problem which has yet to be solved by big Western nations—the adjustment of economic relations of production to the modern technology of production. They have found and established the only economic relations that have a humanistic potential, the *possibility* of a humanistic future, in relation to the gigantic power of the new technology. But they have as yet neither found nor established the moral and political relations that are a precondition to the humanistic future that is possible.

The measure of the present depth and urgency of this problem is the fact that there is evident threat of war between these two socialist giants. There is evidently a power struggle between them which, if fought out militarily, could grow and become the conflict that would destroy the world just as effectively as a war between capitalist and socialist giants or between capitalist giants.

What does this situation mean? Among easy answers are: (a) that one or both of the giants called socialist should not be so called, because true socialism is incompatible with such a situation, and (b) that socialism is no more of a guarantor of peace and a humanistic future than capitalism is. Both possibilities, as put, are oversimplified and too sweeping, for "socialism" is not an absolute, but a matter of degree, of different stages of growth. In any case, we are left with the present threats of war, and the present problem of peace—the need to pose the right questions, and find the right answers.

Still another easy but unhelpful answer is that these unfortunate possibilities of war exist because not all countries of the world are socialist. That is, existing socialist powers have to compete economically with capitalist powers, which means in a non-socialist context, and have to defend themselves militarily from attacks and encroachments by big capitalist powers that are constantly working to seduce, subvert, and divide members of the socialist bloc, constantly working to form overt or covert alliances with certain members of the socialist bloc in order to weaken and destroy the bloc as a whole. There is no doubt that capitalist powers are constantly working to that end, but all this only accentuates the peace problem, and the present unrealism of the traditional, pre-atomic "orthodox" Marxist attitude: that we must accept the possibility of an all-out military conflict, with no holds barred and all weapons used, in order that the world as a whole may become socialist, after which the only real foundation for solving the peace problem would exist. But, unfortunately, the only real foundation of the human race would no longer exist, after all weapons had been used.

The peace problem evidently must be solved in a world not completely socialist, or there will be no world at all. It cannot wait. It cannot be subordinated to something else. Moreover, nothing could be more in the spirit and the letter of Marxism than the realization that the new material powers of production, the new atomic technology, demand new political and moral attitudes and evaluations. In the present world, a secure peace can be built only on foundations which include cooperation between capitalist and communist governments, and on principles shared by these governments. These foundations must also include, on each side, operative channels through which people as people—individuals and minority groups, as well as actual or potential majority groups—can resist their government, dissent from it, or change it. A humanistic future cannot be built on the infallibility of any government or party, or on the conclusion which follows from such presumed infallibility: that the people must always obey the leaders of the established order, as long as that order calls itself by the right name. When governments possess the physical power to destroy the world, the less they can be criticized by people, the greater is the danger to the world.

I would argue, as I have done earlier in this work, that this line of thought does not involve or lead to the conclusion that no government or nation in the present world has the right to take military measures in its own defense. In the present world I do not feel I have the right to advise either individuals or nations to use no violence whatsoever, irrespective of conditions. But I feel I have the duty to emphasize that no nation and no individual has the right, under any conditions whatsoever, to commit biocide, which in practice means that the right to enter into any military conflict is inversely proportional to the likelihood of its becoming thermonuclear war, assuming that the other applicable moral standards are met. In the light of this principle, I have discussed and evaluated various military actions of my own country. I have also, to a certain extent, applied this principle of nuclear pacifism, as I understand it, to the Soviet Union, arguing that this principle was actually what guided the conduct of the Soviet government in the Cuban missile crisis. In regard to later events, I have argued elsewhere that the Soviet invasion of Czechoslovakia should be condemned, not because there was any great risk of its precipitating a thermonuclear conflict under the given conditions, but because it was a clear violation of the right of self-determination without sufficient evidence of any cause that would justify the violation. In my view, this judgment does not apply to the Soviet action in Hungary. There was an actual armed conflict going on in Hungary, and the Soviet government had the legal right to make the decision to give military assistance to the established government, in putting down the attempt against it. Again, there was no evident risk of this becoming a thermonuclear conflict.

In any case, a peace revolution is not a revolution against technology.

It is a revolution against an authority system that allows and necessitates the use of technology by a small group of people in a way that runs counter to the survival-needs and development-needs of the human family as a whole, including themselves.

NOTES

[1]Karl Marx, *A Contribution to the Critique of Political Economy* (Chicago: Kerr, 1904). In Somerville and Santoni, *Social and Political Philosophy: Readings from Plato to Gandhi* (New York: Doubleday, 1963), p. 379.

[2]Ibid.

[3]Ibid.

[4]Ibid.

[5]Theodore Roszak, *The Making of a Counter Culture: Reflections on the Technocratic Society and Its Youthful Opposition* (New York: Doubleday, 1969), p. 5-6. © 1968 by Theodore Roszak. Reprinted by permission of Doubleday & Company, Inc.

[6]Jacques Ellul, *The Technological Society* (New York: Knopf, 1964), p. 138.

[7]Roszak, op. cit.

[8]Karl Marx, op. cit., p. 379.

[9]It is significant that Eastern European countries such as Yugoslavia and Poland, which historically had more contacts with Western European countries than Russia had, and were more influenced by such contacts, reflected a greater degree of the civil liberties tradition of "pluralism," as they built up socialism, than the Soviet Union did. This is most directly manifested in the relative diversity of philosophical currents in Yugoslavia and in the continued existence of Catholic universities and influence in Poland. Of course, where the early stages of building socialism are characterized by armed struggles and the threat of foreign intervention, it is natural that whatever form and degree of civil liberties had previously existed should be temporarily suspended. Apart from such necessities of struggle and self-protection, historical experience suggests that the socialism built up in a given country will tend to reflect the degree (but, of course, not the class orientation) of whatever tradition of civil liberties had been actually operative in the life of that country.

9

The New Human Individual

The best way to gain insight into a new individual is through first-hand contact—by hearing his thoughts in his own words out of his own mouth, seeing him in action in the flesh, making friends with him. This has been my privilege, in the present case, for a dozen years. I say a dozen, though I have been a teacher in daily contact with the student youth for thirty years, because the new individual I refer to began to take on significant dimensions of reality with the decade of the sixties. As a professor of philosophy it has been my practice throughout to begin most courses by asking the students, before they have gone into the ideas in the readings, to set down their own present ideas on some of the important problems of life. Both in the reality I could see and feel, and in such papers written by the students in recent years, new qualities became more distinct, more widespread, and took on increasing strength. Perhaps the best way these qualities can be communicated on the printed page is through selections from some of these papers. I here divide them into two groups: Views on Life and Views on War. Each selection is by a different author. The headings are mine.

VIEWS ON LIFE

Without Preconceived Notions

''The primary criterion to be alive is to understand and appreciate the life-time-space one presently occupies. To understand and appreciate this position is to love it. To love it is to be infatuated by life, to 'grok' every moment, and to encounter it without preconceived notions about persons, places and things. With preconceptions about any of these, objects assume labels; one becomes 'good' or 'bad,' 'liberal' or 'patriotic,' 'straight' or 'cool,' and such labels are binding and misleading. Labels do not allow for variations in character, idea, texture and nature. In short, labels are confining, and one who employs them limits his perceptions of his life-time-space. If there is any lesson to be learned from Adam and Eve in Genesis, it is that once you assign labels, that is, 'tasted of the fruit of the tree of knowledge of good and evil,' you limit your perceptions of the world and each other. You lose Paradise and recognize the differences and imperfections of man. You create a gulf between yourself, other people, and your respective worlds.''

To Explore All the Possibilities

''The imposition society can make in one's life can at times be very overpowering. Very often a particular life style is felt to be cramped by the ever-tightening grip of the social machine. I believe that institutions can only be a threat when one catches sight of something that encompasses so much more than they are equipped to reckon with. There are really two realms of existence: the natural environment and the structure that society produces and wishes us to conform to. Seeing the human predicament in its purest, most natural aspects gives the beholder a freedom and sense of purpose that is not possible when the mind has been molded by conventions. This presents to me a problem, for I recognize the fact that an individual life must be lived alongside the existing institutions. It is my concern to explore all the possibilities, and then choose a mode of life that gives me the freedom I desire. This quest promises to occupy my complete attention during the next few years. Only after much preparation will there be a foundation to build upon.''

Morality and Love-Power

''My morality is based on love: love of oneself and of mankind, an unselfish and unexclusive love. All human beings have certain basic needs which must be satisfied if the individual is to be healthy. I feel that love is the prime psychological need. A sense of love gives one self-esteem, hence the ability to love others. Consider love as positive energy generated from human beings who possess love. A constant state of this energy-flow builds the resources of the individual. His energy is received by others who in turn return his love, building and containing the store of power energy within all those involved. When an individual becomes selfish or narrow in his love of others or acceptance of their love, his energy is diminished. A need will again arise, and if that need is filled through anti-love or evil-hate, it will drain the energies of others. I feel as long as an individual is true to a philosophy of love for himself and his fellow-man, he will continue to grow in wisdom and perpetual joy.''

Love and Lust

''The greatest manifestation of beauty is love, specifically that of a man by a woman or vice versa. All senses—emotions involved to the fullest. Emotions of happiness in being with somebody you enjoy. All the physical senses—touch, see, hear, taste, smell. Touch or be touched, smooth part of a body or rough, makes no difference for it is beauty since it makes you feel good/happy. See a part or whole of a body—pure happiness—look into eyes—direct communication not by sound which can be distorted to deceive, but by eyes—can only tell what real thoughts are. Hear—voice of the other pleasant to hear can only cause goodness. Taste—lips or other parts of a body can cause happiness. Smell —sweat—sexual smell—artificial—all relate back to one per-son—causes happiness of being.

''Problem occurs since lust and love are often confused. They are so close, lust can be part of love but love not part of lust. Lust only involves intimate sexual relations—not a deeper inner happiness and contentment. Relationships based on lust only eventually turn out to be disasters, for physical lust cannot bring on emotional attachment or love. After a while physical ''love'' loses its enjoyment—it becomes a habit expected of each partner. This is the only thing holding those people together—when one gets tired of his/her partner the relationship falls apart, both have nothing only memories of physical contact—not anything of an inner lasting value.

''Love can and usually uses lust as part of its being. It should follow after two people become emotionally one—feel happiness together purely emotional (spiritual) not physical. Later if both want to include lust as part of their relationship it can be used to heighten love of each other, but if the couple let lust control their relationship and they lose sight of inner happiness (just by being with another person—not in a sexual way) their relationship often ends as a pure lust relationship, each with nothing—only memories—painful ones which are even worse than those of pure lust, for one knows love could have and probably should have survived but the couple themselves destroyed it, not something else.

"Love can break up as a result of the parties themselves also. One or both parties decide they have lost inner happiness and contentment and the relationship would lower itself into lust. This decision can be hard to take, and memories, often painful will occur but these are much better than those suffered by one whose love ended in lust, for memory of love stopped when in love is infinitely better than that of knowing love was debased to lust and it was your fault the love died—greediness—selfish, not sharing.

"Lust itself is not bad, just when a couple does not accept it as it is. If two people enter a purely lust relationship and they realize what it is and they both agree to it, there is nothing wrong with it. But if the couple is under the illusion that love comes from lust, that couple is to be pitied, for their relationship will end in total disaster. Sex can be healthy if both parties go into it in a frame of mind for what it is, physical pleasure. If only one party really wants to do it the situation can become dangerous, the party who wants it may force it on the other party, this party will become shocked and will become first fearful then hateful of the other party—thus ruining any type of relationship the two might have and perhaps altering the way both parties effect future relationships."

By Holding Hands They Are Showing Trust

"There are several things in life which are beautiful to me. One is seeing a guy and girl holding hands walking down a barren beach at sunrise. Symbolically speaking, as the day is to begin so is their relationship. By holding hands they are showing trust and love for each other, which to me is real beauty, not being afraid to show a real and true love, the boy, as is the girl, showing respect for the other person. Being truthful and trustful toward each other puts them in a world of their own, naturally in their eyes and mine a beautiful world. Every day they are living toward a better life and relationship. But the true beauty in this relationship is the truthfulness toward each other. It is so beautiful to know that a person loves you as you love them, a person needs you as you need them, and a person wants you as you want them.''

One of the Most Beautiful Experiences of Life

''I believe that people are capable of truly being themselves, without playing games in their relations with other people. It is very easy for us to put on a mask, or play a role, because that is what we have been taught to do. And this is deeply internalized within human beings. It is very hard for a person to even attempt to expose his naked self, his inner feelings, his good *and* bad points, his real self, to another. But I feel that this can be done, and that it is for the best. It is a fantastic feeling to have someone's innermost fears and joys shared with you. I am not proposing that everyone tell everyone else all his thoughts, but I think it would be beautiful if everyone could truly open up to several people during their lifetime. Sayings such as 'Don't let him know how you feel,' 'Big boys don't cry,' 'Pretend you don't care,' 'Act like nothing is wrong,' are much too common in our society.

''I have found so far in my life—which I realize is not even a speck in time—my most successful relationships have been those in which I was most honest—those in which I stated how I felt even if it was silly. Something which always seems to work is when one's primary concern is someone else's happiness, because one is more pleased by this than by any possible selfish actions. To me, this type of unselfish, honest, real relationship would be one of the most beautiful experiences in life.''

A Spiritual Development

''A man's obligation after first discovering that he is ignorant and small is next to develop his intellectual and communicative capacity, (e.g., science, math, language, vocabulary) together with a spiritual development. I have recently had certain personal experiences which have made the above more meaningful to me. This Christmas vacation two friends and I drove 2,000 miles to Vancouver, B.C. During the trip I met many brothers and sisters. We picked up hitchhikers along the way; one in particular was a long-hair in Berkeley. This man's name escapes me at present, but I do remember he stuttered with eloquence and exemplified brotherhood. . . .

"Another human being whose acquaintance marked my memory was Jacob. This man previously ran drugs from Mexico to Canada approximately five years ago. He had taken LSD, reds, uppers and other forms of drugs in the past, but was now off of them. His reason for stopping, he said, was Jesus Christ. He and many other friends living in a West Vancouver commune were all "Jesus freaks" or "children of God." They gave us a place to sleep for two days, as well as offering their food. In Vancouver, men, women and girls hitchhike freely, without harm, and we gave them rides. This city and a minority of its population showed me another form of brotherhood, somewhat different from our hippie brother in San Francisco; theirs was driven by a total love of Christ and his teachings. After this beautiful experience in Canada we returned home."

A Vast Number of Churchgoers Are Fakes

"Religion is another good example of man contradicting himself. Children born into a churchgoing family believe and accept as fact Biblical stories, church creeds and the Father, Son and Holy Ghost. As they grow older and learn to reason for themselves, many of the old beliefs are doubted, and church becomes a boring ordeal, to which they're dragged on Sunday mornings. Many discontinue their churchgoing habits until later in life when the thought of old age and death creeps into their minds. Even now many aren't sure of the existence of a Supreme Being, but are trying to believe for the sake of insurance. If there isn't a God, then the few hours they spent in church didn't hurt. But if there is a God, they have saved themselves from eternal punishment. In short, I believe a vast number of churchgoers are hypocritical fakes, too lazy to believe and too scared not to."

So Much America Could Do

"To me, to kill another human being, for whatever reason, be it murder, an act of war, or an act of retribution, is totally inconceivable. How can anyone tamper or play with a life which should be left alone to come to its own end? I am revolted inside when I read of bizarre and horrible murders or inhumane tortures and killings concerned with the Vietnam War. My parents and I have had many long and fervent discussions concerning this war; and to me they seem so hypocritical to condemn Charles Manson for murder, yet in the same breath condone the killing that goes on in Southeast Asia. I will always feel most strongly about this, and no one will ever convince me that war, or killing, can be *in any way* justified.

"I am very disappointed with the American political and economic systems today, yet I have no alternatives for them. I am made very mad by the fact that the economic system as it is today encourages men to dupe and deceive others in order to procure more money for themselves. It upsets me terribly that money and power play such a commanding role in American society. There are so many things in life more worth striving for than wealth and glory. It also upsets me to know that many of our problems today could be solved were it not for the greed of men. America has the technical knowledge to make an automobile that wouldn't pollute the air, but the automobile manufacturers would lose money if such a car were developed. Electric companies could easily make light bulbs that would last a lifetime, but people would stop needing them and wouldn't buy them. The sardine is now gone from the coasts of Monterey and Carmel because of man's greed, even though, with maximum limits for catches, it could have been saved. So much America could do if she had not instilled in her people the lust for the dollar. It seems to me that the system of economic and political priorities has gone haywire and something desperately needs to be done, but I don't know what."

Cooperative Society

"The first American colonies tried to implement a system of government similar to the Marxian concept, 'From each according to his ability, to each according to his need.' The colonies having certainly one of the prime opportunities throughout history for a 'fresh start,' found that they must resort to other incentives in order for work to be done. In addition many communal living situations similar to the above in design, have been attempted throughout history, most of which have failed. I do not allow these failures to discourage me.

"Man is yet in the early stages of his development as a species, and even shorter lived in his ability to communicate from one generation to the next. Here lies the answer to a social system based on brotherhood: education. Since the development of the written word, man is constantly progressing and in a sense evolving. He is no longer the same being he was even two hundred years ago. It is my faith in man that through his analysis and observation of past and present, he has the potential to realize the imperatives of peace and brotherhood.

"The acquisition of wealth is the major deterrant to the aforementioned cooperative society. The incentive which compels man to acquire wealth, as it appears to me, is enjoyment, and naturally he wishes to continue it. I believe, however, that the personal creativity which would result naturally from the lack of finance, creativity which would produce other means of enjoyment in the cooperative society, would be more enjoyable and fulfilling."

The Best in the World

"I have grown up believing that our government was the best in the world, that we were a free people with the right to choose our own destinies. When I became more educated, and started thinking about this, I found out we weren't as free as I had thought. I went to Europe for a summer. There I learned that many things had been repressed during my schooling, and that the U.S. government was one large propaganda machine, trying to convince me and the world how right America is. I now see the need for improving our government and feel that it should be done in a peaceful effort if possible.

"Finally people have turned their attention to ecology, mainly because they are starting to feel how it is to suffer in their own filth. I am glad this has happened because I feel nature is our last hope for survival. Without nature we would be no better than caged animals, and the consequences of this would probably be either mass suicide or war. I have grown up surrounded by nature and I would hate to see it destroyed. Nature, to me, is my life-blood; it comforts me and pleases me and provides an outlet for me from this insane world. I love nature and nothing can replace it; no machine or toy can make up for it if it's lost. The beauty of nature can't be measured in terms of money or amount of resources but only in the eyes of the beholder, and no one has the right to say which part of this beauty should be destroyed and which part saved.''

A Change Is Going to Come

''A change is taking place in the United States as well as the rest of the world. A new generation is coming to life and I want to be a part of it. A Utopia we will never find, but a better life would be impossible to avoid. There are so many places where improvement would not be difficult. I truly believe that in time the change will come.

''The first step in achieving our goals will be to educate ourselves. Through an education we will be able to compete with the people who at present call themselves our superiors. The trend is no longer toward big business, and they seem to be in trouble; recruiting is becoming more and more difficult. More of us are going into government work and teaching. I do believe that money is no longer the driving force, for who really needs it. To be happy and content, to be able to get the things your family needs and live comfortably should be so much more important than salting away a million dollars in a bank and dying before you can spend it.

''We have been brought up in a world of distrust and discrimination. For so many years our parents hated, and in return were hated themselves. The idea of helping others was almost unheard of. Nigger was a common word, and I might add is still prevalent in our parents' vocabulary today.

''Our constitution stated that all men are created equal. This is a document we are to respect and live by. The generation of yesterday had no use for this piece of parchment, but I think we do. It's not hard to live near a yellow person or a red person or a black person, yet so many narrow-minded, white-collared, middle- and upper-class racist slobs think their world will come to an end if they do. How many times have you heard, 'They're dirty, they spread disease, they'll teach my kids dirty words, or they'll rape my daughter,' and it makes me sick. Sure property value goes down, but only because they made it that way. What a blessing when we can all live together like brothers and sisters as we were meant to be. What will it take to open the eyes of the stagnant generation?

"I feel it will take another ten years before we can establish ourselves in the system as we know it today, that is, political as well as economical. The revolution is starting, the goals being set, the new ideas being made ready to put into use, and a completely new system being prepared to take over. Imagine what it would be like without war, cold or hot. And how it would be to not sit and wait for that day when we all blow up together. How great will it be when freedom of speech is restored, the right to assemble is returned to us, and no matter how you look or what your beliefs are, you know some cops are not going to crack your head just for being alive.

"Too much power has been given our executive branch of government, and whether it's legal or not, no one is doing anything about it. Our government by the people and for the people has fallen by the wayside. They no longer respect our wishes. Take Vietnam for example: all polls show the general public wants out of that conflict. But are we? Hell, no. Well I'm sick and tired of it, and a change is going to come."

II. VIEWS ON WAR

To the Last Man, Woman, and Child

"If attacked by someone, I would defend myself as long as I could. However, if the attacker gave me the choice of either being raped or dying, I would gladly consent to the rape. If my family was threatened, and the offenders gave us a choice between slavery and death, we would go willingly to the cottonfields. As long as I am alive I can live through anything; but as soon as I am dead I will have to sleep through everything.

"This is only my personal feeling about dying. There are probably hundreds of thousands of people running around who do not give a damn about their lives. They would die for anything or for nothing at all. Somehow I feel that these are the people in industry and in the military who claim that we need nuclear weapons, that, 'my country right or wrong,' we must defend ourselves to the last man, woman and child. Is there anything so valuable that it would be worth the destruction of the entire earth?

"Preparing for war should be just as unlawful as war. The more we stockpile, the bigger the odds for a mistake or a misunderstanding. A contemporary nuclear war would leave little or no time for an apology. It bothers me when I hear people talking about 'limited' war. Who is going to limit the war? Who is going to play referee and call 'out of bounds' or 'roughing the player'? The countries involved? The United Nations? Some innocent bystander on Mars? God?

"War is an international problem. It is going to require an international solution. The prevention of war should be of primary concern to all the peoples of the world, regardless of age, race, creed, color, religion or size of country. International laws must be given strength. They must be enforced with equal pressure on every country including the two biggest ones. That the lives and welfare of so many are in the hands of so few is a situation that must be rectified as soon as possible."

What I See I Don't Like

"To die by natural causes is a decision that should be made only by one's own self. Neither another man nor a man's country has the right to say, 'You must go to war and possibly die, because it is for your own good and the good of our country.' There is no way in hell that the possibility of my death is going to be in the best interest of myself and 'my country.' Especially today. 'We, the American people,' are in Vietnam because a few men felt that a small incident, in which no one was killed, was just provocation to escalate 500,000 men and billions of dollars into a country where, (1) we are not at war, (2) no American blood was to be shed. Today about 40,000 boys have thus far lost their lives. I cannot judge the past nor predict tomorrow; I can see what it is today. What I see I don't like."

As the Mushroom Cloud Hangs Overhead

"War has been taken for granted so long that it is only recently that a vast majority of the people have finally begun to question the killing. Life is the most precious and important commodity that we have; however, we destroy this for such comparatively worthless values as fear, pride, prejudice, blind loyalty, greed, and of course, for most of us, the all-important dollar. Our lives revolve around the materialistic rewards of our society, with the truly important values, such as honesty, sincerity, compassion and gentleness almost always forgotten.

"With the advent of the nuclear bomb the total destruction of the world could be a distinct possibility. As the mushroom cloud hangs overhead it is now possible for war to not only morally destroy our society, but to physically destroy it as well. Our technical knowledge has advanced above our spiritual side of life, and until we take actions to change our priorities people will face an endless line of wars.

"War is the most unnatural, immoral and evil force working within our society. It has for years destroyed the moral fiber upon which our country is based, and if allowed to continue will ultimately destroy all living beings. It is time all peoples of the world resist, for the time has come to 'study war no more.' "

The New Barbarians

"It is my feeling that we are now living in a weapons culture in which a technological elite in this country are using propaganda to serve the purpose of lining their own pockets with money. They are using the self-survival instinct of the American people to perpetuate the arms race. The bomber gap was the first example of the fear propaganda of which I am speaking. The American people were led to believe that the Soviet Union was surpassing the United States in bomber capabilities. The American people were automatically horrified at this prospect, and we increased our production of bombers at a time when bombers were becoming obsolete. The missile gap was the next great swindle which involved a production of missiles in order to catch up with the Russians. Statistics were published of Russian missile capability which were later proved false by our satellites which clearly showed that we were way ahead of the Soviet Union and no such missile gap existed. Now we come to the megaton gap which in the same way led to the unnecessary production of arms simply because Russia had larger bombs than the United States, which means absolutely nothing in terms of nuclear capability.

"The American people are still swallowing much of the garbage handed them by people who profit from fear. This can be seen today by the adoption of an anti-ballistic-missile system which in reality has no practical use because there is no possible defense against nuclear missiles with multiple warheads.

"As I said earlier, the very concept of war changed the moment the Soviet Union achieved nuclear parity with the United States. Not only is it futile to hope for victory in nuclear war, but the United States cannot hope for even a slight advantage of nuclear superiority when the entire world represents a powder keg in which making more armaments only adds to the concept of overkill.

"Turning to the limited war we are now engaged in, I must point out that for the masses of people to identify themselves wholly with such a war is obviously impossible. For such an identification a moral issue was needed for whose defense or attainment war was to be waged. In other words, war had to be just on one's own side and unjust on the side of the enemy in order to evoke moral enthusiasm in support of one's own cause and hostile passion against the enemy. Taking this into account I wonder how many Americans feel a hostile passion against Vietnam, which is being physically, morally and spiritually destroyed. I wonder how many Americans are appalled when they watch the news and see the levels of suffering of the Vietnamese people. Of course, after watching John Wayne and our gallant men fighting to make the world safe for democracy on channel nine I doubt if many Americans can see the present tragic image of the United States, one of the world's most powerful nations, raining bombs and chemicals and napalm on the rice fields and bamboo huts of one of the poorest and most defenseless countries, which is trying to drive the foreigner from its soil, while the U.S. fights only to sustain the power of a corrupt military clique. In my opinion the American people have become the new barbarians."

Hitler in the Midst of His Rampage

"I cannot accept the use of sadistically devastating weaponry such as napalm and white phosphorous on any human being, regardless of color, religious or political beliefs. To wilfully maim, disfigure and torture men, women and children is the act of madmen, no more sane than Hitler in the midst of his rampage.

"The quest for new territories is over. Why must this economic and political plundering go on? Have people become so afraid of each other and themselves that peaceful coexistence and economic cooperation have become only a utopian ideal?''

A Way Other Than War

''What we face now is a situation that is new to us and yet so important that we cannot waste time debating the insignificant issues. It is a hard, cold fact that we, and others, have the power to end all forms of life with very little effort. If we said before that peace means freedom, and if freedom is violated, that justifies war, we no longer can. We have to seriously ask ourselves the question of whether or not war is necessary to have peace, and then find some way to answer the question negatively. Under the circumstances, if we want to be around to enjoy this peace and freedom we will have to find a way other than war to achieve it.''

The Effects Do Not End on the Battlefield

''War to me is a mass all-out effort, a thing which seems to generate its own power. This I am afraid of! Because the effects do not end on the battlefield or at the military level, but permeate the entire society if not the entire world. Whole institutions are set up, maintained and survive only as a function of war and its products. It has reached the point of irony where war has become responsible for people's and even countries' survival. War itself has been established as an institution. This is why I say that war generates its own power. I'm not only talking about Cambodia or the professional soldier; I'm also talking about my uncle who works at Lockheed.

''So why is the system here? It appears not for the maintenance of reason and rationality. Only violence and destruction seem compatible with the maintenance of a weaponry which could destroy humankind multifold. In a society that condones war by its very action what fact of reality has so distorted its values? What happened to the Judeo-Christian tradition? What has happened to human values as a whole? 'Thou shalt not kill'? Ideology appears to have become more nationalistic than personal. Does the state have the right to use its own subjects to make war on other states, to employ their property and even their lives, and expose them to hazards and danger, and in such a way it does not depend on their own personal judgment?

"Is it not just as bad to be a slave of one's own state as it is to be the slave of another? Many terrible wars have been the result. In such a state war is glorified as strength, and the society's heroes are warriors. Indeed, when an entire society becomes conditioned to such an existence it takes a great step backward. War has a dehumanizing effect, especially on those who are killed and must kill. For the value of human life becomes secondary to the cause. An inertia or mania is developed when the results surpass the objectives and countless innocents are killed. Man has shown himself to be the only animal which systematically annihilates its own kind. This, of course, directly contradicts the highest of all human goals—survival."

Such Putrescence Shall Cease

"War is the systematic destruction of human beings. Subjectively I feel this is wrong and rationally I know it is illogical. Why then does war exist? How can it be overcome?

"It appears to me that wars occur because of weaknesses in the institutionalized structures created by man. Essentially war and the preparation for war result from the inability of two different groups to reason and communicate meaningfully; or, secondly, the nature of one group may be materially exploitive and aggressive, encouraging war for oppressive purposes. I view war then as the most brutal form of persuasion; engaged in by mutual agreement of two organic groups with opposing values and/or material needs.

"In the past (before the nuclear annihilation age) wars could be justified by claiming that a supreme moral principle or objective goal was worth human expenditure. Life could continue—with the "victor" reaping the benefits of his engagement. But today war carries with it the potential threat of death to all persons. No one might survive to enjoy anything. If one believes values exist only in the context of human experience, then one can only conclude that "the" supreme value of man must now be the preservation of mankind. Conclusively one cannot engage in war or even in its preparation risking such destruction.

"It is possible that the risks involved in modern warfare will be the prime mover in establishing more humane methods and systems of human relations. Ultimately nation-states must recognize that more is at stake in war than their petty national identities. Just as warring groups in the feudal past sacrificed their sovereignties to form more stable states, so must the present states unite cooperatively to achieve today's supreme value, the survival of mankind.

"The nation-state system is a weak institution for dealing with atomic weaponry. The international system to date is so primitive that it, too, cannot control the potential use of nuclear destructibility. Communication and reasoning between 'opposing' groups are insufficient and inadequate. The time is ripe for war and more war.

"Since the institutions appear to be incapable of preventing war, the logical control factor exists within the individual, from whom, ultimately, all power is derived. Renouncing war at the individual level, however, is a tremendously difficult task. Most individuals of a population, propagandized (educated) to respond to narrow 'patriotic' ideals, do not recognize the very real threat of omnihomicide or biocide in warfare. National integrity and defense remain the motivating forces promoting more war. Because the state and its leaders have these values at stake, methods of compelling young men to sacrifice their lives for these secondary values are necessary. As a consequence, men who lack reciprocal influence are literally "forced" to bear arms regardless of their personal preferences. These individuals face such physical, social, economic and political degradation that the inevitabilities of not fighting appear worse than to do so. And war continues.

"However, such putrescence shall cease. Men will recognize that human relations *can* occur without war when they begin to realize, as Margaret Mead put it, that "the killing of an enemy is not qualitatively different from killing a neighbor."

A Handful of Men

"The one thing about war that disturbs me the most is that a handful of men can decide *our* future for us, where nuclear weapons are concerned. War involving guns is bad enough, but when the whole human race and all plants and animals become involved in military affairs between countries, and their lives are being used to finalize some argument, I believe that that handful of men are themselves committing the worst crime in the history of mankind.

"I cannot understand why grown men, who themselves have a life to live, cannot *discuss* disturbances they have, and through peaceful tactics settle any disagreements at hand. Why must they use violence to end their differences? And the point is, their differences will never come to an end through violence. They will keep on and on until the only thing left to do is to push that fatal button. How absurd is this thing called war. It is the most disgusting thing I know.''

Before It Is Too Late

"Both sides view each other as the enemy out to destroy 'our' way of life. In order to achieve this perspective, governments try to create strong feelings of nationalism. Our side is morally right and justified—we have God and freedom on our side. We are raised according to the Golden Rule and the Judeo-Christian ethic, yet if we believe in being a Christian, and in peace, we are labeled traitors, peace creeps, and the 'enemy.' We are taught Thou shalt not kill, but then are told later that this refers only to our allies—it is necessary and right to kill the 'enemy.'

"Each day a state of tension exists which could lead to the total destruction of our world. In a nuclear world there can be no such thing as a limited nuclear struggle. The time has come for us to learn to live together before we all die together. Never before in history has the challenge been so great. To meet this challenge of world peace, we must find inner peace and harmony within ourselves, for only through inner peace and harmony can we come to find and establish peace in the world. There can be no external peace without first establishing internal peace. I only hope that we all can make it before it is too late."

10

Prospects and Conclusions

WHAT THE FUTURE DEPENDS UPON

To ask today, "What are the prospects for peace?" is to ask, "What are the prospects for the survival of the human race?" "Can we look forward to world peace?" means "Can we look forward to a world?" The first thing that the answer to such questions depends upon is the degree to which those who raise them understand what the questions actually mean under the conditions that now exist. That is one of the factors—in this case it could possibly be the decisive one—on which the future depends. What we are referring to may be called the social consciousness that underlies public opinion on these matters.

By whatever name we call it, the thing itself is made up of so many different elements, and changes its content in response to so many different kinds of causes, that it must be broken down into its main parts if we wish to deal with it effectively. In other words, if we wish to inform and change public opinion on these matters, to deepen and sharpen social consciousness—as we must do, or perish—it is necessary to work along many different lines, and through many different social institutions.

At the same time, since social consciousness about world peace is focused, deepened, and sharpened by impacts and influences that come through social institutions (or processes) such as education, politics, economics, morality, religion, mass media, and the arts, these institutions or processes themselves must be pressured by social consciousness to act in certain ways along certain lines if world peace is to be maintained. It may seem paradoxical to demand that social institutions should be used to influence social consciousness so that social consciousness should better influence social institutions, but it is no more paradoxical than to say education should influence people so that people should improve education, or that politics and mass media can be used to influence people to demand and create better politics and better mass media.

These seeming paradoxes are functional, not only because causal influences can work reciprocally, but also because any one institution is made up of diverse and conflicting tendencies, interests, and viewpoints which are capable of influencing social consciousness in opposite directions. Thus a battle is always going on within any one institution, over what kind of change *it* ought to undergo, and what kind of change it ought to bring about in society. In these battles efforts are made by the various contending groups to enlist the aid of the general public. Specifically, the maintaining of world peace depends, in the direct and immediate sense, on decisions taken by governments in power. But these decisions are in turn a consequence of the ''foreign policies'' adopted by the given governments, which in their turn are influenced by economic, educational, moral, psychological, and other factors.

So the future, by which is meant first of all whether we humans are to have any future, depends mainly upon the interrelated action of a number of leading variables. Among these are: our foreign policy; our education, insofar as it relates to the areas of foreign policy, war, and peace; our economic system, insofar as this influences decisions and attitudes in relation to foreign policy, war, and peace; our moral and religious beliefs, insofar as these are taken seriously and applied to living problems; and our social consciousness in relation to the foregoing variables, which in this case means the extent to which we as individuals are prepared to change the content of such variables for the better in relation to peace. Let us take a reckoning as to where we now stand in relation to these variables, and what we must now do in order to make the continuity of the human race more likely. I say ''we'' first of all in relation to our own country, wherein we Americans have primary responsibility for what happens, and maximum potentiality of effective action.

FOREIGN POLICY

There is no doubt that the most immediate danger lies in the readiness of our government leaders, especially the Chief Executives and their chief advisers, to initiate acts of war, or to threaten to initiate acts of war against other nuclear powers in order to gain some advantage in international relations and world competition. The most dramatic instance of this can be seen in the Cuban missile crisis of 1962, which we have examined in some detail. Subsequently, United States policy in relation to the Vietnamese war showed, unfortunately, that this readiness remains as great as ever. In this connection it is very instructive to note that a leading figure among President Kennedy's advisers in the Cuban missile crisis, Theodore Sorensen, publicly argued in 1972 that President Nixon's mine blockade of North Vietnamese waters, explicitly directed against the Soviet Union and China, involved a much greater risk of the final thermonuclear holocaust than President Kennedy's actions.

In a special article for *The New York Times* of May 12, 1972, Sorenson wrote that President Kennedy's naval blockade of Cuba "was, like President Nixon's mining of North Vietnamese harbors, an interdiction of Soviet shipping that risked the nightmare of nuclear war. There all resemblance ends."

Interdiction of another country's shipping by force of arms is of course an act of war, and if these two cases were alike in that respect, and in the further respect that each "risked the nightmare of *nuclear* war," the realistic reader can only wonder how much importance could be attached to the qualifying statement, "There all resemblance ends," since that much resemblance can mean the end of all.

In any event, Sorensen proceeds to point out differences in the two cases, arguing that these differences are such as to lend greater justification to President Kennedy's thermonuclear nightmare. He makes the point that the Soviet missiles in Cuba were but ninety miles from our coast, whereas the weapons the Soviets were supplying to North Vietnam were some 9,000 miles away and they represented a natural Soviet desire to make available to Hanoi at least "a fraction of what our own country is supplying its allies in Saigon."

Thus, when Sorensen, a Democrat, is scrutinizing the actions of a Republican Chief Executive, he takes into account those factors that bear on equality of rights among nuclear powers, and the reckless danger of trying to prevent another nuclear power from doing on a relatively small scale what we ourselves were already doing on a much larger scale.

However, Sorensen does not mention in his article, nor did he emphasize to President Kennedy in 1962, in the same spirit of reasonableness and regard for equal rights which he urged upon Nixon, that while the Soviets were setting up missile bases in Cuba, we already had missile bases in Turkey, ninety miles closer to the Soviet border than Cuba is to the United States, not to speak of our missile bases in Italy, and a number of other countries within easy range of the Soviet Union. The truth is that the actions of both Presidents represented reckless denials of equal rights, infinitely dangerous attempts to prevent a fellow nuclear power from doing on a relatively small scale what we ourselves were already doing on a much larger scale, but Sorenson only sees the danger when some other executive is carrying out this policy.

He further argued that "President Kennedy obtained a unanimous vote in the Organization of American States authorizing his action and the participation of Latin American vessels in the barricade. He invoked the Treaty of Rio as well as a new and specific joint resolution of Congress. President Nixon prefers to act alone, without authorization or participation by either allies or Congress."

Sorensen did not mention that President Nixon (and President Johnson) had the same hollow facade of "allies," regional "organization," "Treaty," and "resolution of Congress"—everything except what the Constitution of the United States explicitly lays down as the sole legal authorization to *initiate* war: a declaration of war by majority vote of the Congress. President Nixon (and Johnson) had, as did Kennedy, no more than small, insignificant military help from small powers, "token contributions," as they were rightly called. Nixon and Johnson had the Southeast Asia Organization, as Kennedy had the Organization of American States. They had the Seato Treaty, as Kennedy had the Rio Treaty. They had the Tonkin Gulf Resolution, as Kennedy had a joint resolution. But neither of these congressional resolutions, nor any treaty with other countries, nor any action taken by any outside organization can ever substitute for a specific Congressional declaration of war if the United States is to *initiate* war. When President Nixon proceeds to initiate war that can easily become thermonuclear, and does so on the basis of such transparently flimsy pretenses to "legality," Sorensen sees through them, and says Nixon really acted alone, and without the proper authorization of Congress, which is precisely what Kennedy did. Neither

Executive was willing to let Congress play the role the Constitution gives to it as the nationally representative deliberative body—the role of deciding whether the specific circumstances really necessitate the bloodshed and destruction of war—deciding *by its majority vote,* so that "*no one man* should hold the power of bringing oppression upon us," as Abraham Lincoln put it. "Kings had always been involving and impoverishing their people in wars," Lincoln explained, pointing out that our forefathers who framed the Constitution well understood this to be "the most oppressive of all kingly oppressions."[1]

Sorensen ended his article with a warning that points to the future. While we "all had reason to be fearful in 1972," he writes, the danger is much greater now because of the following factors: the Soviet Union is stronger than it was then, its leadership is less likely to continue to yield, our support from abroad has become weaker, and "finally and frankly, we may not be as lucky this time as we were in 1962. . . ." Therefore, "before it is too late, both sides must be urged to get back on the 1962 track; secret negotiations and communications, contacts at the United Nations, more cautious rhetoric in public, and above all, the exercise of military restraint. One mistake is all it takes; and saving one's face is not worth losing our planet."

It is not strange that Sorensen should say we all had reason to be fearful in 1962. As Robert Kennedy's posthumously published memoir of the crisis has revealed, President Kennedy *expected*[2] that the Soviets would not comply with his ultimatum to remove their missile bases or else have them destroyed by American bombing, *expected* that he would have to order them bombed, that the Soviets would bomb in return and that the ensuing thermonuclear holocaust would engulf the planet and destroy mankind. As that is what he and presumably his closest advisers consciously expected, it is also not strange that Sorensen should emphasize how "lucky" we all were in 1962, which means how lucky the whole world was that President Kennedy and his advisers made a capital mistake about what the Soviets would do. Here is a fact stranger than all fiction. Since the advent of themonuclear weaponry we have grown accustomed to reading stories about how the world could be destroyed, based upon one or another kind of unexpected mistake that could result in triggering off the ultimate weapons. But the actual record of nuclear

history must now include the fact that in 1962 the world was unexpectedly *saved* from nuclear destruction by a mistake. That is, an American
President who expected that the Soviet Union would defend its missile
bases was all prepared to drop the bombs that he expected would bring the
end. But as it turned out, he was mistaken about the Soviet Union, which
decided not to defend those bases, so the end did not come on that
occasion.

Sorensen, however, while in one breath admitting how blindly lucky
this was, in the next breath says we ought to get back on that same track,
which he characterizes as that of "secret negotiations," which it
certainly was, and of "military restraint," which it certainly was not. It is
plainly absurd to use the term "restraint" to characterize the decision to
bomb the missile bases of a fellow nuclear power becuase he set them up,
quite legally, ninety miles from your shore while at the same time you
have your bases on his very border, meanwhile rejecting his offer to settle
the matter by a simultaneous removal of both missile bases, even though
you acknowledge your own bases are "obsolete."[3] When, in such
circumstances, you *expect* your bombing of his bases to result in the
nuclear war that will annihilate mankind, and you still decide to deliver
the ultimatum that you expect will start the war—all without declaration
of war by Congress—surely this is as far from "military restraint" as
anything can be. The plain truth is, it was the other side alone that showed
any military restraint, by refraining from defending with military means
its equal legal rights in the matter of missile bases.

The closing sentence of Sorensen's article expresses the most important truth in the entire matter, but he seems incapable of applying it to
the very crisis through which he was lucky enough to live: "One mistake
is all that it takes; and saving one's face is not worth losing our planet."

In the context this is meant as a condemnation of Nixon's conduct.
Apparently, Sorensen does not see that it equally condemns Kennedy's.
For the latter's decision was that it *was* worth losing our planet if that was
the only way to get the Soviet missiles out of Cuba *without simultaneously removing ours from Turkey.* The President insisted that the Soviets
must remove their missile bases without any "quid pro quo or any
arrangement,"[4] *even though the Soviet proposal of simultaneous removal was privately recognized as reasonable on its face, and even though*

the President and his advisers also acknowledged privately that our missiles in Turkey were obsolete. This is what Robert Kennedy himself reveals in his memoir:

> The fact was that the proposal the Russians made was not unreasonable and did not amount to a loss to the U.S. or to our Nato allies. On several occasions over the period of the past eighteen months, the President had asked the State Department to reach an agreement with Turkey for the withdrawal of Jupiter missiles in that country. They were clearly obsolete, and our Polaris submarines in the Mediterranean would give Turkey far greater protection.[5]

But, as Robert Kennedy adds, the President "did not wish to order the withdrawal of the missiles from Turkey under threat from the Soviet Union."[6] Kennedy is of course not referring to any explicit threat, but to the setting up of the missle bases themselves. Thus the decision to insist on the ultimatum, and to reject the idea of simultaneous removal of the two sets of missile bases was admittedly not grounded on reasonableness, or on the objective truth about the missile bases, but on the desire to save American face as the image and symbol of the strongest power in the world, even at the cost of destroying the world. It is thus clear from the record left by Robert Kennedy that the Soviet missiles could have been removed without any risk or expectation of a nuclear holocaust simply by the simultaneous removal of our admittedly obsolete missiles from Turkey. But our leaders were so afraid that the United States might seem to lose face by this admittedly "not unreasonable" action that they consciously chose an uncompromising course even though they expected it to end in the final holocaust. Thus a foolish pride would have destroyed the world for a set of obsolete missiles. Never was so much risked with so little justification.

This is not a problem about John Kennedy, Richard Nixon, Lyndon Johnson, Dwight Eisenhower,[7] or Harry Truman as *individuals.* It is a problem about a state of mind which obviously still exists as a widespread reality, as the basis of an ongoing foreign policy. In a sense, the problem about this state of mind begins with the fact that the great majority of the American people have not yet faced the truth about what that state of mind can lead to—specifically, that it has already led to a Chief

Executive and a few appointed advisers, behind closed doors, taking decisions which they admittedly expected would result in the extermination of the entire human race, in "the death of the children of this country and all the world—the young people who had no role, who had no say, who knew nothing even of the confrontation, but whose lives would be snuffed out like everyone else's."[8] Robert Kennedy tells us that this was the very thought of President John Kennedy about what would happen in a nuclear war with the Soviet Union, and then goes on to tell us that President Kennedy and the majority of the small group of top executive advisers behind closed doors decided to order the Soviet Union to remove its missiles from Cuba or else the President would order them to be bombed by American forces. He further tells us that he and the President, (and presumably the other top advisers) "hoped"[9] that the Soviets would comply with this demand, but "expected"[10] they would not, and that the President (without consulting Congress) expected to order the bombing which would begin the war that would end the world.

All this is put down, black on white, under the signature of Robert Kennedy, with a Foreword by Theodore Sorensen, and published by *McCall's* in its November 1968 issue with the title in huge black letters against a flaming red background THIRTEEN DAYS BY ROBERT F. KENNEDY THE STORY ABOUT HOW THE WORLD ALMOST ENDED. Millions of American parents have read the story in *McCall's* or in the paperback editions that speedily followed (Norton, New American Library). They must have read it, and understood it. But the problem is that somehow they did not really believe it. They understood that Robert Kennedy was telling them that President Kennedy *wanted* to remove the American missiles from Turkey, knowing they were really *obsolete,* that President Kennedy recognized that the Soviet offer of a simultaneous removal of their missiles from Cuba and ours from Turkey was *not unreasonable,* but that President Kennedy nevertheless rejected the offer, told the Soviets they must remove their missiles without any conditions, did *not* expect them to do so, *did* expect to bomb their bases as the beginning of nuclear world war that would wipe out everybody. The American people understood that they were being told by Robert Kennedy that, in all this, "The thought that disturbed him (President Kennedy) the most, and that made the prospect of war much more fearful than it would otherwise have been, was the specter of the death of the children of this country and all the world—the young people who had no role, who had no say, who knew nothing even of the confrontation, but whose lives would be snuffed out like everybody else's.''[11] But the American people could not, did not, connect this with reality. They were unable to *believe* that men like President Kennedy and his advisers could really decide that the incineration of all the children in the world, along with all the adults, was preferable, not only to the presence of Soviet missiles in Cuba, but even to a simultaneous removal of Soviet missiles from Cuba and *obsolete* American missiles from Turkey, that is, that Kennedy and his advisers could really decide that the world and the human race were simply not worth continuing unless the Soviet Union removed its missiles *unilaterally,* ''without any quid pro quo or any arrangement.'' It was *not* sufficient that the Soviet missiles should be removed from Cuba in exchange for the removal of ''clearly obsolete''[12] American missiles from Turkey, which the President had long wanted removed anyway, and had actually directed the State Department to remove ''on several occasions over the period of the past eighteen months''[13] because they were ''antiquated and useless.''[14] But the State Department had delayed, and now the President was ''angry,''[15] especially because the failure to remove those missiles from Turkey was admittedly ''our own fault.''[16] The American people understood they were being told by Robert Kennedy that in spite of all this the President and his advisers decided they must not accept the Soviet offer because it might seem like acting ''under threat,''[17] and that it was better to demand the *unconditional* removal of the Soviet missiles on *threat* of American bombing of them, which demand they did *not* expect the Soviets to comply with. What they *did* expect was that they would bomb the Soviet bases and thus start the war that would incinerate all the children and everyone else. It was a conscious expectation of what would result from a deliberate decision in which they faced all the consequences: the extermination of the human race, the end of the world. But they actually decided it was worth it. (I trust the reader will forgive me for repeating these central facts so many times. My only excuse is that they are so hard to believe.)

The American people understood that this is what they were being told by Robert Kennedy, as the President's closest adviser, who was in the best position to know. They understood it, but the great majority of them obviously did not believe it. Any human beings who really believed that those events had taken place in that way would never have accepted them as normal, sane, or tolerable. Our first task can be expressed very bluntly: we must make them believe that these things really did take place in the conduct of our foreign policy, and not in the Kennedy Administration alone. We must make the American people see that the future—that is, whether there is going to be any human future—depends first and most upon whether the foreign policy of the United States continues to be conducted in this way, and that if it does so continue, the human race will not continue. It is a clear case of one or the other.

When we speak of the foreign policy of the United States being conducted "in this way," we are not referring to goals or objectives. We are referring to the state of mind of those who have been conducting it, especially since World War II, in regard to the *means and methods* employed in pursuit of the goals and objectives. The goals and objectives naturally include victory in the competition with rivals and opponents, the most powerful of which are the Marxist socialist-communist states. But the means and methods being used in the effort to secure "victory" are maximally stupid as they would destroy the very things we are competing for, and the entire human race, in a way that would bring about more suffering and agony than ever took place in the whole of preceding history. This state of mind moreover includes an habitual acceptance of what is plainly illegal and unconstitutional: initiation of war by the Executive, by one man. As Robert Kennedy put it, and accepted it: ". . . the President was deciding, for the U.S., the Soviet Union, Turkey, Nato, and really for all mankind."[18] The replacement of this whole state of mind by one more compatible with a human future and with respect for our basic law necessitates not only strong political effort but strong effort in every sphere of social concern.

EDUCATION

Just as politics is the social process in which foreign policy is most directly expressed, so education is the social process in which states of mind are most directly shaped. It would not have been possible for Kennedy and the other Chief Executives since World War II to acquire the state of mind which became habitual to them unless the American educational influences as a whole had been such as to induce and encourage it.

Concretely, this means that communism as an idea and communist countries as sovereign states must have been presented to them in such terms and in such a way as to leave the net impression that these ideas and nations were not parts of human culture and mankind so much as enemies of human culture and mankind, monstrosities and criminals whose central purpose is to destroy all that is good in human life. Only this could account for the fact that it became habitual for these individuals who eventually occupied the office of President of the United States, along with the great majority of their fellow countrymen, to accept the idea that, in dealing with communism and communists, normal human restraints cannot operate: anything goes. If you are realistic, you must expect the worst, and you must never hesitate to draw first. Albert Einstein, one of the creators of the atomic bomb, made a very keen observation with profound regret when he said that the bomb changed everything except our way of thinking.

Our first and most necessary objective in education can, like that in politics, be put bluntly: We must from childhood educate people in such a way that they do not consider it natural to prefer the extermination of the human race to granting equal rights to communism and communists. There is no need to dwell upon means and methods of doing this, upon detailed programs of instruction, for the means and methods are in no way difficult or extraordinary. What is difficult, what requires extraordinary efforts of misplaced creative imagination is to continue "educating" about the theory and practice of communism and communists as if they were by definition forms of crime and criminals, sworn enemies of the good, rather than a competing social philosophy and form of government with practical successes and failures, strengths and weaknesses, but in any case a fellow member of the United Nations.

The problem is not one of devising new pedagogic techniques, but of realizing the absurdity and danger of an absurd and dangerous state of mind. The problem is to look at facts without a double standard, and to act normally in the light of them. If we cannot measure up to this situation in education, then we cannot expect our political decisions, especially in foreign policy, to be realistic enough to allow for the continuity of the human race, the human adventure. For us to measure up to this situation would by no means require that we should force ourselves to become a politically radical nation or to undertake great new experiments in education. All we need do is look around us in the world of today and compare what takes place in our own country on the plane of education and politics in relation to communism and communists with what takes place in other leading capitalist countries such as France, Italy, Japan, West Germany, or Britain. Taken all in all, it is the difference between self-destructive fantasies and recognition of realities. The only ''détente'' that will have meaning for survival must include thorough house-cleaning in education.

ECONOMICS

Of course everything, including fantasies that encourage war, has causes, sources, roots. It is well established in modern economics and sociology that economic rivalry is one of the major causes of wars between nations. It is also recognized that capitalism is the kind of economic system that not only emphasizes and intensifies economic competition, but in so doing can give rise to a system of culture, a set of mores, and a general state of mind in which everything in human life becomes unduly subordinated to the power of money. Private money becomes not only public power, but also the major need of the individual for survival. As money is the precondition for obtaining the necessities and luxuries of life, it is not strange that life itself is risked and taken in the pursuit of it. Money, says the proverb, is the root of all evil, and the creative literature of capitalist civilization has documented this in thousandfold detail.

The *moral* point of socialism and communism as *theories* is to make all economic relations between human beings socially cooperative in a sense that allows for competition but reduces and precludes its destructive forms. The effort is to bind all human beings together as joint owners rather than to divide them into employers and employees, so that people will not have to exploit *people* in order to obtain the necessities and luxuries of life. As science and technology increase the abundance and efficiency of man's economic productivity, it becomes more and more realistic to think of such possibilities as producing an abundance of physical commodities, social services, and cultural opportunities that will reach everyone on the basis of only a few hours of necessary labor per day or week. Provided all were joint owners, involuntary unemployment and poverty would be impossible. Provided the system were world wide, with rational economic and ecological planning, destructive competition would be unnecessary. Given scientific progress, a point could probably be reached at which the level of abundance was such that private money would be unnecessary. In a world unified on the basis of such a system, the major cause of wars between nations could be expected to disappear.

Something of this kind could conceivably be the long run solution of the war problem. It could conceivably become the foundation of a kind of human culture, set of mores, and general state of mind in which the old ideal of brotherly love would no longer be accompanied and frustrated by the economic reality reflected in the proverb, "man is a wolf to man." However, the problem of peace as that problem exists today is, to speak in comparative terms, not as simple as the problem of replacing one economic system with another economic system, even though that problem in itself is of course tremendously complex. The empirical situation today is one in which there is not only a group of capitalist nations in hostile confrontation with a group of socialist-communist nations, each group possessed of an overkill nuclear arsenal, but even within the respective groups there are confrontations charged with the possibility of nuclear extermination.

In other words, basic economic rivalries of the kind that have always produced wars in the past continue to exist, while the weapons with which wars can now be fought will, if used, end the world. History did not wait until the human race was unified by an economic system free of destructive competitiveness before supplying it with weapons which could annihilate humanity. Before such weapons were brought into existence it was possible to conceive that some final and decisive world war, fought out with all the strongest weapons between the bloc of nations representing the old economic system and the bloc representing the new system, could be won by the new system, after which it could become the basis of a human future of peace and prosperity on earth. But we now know that such a scenario is impossible because a final struggle fought out with the weapons now permanently available in terms of scientific knowledge would destroy all life; no habitable earth would be left, nor any victors or vanquished to inhabit it.

What, then, can we expect to happen at the sensitive and fecund economic level where the roots of war so thickly thrive? We cannot realistically expect the leading holders of power within any economic system to relinquish their power in favor of some other system without a tremendous struggle. The competition between the economic systems will therefore run its course with the threat of nuclear war hovering in the background. The hope for a human future depends on the extent to which the leaders and the people on either side are convinced that nuclear war, or war with any weapons of similar destructiveness, is the worst of all possible alternatives, and that such a war must never be initiated no matter what the circumstances, and if initiated, never joined under any conditions.

The leaders—capitalist leaders in the first instance—must be convinced of what they are evidently not yet convinced of: that nothing would be gained by destroying the world. They must be convinced that, since nothing could possibly be less profitable than that, that is the one tactic that must never enter the competitive game. The people must be convinced that their leaders are not yet convinced of this simple truth, and that they, the people, must keep unremitting pressure upon their leaders, so that the leaders are constantly aware that the people on whose support they are counting know what has already happened in regard to these matters, and understand the infinite criminality and stupidity of it. The established leaders must be kept aware that they, the people, would refuse to tolerate, cooperate with, support, or obey anything that suggested the renewed beginning of the patterns of decision that characterized the Cuban missile crisis, the escalation of bombing in North Vietnam, the invasion of Cambodia, the mine blockade of North Vietnamese waterways.

At the present time there is not a sufficient proportion of either the leading holders of power or of the general public who are actually convinced of what they must be convinced of in order to afford a reasonable guarantee of a human future. The proportion can become sufficient only if those already convinced are successful in convincing more and more of the others. The process of reaching the leading holders of economic power can and must take many different forms. This will challenge creative effort, practical ingenuity, and constant courage not only in politics and education but in morality and religion.

MORALITY AND RELIGION

What precisely is the nature of the task that must be carried out in the fields of morality and religion in order to ensure that there will be a human future in this world? Paradoxically, the task is to convince people that their own selfish material and physical interest *now* coincides with their highest moral duty. In all past history the great difficulty in teaching morals arose from the fact that the world was filled with so many examples of people who obviously did not live by the moral commandments, but in spite of that, indeed, because of that, seemed to live so very well. The moralists had the hard job of arguing that, though these people *appeared* to live very well, to prosper and enjoy happiness, this was not really true; the real truth was that their disobedience to the commandments, their violation of the rights of their neighbors, their killing, stealing, and the like polluted their *souls* and destroyed their happiness *inside,* no matter what the outward appearance might be.

No doubt one of the main reasons this argument was of limited effectiveness, however true it might have been, was that there always seemed to be so much visible evidence that the greater the scale on which the commandments had been violated, the greater were the rewards and the less were the penalties. It was clear, to take prime examples, that the punishments laid down by the state for disobeying the commandments against killing and stealing did not apply to the state itself. Everyone saw that the state itself habitually commanded, in the form of war, wholesale killing and wholesale seizure of the lands and goods of others, and punished disobedience to *those* commands. When the wars were over, when the seizure of lands and resources had been successfully carried out, and an "empire" established, the whole nation was taught to rejoice in its good fortune, and the highest pinnacles of honor, glory, and power were reached by those who had done such deeds. Whatever the religious moralists might teach about punishments in a life after death, where those who disobeyed the commandments were eternally tortured (which again was hard to make credible because it could never be seen) in any case did not appear to apply to the large-scale killings, the wholesale stealings, the mass indiscriminate violation of rights which took place in war, carried on in the name of the state.

What a tremendous help it would have been to the earlier teachers of morality if physics, chemistry, and sense evidence had cooperated with them in such a way that, whenever anyone killed his neighbor, he automatically and visibly killed himself also, that whenever any nation made war upon another, destroying it with the most powerful weapons available, it automatically destroyed itself also! This would have been a superlative teaching aid in relation to the commandment on which the survival of man most directly depends: "Thou shalt not kill." This teaching aid, this visible model, is now available on the largest possible scale.

It is now possible, with the help of a multiplicity of audiovisual instrumentalities, to drive home the truth that has not yet been driven home, the truth on which everything else now depends, the moral truth which is now one with the physical truth, as unmistakable in sense evidence as in the light of pure reason: you cannot destroy the world for your neighbor without destroying it for yourself. The power to destroy the entire world, which never existed before, now unites the entire world. Now I *must* be my brother's keeper if I want to keep myself. To the extent that it was possible in the past for me to destroy my neighbor's world without destroying my own, we really did not live in the same world, he was not really my brother, and I did not really need him. To the extent that it is now not possible for me to destroy my neighbor's world without destroying my own, we really live in the same world, he really is my brother, and I really need him.

The old pre-atomic world *needed* the morality of brotherly love in order to become better, but it did not need this morality in order to exist. It existed for millenia as many separate worlds, doing violence to one another with weapons of ever-increasing destructiveness, until the ultimate atomic weapons that can destroy the entire world of living things were finally reached. Hence this new, atomic world needs the morality of brotherly love, first of all at the highest levels of power, in order to exist at all. There is no doubt that the old world would have been a better world if more of the people in it had been able to turn the other cheek, as individuals, to refrain from returning blow for blow, violence for violence. As it nevertheless could exist in spite of its violence, so also the new, atomic world could continue to exist even without persons in their individual relationships rising to the level of habitual non-violence. But the truth that now underlies all other truths is that the new atomic world cannot continue to exist at all unless the nations are able, *as nations*, to refrain from collective thermonuclear violence, and collectively to turn the other cheek rather than reply to thermonuclear violence with thermonuclear violence.

The new, atomic world has survived its first crisis—the Cuban missile crisis—in which one nuclear power, in order to maintain an advantage over a second nuclear power, delivered an ultimatum to the second which it expected the second to refuse, and upon that refusal, expected to start the nuclear war that it expected would end the world; but the world was not ended because the other nuclear power unexpectedly complied with the ultimatum. The second, far graver crisis will come about when some nuclear power actually uses nuclear weapons against another nuclear power, in order to gain some advantage. Such a first strike would not of itself end the world, but if replied to in kind, would be the beginning of the end, which would not be long in coming, though every day before the end would seem like an eternity of torture to the billions of crazed humans exposed to the unspeakable agonies of global thermonuclear incineration. The planet might take years to die, and half killed humans might stagger, crawl, writhe, scream, and moan for months, but that would be the end of the story of human beings, more horrible in its moral implications than anything ever imagined in the tales about a life after death. This is the crime so unspeakable that it does not even have a name, the utter destruction not only of the human past and present, but of the human future. Because only the future is infinite in its potentialities, this is the only infinite crime that humans can commit against themselves, and it can be committed only once.

Unless there is a peace revolution, a revolution in ways of thinking and acting about war and peace, this crime will be committed. The enormous danger of the present situation is perhaps most clearly defined by the fact that the leaders in each of the nuclear camps, capitalist and communist, say *they* will never be the first to strike with nuclear weapons against the other; but each set of leaders says this in a way which always implies and often explicitly states that if the other side should strike first, a nuclear reply, only stronger, will be made, and each side conditions its people to think of this attitude as patriotic, manly, courageous, and highly moral.

Actually, the moral level of this nuclear stance is the same as that of a man who would take his wife and five children for a drive on the freeway, and say, ''I understand that if two cars have a head-on collision on the freeway, all passengers in both will be killed. I will never be the first to drive in the wrong direction in a given lane. But if someone else is driving in the wrong direction in my lane, I'm not going to surrender that lane. Unless *he* turns aside, I'm going to plow into him at increased speed.'' It is the same moral stance as that of a man whose home is broken into by a gang of thieves throwing a hand grenade that destroys part of his house and kills two of his five children. With his wife and remaining three children he retreats to a room where he himself keeps a supply of hand grenades. He understands that if the thieves follow them into this room, and he throws a grenade at the thieves, everyone in the room will be killed. The thieves enter the room; he throws the grenade; everyone is killed, including the whole of the remaining family, and the house burns to the ground. If we recognize that this kind of behavior would be abysmally stupid and immoral in relation to a father, a mother, five children, an automobile, and a house, what are we to call it in relation to the entire human race and the only human planet?

It would be most comforting, if only it were realistic, to think that this problem could be solved simply by treaties among the big powers outlawing all nuclear weapons and any other weapons of similar destructiveness. But, even if such treaties should be signed, which in itself would be a step in the right direction, they could not be relied upon unless they were accompanied by qualitative changes in ways of thinking and habits of action. No matter how many such existing weapons are destroyed by treaty, they can never in reality be permanently destroyed, for there is no feasible way of stopping the scientific and technological progress on which the development of nuclear and biochemical weapons depends. We must expect that utterly new forms of such weapons, not now imagined, and of ever increasing destructiveness, will become possible as time goes on, simply as a by-product of normal and general scientific and technological progress. Moreover, unless ways of thinking and habits of action are sufficiently changed, we must expect that when a crisis arises treaties will be disregarded. The Charter of the United Nations is in essence a treaty among big and small powers alike, in which all the signatories pledge themselves to renounce the use or threat of force in their dealings one with another, yet this was disregarded by our government in the Cuban missile crisis, though nuclear disaster, admittedly expected, was to be the cost of disregarding it. This is only one instance, and if it is argued that other governments are no better, or even worse, that only makes it less realistic to think that the problem can be solved simply by treaties among nuclear powers, or among all governments. If the treaties that already exist had been observed by the governments that exist, this problem would not exist. It can be solved only to the extent that a peace revolution is carried through.

At the present time and for the foreseeable future the greatest danger does not lie in the possibility that a nuclear power on one side or the other of our ideologically divided planet may use nuclear weapons against an opponent. That is Step I, very destructive, but not likely by itself to exterminate mankind, as the grenade thrown by the thieves did not wipe out the family. The human race would be wiped out only by subsequent steps of retaliation, counter-retaliation, and so on. Precisely how many such steps would bring the end would of course depend upon the degree of effectiveness attained by the weaponry up to the given point in time. It is therefore obvious that the morality which is needed cannot be that fatally limited kind that applies itself only to Step I. It cannot be the idiot morality that says, ''I will not destroy the world unless someone else begins it,'' ''I will not kill off my family and myself unless someone else begins it,'' ''I will not drive my car head on into another car at sixty miles an hour unless I have the right of way.'' It must be the common sense morality that says, ''Though he is wrong, though he attacked me, I must not reply *in kind* if that kind of reply would destroy everything, including myself.'' This is the irreducible minimum, in relation to nuclear weapons, that people must demand and obtain from their governments today in order to have any tomorrow whatsoever. It is suddenly clear in the visible world that the biggest crimes, even when committed in the name of the state, can no longer pay, that the wages of sin on the largest scale are really death on the largest scale, and that if a better morality is not practiced at the top, both top and bottom will disappear.

Though all this is clear, though human beings understand, in the purely intellectual sense, that if they wish to have any future, they cannot make war with the weapons now available, any more than they could have a future if they continued at sixty miles an hour into another car *even though they had the right of way,* or if they threw the grenade *even though a grenade had been thrown at them,* they are genuinely bewildered by this situation when it presents itself in nuclear form. This bears witness to the strength of the conditioning processes associated with patriotism, the right of self-defense, courage, the duty to defend one's country, and the like. The tremendous psychological strength of these concepts was, over the centuries and tens of centuries, built up in and associated with a context in which the most destructive weapons could be used without any fear of exterminating the human race or atomizing the planet earth. That context has now disappeared forever, but the emotions associated with it have not yet been modified in the new context. That process of modification is obviously not impossible. In fact, it cannot even be said to be difficult, once it is seriously undertaken. But until it takes place, the individual is genuinely bewildered: he both understands and does not understand why he cannot use the most powerful weapons he possesses to defend himself and his country when he and his country are attacked with the same weapons. When it is a case of automobiles on the freeway, or hand grenades in a small room, he is not bewildered, at least, not to the same degree, and he usually survives.

In the nuclear situation the bewilderment of the individual takes a further form, in which he finds it difficult to imagine how he could live a life of any value if, in effect, his country "surrendered" in the face of a nuclear attack, if it were "taken over" by the nuclear aggressors. This difficulty is probably greater for Americans than for most other people, since our national history so far has been a very short one, in which we have not experienced invasion or surrender, at least of our own country. Yet the history of the rest of the world is replete with examples of surrendering and being invaded without life ceasing to have value. Every major power in the world today, with the exception of the United States, has gone through these processes repeatedly, and it would certainly be absurd to argue that each of them should have committed suicide rather than accept such alternatives.

What all history shows is that surrendering or being invaded is not the end of a nation, but the beginning of a new kind of struggle, a new kind of warfare fought out with weapons that do not destroy the world but are capable of denying the fruits of "victory" to the invader. Sheer physical force has never been the only weapon or even the main weapon success-fully used against invaders and occupiers. In any case, the peace revolution is not against struggle, resistance, courage, or patriotism. It is against the stupidity that would destroy these very things, along with all else, in their own name.

NOTES

[1] *The Writings of Abraham Lincoln,* Arthur B. Lapsley, ed., vol. II (New York: Putnam, 1905), p. 51, 52.

[2] Robert F. Kennedy, *Thirteen Days: A Memoir of the Cuban Missile Crisis* (New York: New American Library, 1969), p. 109.

[3] Ibid., p. 94.

[4] Ibid., p. 108.

[5] Ibid., p. 94.

[6] Ibid., p. 95.

[7] It is important to note the statement made by Pierre Mendès-France in June of 1954 in the French Parliament, in which he referred to Eisenhower's willingness to launch an atomic attack against the Vietminh forces in order to stave off the defeat of the French at Dien Bien Phu (if Congress and the British government would agree). In his speech directed against M. Bidault, then Foreign Minister in the Laniel government, Mendès-France said: "You had a plan which was revealed at the beginning of May: the large-scale intervention of the American airforce at the risk of provoking Chinese intervention and starting a general war. Parliament had adjourned on April 10, but M. Laniel had undertaken to call it if there was anything new and important. The American intervention plan had been prepared, and was about to come into action—at your request, too. The attack was to be launched on April 28, and the ships with the aircraft and the atom bombs were on the way. President Eisenhower was going to ask Congress on April 26 for the necessary authority. The French Parliament was going to be faced with a *fait accompli.* Fortunately, the plan was rejected by Britain and by public opinion in the USA—at least for the time being." Quoted in Alexander Werth, *The Strange History of Pierre Mendès-France and the Great Conflict over French North Africa* (London: Barrie, 1957), p. 82, 83.

[8] Kennedy, op. cit., p. 106.

[9] Ibid., p. 109.

[10] Ibid.

[11]Ibid., p. 106.
[12]Ibid., p. 94.
[13]Ibid.
[14]Ibid., p. 95.
[15]Ibid.
[16]Ibid.
[17]Ibid.
[18]Ibid., p. 99.

Index

Albania, 125
American Revolution of 1776, compared to Bolshevik Revolution, 7-8; compared to Peace Revolution, 9-15, 20-21; measured in terms of range and depth, 6-8
Anti-communism, effects of on American statesmen, 105-13; influence of on education, 105-13
Archimedes, 136
Aristotle, on slavery, 70, 71
Atomic blackmail, 28-30; in Cuban missile crisis, 28-30

Bacon, Francis, 135-36
Ballou, Adin, 73, 78-81, 92
Biocide, 116-18
Blackmail, atomic. *See* Atomic blackmail
Boston Evening American, 110
Brown, John, defended by Thoreau, 77
Bulgaria, 125
Bundy, McGeorge, on bombing North Vietnam, 56-57
Burtt, Edwin A., 157

Caesar, Julius, 116
Cambodia, invasion of, 215
Capitalism, and competition, 67-69; contribution of, to social progress, 67; increasing dysfunctionality of, 175-79; in relation to war, 64-70; and technology, 175-79. *See also* Profit
Chaplains, attitude of in relation to Vietnam war, 92
China, People's Republic of, 125; U.S. objective in Southeast Asia to contain, 46-48; U.S. opposition to entrance of into United Nations, 86-87; U.S. readiness to initiate war against, 46
Christianity, in relation to civil disobedience. 25, 78-81; in relation to non-violence, 78-81; morality of, 73-81
Civil disobedience, 24; and Christianity, 25, 78-81; as defined

227

Liberation, Marx's view of,
164-65
Lincoln, Abraham, 134, 206; as
opponent of Presidential war,
21-22
Locke, John, as political and
philosophical mentor of
Jefferson, 16; his reasoning
about right of revolution,
16-18
Louis XV, and revolution, xiii
Love, ethics and morality of, 73-
81, 186-90; and lust, 197-88;
needed for survival in atomic
age, 216-18

Mao Tse-tung, 87
Marx, Karl, 111, 125, 126; his distinction between powers and
relations of production, 158-63;
his predictions and the actual
course of history, 172; role of
technology in his outlook, 158-
63; his theory of history, 158-
63; his view of the genesis of
significant revolutions, 161-64;
his view of moral progress,
163-65
McCall's magazine, 119, 209
McCarthyism, 36, 45, 133-34
McNamara, Robert, 24, 85, 105,
122; on policing Southeast
Asia, 52; on U.S. objectives in
Southeast Asia, 49
McNaughton, John, 57-58
Mendès-France, Pierre, statement
of in relation to Eisenhower's

willingness to wage atomic war
against Vietnamese, 222
Mongolia, 125
Moral progress. *See* Progress,
moral
Morality, of civil disobedience,
73-81; of Gandhi, 73-75; of
love, in youth rebellion, 73-81;
and power interests, 81-91;
psychological basis of, 72;
teaching of, in relation to peace
today, 216-22; and technology,
161-65; theory and practice in,
72-73; and Vietnam war, 81-91.
See also Declaration of Independence.
Morse, Senator, 52; and Tonkin
Gulf Resolution, 45

Napoleon, 116
Nato, ideological and material
basis of, in Eisenhower's view,
66
New politics, and democracy, 34-
36; legal and illegal action in,
37; short-run tasks of, 36-38
Newton, Isaac, 136
New York Times, The, 46-49; 51,
53, 57, 70, 82, 90, 92, 134, 204
Nixon, Richard, 40; his mine
blockade of Vietnam, 204-8;
and "new American Revolu-
tion," xiii. *See also* Presidential
war
Non-violence, philosophy and
morality of, in Ballou, 78-81; in
Gandhi, 73-75; in William

About The Author

John Somerville, Professor Emeritus of the City University of New York, is the author of nine books and joint author of another fifteen in the field of contemporary social problems. His works appear in numerous anthologies and have been translated into all major languages. He has been author-participant in three of the international research projects of UNESCO and has presented papers at twelve international congresses. Under grants from Columbia, Stanford, and the Rockefeller Foundation he did three years of field research on Eastern Europe. A pioneer in peace studies and the development of peaceful coexistence, he arranged and chaired at three World Congresses of Philosophy the first large-scale dialogues between American and Soviet philosophers. His *Philosophy of Peace* (1949), the first full-length book on this subject, appeared with Introductory Letters by Albert Einstein and Thomas Mann.